Patriarchal precedents

Patriarchal precedents

Sexuality
and social relations

Rosalind Coward

Routledge & Kegan Paul

London, Boston, Melbourne and Henley

First published in 1983
by Routledge & Kegan Paul Ltd
39 Store Street, London WC1E 7DD,
9 Park Street, Boston, Mass. 02108, USA,
296 Beaconsfield Parade, Middle Park,
Melbourne, 3206, Australia, and
Broadway House, Newtown Road,
Henley-on-Thames, Oxon RG9 1EN
Set in 11/12 Journal by
Academic Typing Service, Gerrards Cross, Bucks
Printed and bound in Great Britain by
T.J. Press, Padstow, Cornwall

Library of Congress Cataloging in Publication Data

Coward, Rosalind.

Patriarchal precedents.
Bibliography: p.
Includes index.
1. Feminism – Philosophy. 2. Social sciences –
Philosophy. 3. Patriarchy. I. Title.
HQ1206.C727   1982   305.4'2.   82–12206.
ISBN 0-7100-9324-1

Contents

v

Acknowledgments

I am extremely grateful to all the people mentioned here; to John Ellis who suffered the production of this book first hand with unfailing kindness; to Barbara Taylor and Maria Black for their immense help; to Jeffrey Weeks, Annie White-head, Olivia Harris, Diana Adlam, Judy Holder, Philippa Brewster, Janet Montefiore and Barry Hindess who all gave invaluable help at various moments; to all the members of the Social Policy Groups who were a constant source of support – Fran Bennett, Wendy Clark, Margaret Page, Ann Wickham, Sue Lawrence, Maria Black, Rosa Heys; and to Pam Taylor who gave me the idea for this book.

Finally, I am grateful to all my family (and ex-family) for their help, especially to my father who helped with some of the typing and the bibliography. This book is, appropriately, dedicated to them.

Introduction

When we turn our attention to theoretical discourses, our gaze falls on what the discourse itself sees, its visible. What is visible is the relation between objects and concepts that the discourse proposes. This is the theoretical problematic of a given theoretical discipline.[1] It will render visible only those objects or problems that occur within its horizons and upon its terrain. Only these objects and problems are significant for the theoretical discipline, and have a place within its overall structure. Other objects and problems are therefore insignificant; they fall into the interstices of the structure, they become invisible. The theoretical problematic, through its criteria of relevance or appropriateness, defines what is excluded from the field of visibility.

A certain relationship of necessity exists between these two moments. The invisible is not simply anything at all outside the relationship between objects posited by a discourse. It is within the discourse, it is what the light of the discourse scans without picking up its reflection. In the fullness of the discourse, there are oversights, lacunae, the 'blanks on the crowded text'.[2] To see these blanks, something more than close attention is needed. What is required is a new gaze, an informed gaze, itself not the product of any one individual, but made possible by changes on the exercise of vision, changes in social and political conditions.

This metaphor of the 'informed gaze' is usually used to describe a 'science' regarding its ideological predecessors. Without making such grandiose claims, however, the metaphor

1

can be extended to encompass the effects of a shift in political and theoretical concerns which then reveals blanks in previous theories. In recent years, a new form of attention has been turned on social and political sciences. It is a gaze arising from the politics of feminism, a gaze which has turned to these discourses requiring illumination about the social position of women. From this informed gaze there has not shone back the required light of illumination, but a light from the lacunae of the discourses. Instead of light from the plenitude of these discourses, a light has shone back from places where only darkness was suspected. What has been exposed are the absences, the questions not asked, and the answers not heard in these theoretical discourses.

This book is structured around three questions. Why is it that the questions asked by feminism have revealed these absences? What are the terms in the fullness of some discourses within the social sciences which have long hidden the absences? And what are the areas of theoretical invisibility which must be made to appear if any discourse is to be constructed adequate to the gaze of feminism? The introduction deals with the questions asked by feminism. The body of the text is about the history of the social sciences and why sexual relations are thought of in definite and limited ways. The conclusion attempts to develop the implications of this history.

The informed gaze

Contemporary feminism has a strange quality; it always seems to exceed its objects. It almost takes its definition from that excess. A heterogeneous movement, pragmatic when pragmatic action is required, and reformist when reforms are sought, feminism now always means something more than a commitment to piecemeal reform to better the lot of women. It is also a commitment to exploring the problems of being a woman in contemporary society. That commitment is to non-complacency towards these problems. It is rare, not to say impossible, to find a feminism which attributes women's subordinate position to some natural, god-given and therefore unchangeable sexual role. Instead, the commitment to exploring the ways of being a woman is to understanding these as constructions in order that they may be changed. It is a commitment involving a double movement: on the one hand, there is a desire to understand how it is that women as a sex are subordinated; on the other hand, there is a desire to challenge the very idea of natural sex roles. The problem is that of understanding the position of women as a sex without presuming that being a sex entails forms of natural behaviour and position.

This simultaneous quest for understanding women as a sex, and sexual categories as constructions appear contradictory. Surely any attempt to talk about women *as a sex*, distinct from men, automatically entails a form of essentialism? It seems to imply that women have a separate history and distinctive experiences, radically different from men. A suggestion like this would appear to rely on an idea of some radical difference between the sexes. It would appear to rule out the possibility that sexual division is socially constructed. Yet this apparently contradictory position is the one most commonly expressed amongst feminism; women have been treated as a sex, but sexual categories are social constructions. Most striking about this position is that its apparent contradictoriness seems to limit the possibilities for saying much more about the problem. It appears to be a compromise formation between two modes of explaining sexual division which, if further elaborated, would run the risk of falling into the pitfalls of either explanation.

The contradictoriness of this position is, however, only apparent. It results from the impossibility of certain options which are presented to us in current ways of thinking about sexual relations. It is the fact that the feminist quest wishes to explore *between* explanations which has exposed dominant ways of conceptualising sexuality and social relations. The mutual incompatibility of answers about sexual relations make the silences of discourses speak; feminism has revealed the black holes in theories of sexuality. Suddenly, for example, the unresolved status of the so-called natural within the social sciences is revealed. For the dilemma between forms of explanation is produced by a particular dogma of social determination. Sex is either the

3

realm of natural and instinctual — hence to be accounted for by biology or psychology — or sexual relations are thought to be determined by 'social' forms, social here implying technical, demographic and economic instances. From either perspective the study of forms of sexual relations themselves is frequently put into abeyance even in those discourses which seem to make the greatest claim to understand them. Either they can be explained by another discipline (an 'individual' or natural science), or they are uninteresting in themselves, always being the effect of other, more tangible social relations, attended to only as examples of the variability of different cultures.

A series of excluded concerns comes to light behind this lack of resolution in the dispute between forms of explanation of sexual relations. How exactly is the 'natural' theorised in the social sciences frequently subsumed under studies of this space? Why is the study of sexuality when it appears in the social sciences is frequently subsumed under studies of institutionalised (social) forms of sexual regulation, like marriage? Why is there no theory of forms of domination and inequality in the dynamic of sexual relations? Why is there no understanding of the construction of sexual identity or consideration of the distribution of power and status which this identity might entail? In short, why are all theoretical discussions of sex polarised around a dispute between 'naturalism' and 'culturalism'?

Essentialism versus culturalism

Feminism turns these questions about sexual construction to the social and political sciences and the glaring light of the invisible shines back at us. Sociology often answers with a useless tautology — society determines social relations in which sexual relations are included. Marxism answers with a rigorous determinism, already politically discredited within feminism: all forms of social identity, including sexual identity, are determined in the last instance by the economic mode of production. Anthropology answers with a comforting but bewildering proliferation of evidences against the naturalness of any one form of sexual behaviour. But no general analysis of sexual relations in their historical specificity is offered. Turning to areas outside the traditional social sciences, psychoanalysis appears to offer a detailed account of the construction of sexual identity, but it outrages many by appearing to claim the universal validity of its findings.

Each of these discourses appears to address some aspect of sexual relations. Sociology takes on the household, marxism tackles the question of property and class and its relation to sexual division, psychoanalysis tackles infantile sexuality and the form of the unconscious. Even the terms used sometimes appear the same, for example, the use of the term reproduction in marxism, some anthropology and sociology, but their use in each discourse is often widely different. The explanations and terms in these different discourses can by no means be added up to construct an adequate general account of sexual relations.

The situation is one of almost bewildering confusion. There is a multitude of contesting definitions, all appearing to ask similar questions and occupying roughly similar theoretical space. But there appears also a real level of incompatibility between these explanations. Any dogmatic espousal of one form of explanation produces a howl of outrage within academic feminism. Attempts to use marxist definitions provoke the criticism that what is specific about sexual division is being neglected and reduced to other social divisions, such as class. To espouse explanations culled from anthropology and psychoanalysis is to run the risk of applying universalising and therefore essentialising definitions. Psychoanalysis appears to commit the additional crime of neglecting the impact of specific cultures on the individual. To espouse sociology is to invite the criticism that no explanation is in fact being offered other than the claim of a diffuse form of causality whereby the interaction of elements in a given culture determines the forms of households and sexual relations.

The vigilance within feminism against reductionism on the one hand and essentialism on the other has at times become severe and violent. The vehemence of the division between various forms of explanations has often left feminism, from when the questions arose, stone cold. The feeling is, if all academic feminism can produce is a fight to the death over competing explanations, then perhaps theory is left well alone.

But these are more than just 'professional' quibbles, off-putting though they frequently are to women outside academic feminism. Academic feminist theory draws its problems from the political discussion in the women's movement; its solutions and ideas filter back, sometimes fast, sometimes slowly, into general discussion. Political tendencies mobilise forms of explanation suitable to their aspirations.

One of the most vehement divisions within the women's movement has been fed in a most unfortunate way by the impossibilities and incompatibilities of theoretical explanations of sexual relations. The endless cycle of accusations of 'reductionism' and 'essentialism' which flow between socialist feminist and radical or revolutionary feminist positions is fed by the fact that theoretical explanations of sexual relations are hopelessly polarised between essentialist and deterministic explanations. It is possible that there would be more common ground between the two major political positions if there were more advances on the theoretical front.

At the moment, however, there is a very real problem that there really is no ready solution to the double exigency to look at women as a sex, but at sex as a socially constructed category. In such a context it is all too easy to become polarised between two unsatisfactory options. The hegemonic definition within the social sciences, and this is true for marxism, is that there are some practices which are determinant, like the economy, and others which are determined, such as the family and marriage. But for a long time now this has seemed inadequate. The way the domestic is organised, the structures of the family, the ways of reckoning blood relationship, the forms and practices of sexual behaviour, the rigidity of sexual division all have a tenaciousness and dynamic which suggests that, provisionally at least, the organisation of sexuality requires, separate analysis. This rarely happens in any of the social sciences with the consequence that study of the sexual dynamic is almost invariably subsumed to the study of other social practices. But the opposite of this apparent neglect is no less problematic. For the assertion that the dynamic of sexual relations should be studied in its specificity, appears to be irredeemably essentialist. It seems to suggest that there is something autonomous about sexual relations. They are exempted from changes and developments in social institutions. This autonomous level is frequently explained in terms of male control or sexual antagonism which is elevated thereby to the status of a universal truth.

Patriarchy

Even where feminism has begun to develop its own terms, looking outside the traditional social sciences, the discussion frequently returns to this hopeless polarity. It is the term patriarchy which has been most widely used as the foundations for a specifically feminist investigation of sexual relations. Sometimes it is used casually, interchangeably with 'sexism', a reminder that there is one sex which dominates, another which is subjected. But patriarchy has also been advanced as a theoretical explanation for the subordination of women. It describes the political and social control of women by men. Here patriarchy promises both to deliver the history of the relations between the sexes and to explain the form and function of male domination.

A principle reason for the strength of the attraction of the concept of patriarchy is that it is a term with a history in those very theories which appear to be most important for feminism. Marxism talks of the crucial relation between patriarchy and private property. Psychoanalysis cites the history of the patriarchal family as the crucial condition in imposing reproductive sexual identity. Anthropology records the social and political dominance of men in numerous societies and asks whether or not some sort of patriarchy is inevitable. That the term should lie hidden in so many rich fields suggests that its excavation might solve the problem of the divergence between these three forms of explanation. It has been tempting to think that perhaps our inadequate means for understanding sexual relations occurs simply because we have lost or neglected a useful concept. The reinstatement of such a concept would perhaps supplement the inadequate analysis of sexual power in the various disciplines.

So far, however, the various explorations of the concept of patriarchy seem no better suited to avoiding the usual tussle over explanations of sexual relations. Patriarchy frequently comes under attack for implying pre-given sexual characteristics of men and women. It offers itself as an account of the history of sexual relations, but at a certain point the same question has to be asked; why was it men who took control and what were the interests thus served? These questions lead back with an unerring certainty to the same divisions; are there natural sexual differences in which the sexes have distinct interests? Or are sexual dispositions produced by the patriarchal structure itself? If so, how can patriarchy arise and then determine sexual forms if it is premised on sexual interests?

The concept of patriarchy, then, seems no more able to avoid the organising principles by which sex is dealt with by the social sciences. On the one hand, it is subject to the contesting explanations of essentialism and culturalism; on the other hand, a nebulous notion of social determination is often brought forward to try to counter the effects of this division. It is argued that patriarchal structures, being in existence for whatever reason, determine the interests of the sexes.

Confronted with this seemingly inevitable return to this theoretical impasse, we need to ask ourselves two questions. One is just exactly why the study of sexual relations, in a historically specific way, should be so fantastically difficult. Consequently, we need to ask a second question; is it theoretically necessary that any understanding of the relations between the sexes has to run aground on this seemingly impossible dilemma? In order to answer these questions, there are certain things we must know. One is whether the discourses which we have at our disposal have simply paid insufficient attention to the question of power between the sexes, and could be refined and improved upon to deliver an adequate account of sexual relations. If it is not the case that sexual relations have been neglected, then we need to understand the history of the way in which sexual relations have been studied. This is in order to understand whether the forms of explanation now in play are inevitable or have emerged for particular reasons.

The history of the study of sexual relations

My examination of the history of the study of sexual relations has produced a number of surprising results. It is clear that in spite of the multitude of ways in which 'sex' appears in a variety of discourses, there are nevertheless a number of different phenomena merged in this. Sex, sexuality, sexual relations and sexual division are different phenomena. Yet they appear in the social sciences, all merged together and therefore submerged under concepts like, 'the family', 'the household', 'reproduction', 'kinship' or 'sexual behaviour'. Disciplines which deal specifically with sexuality are arbitrarily excluded from the social sciences, designated 'ahistorical'.

The history behind the definitions of sex at play in each discourse and their rivalry with one another reveals another, yet more startling, fact. During the second half of the nineteenth century, a fierce and violent debate took place over the nature of sexual relations, the question of power between the sexes and the role of the family in relation to other social institutions. Crucial to this debate were the concepts of patriarchy and matriarchy. On the understanding of these terms hung a whole series of interpretations of social forms. The understanding of patriarchy became perhaps the key issue in studies of society during the second half of the nineteenth century.

It was during this debate that the theories and practices of marxism and psychoanalysis were formed. And it was in the course of this debate that the characteristic forms of sociology and 'modern anthropology' emerged. Looking back at these debates reveals startling phenomena; all the questions which exercise us now about the organisation of sexual relations, the history and function of the family were all asked at this earlier period. They were asked in crucially different ways. Nevertheless, there is an extraordinary familiarity about some of the issues, and it surely must be no coincidence that these debates occurred at precisely the moment when nineteenth-century feminism made its impact. These debates, and their influence on our contemporary formulations of the problems, are the subejct of this book. The history of these debates and the emergence of definite meanings and interpretations for the terms of 'sex', 'sexual relations', 'the patriarchal family', has important implications for our contemporary approach to the subject.

The subject of this book

Studies of society in the mid-nineteenth century were 'detonated' by evidence of the social organisation of 'primitive societies' being put to new uses. This evidence had long been available, but in this period it was mobilised specifically to put an end to a theory of social and political organisation, known as 'the patriarchal theory'. The new use of data from so-called primitive societies was motivated by several factors, including the emergence of evolutionary theories in natural history and a new imperative to investigate the forms of sexual organisation of non-Western societies.

Debates about social organisation, its history and function, crucially foregrounded the question of sexual and familial organisation. The question was whether other societies, and indeed whether Western society itself had ever been witness to an entirely different ordering of the relations between the sexes. Had it ever been the case that the patriarchal family, so much taken for granted as the fundamental social unit, had in fact not existed? This question provoked the most violent controversy. It engaged virtually every social theorist writing in the second half of the nineteenth century. It produced a mass of speculation not just on the history of the relations between the sexes, but also on the meanings of the different forms of sexual ordering which had been systematically recorded by anthropologists.

Marxism and psychoanalysis, both given certain credibility in our contemporary debates, were importantly influenced by these discussions on the transitions in sexual relationships.

Both theories drew on these debates in significant ways and indeed actively participated in the discussions. Engels, like most communists of this period, was vehement in his commitment to the idea of the universal precedence of matriarchal rule. Freud concocted his own variant of the history of patriarchy and made it central to his account of the development of the individual psyche. The so-called founding fathers of anthropology all speculated on what the history of sexual relations and sexual power within the family had been. Their debates and speculations fed numerous other discourses. Sexology, in the hands of Havelock Ellis, and sociological studies of households, were no less concerned with what had been the history of sexual organisations. Indeed, so general was the interest, so crucial was its answer considered, that it is by no means so easy to draw firm distinctions between these theories in the way it is easy to do so now. Our contemporary division between various disciplines, all appearing to tackle different aspects of the social formation, was partly decided by this debate.

It has been tempting to look at these discussions and conclude that there was a glorious moment when the study of sexual relations flowered, but was then repressed or neglected. Some contemporary feminist work has looked at these debates in this way. Certain theorists of this earlier period have been 'reclaimed'. Bachofen and Briffault, both great adherents to the idea of the historical primacy of matriarchy, have been revived and their work has been used as 'evidence'[3] for matriarchal societies. It is claimed that this evidence has simply been suppressed because of the male bias in subsequent anthropological and sociological theories.

But before leaping to such conclusions and attempting to revive these pieces of suppressed evidence, it is worth looking more closely at the context in which these ideas emerged, what exactly these ideas were, and why they were largely abandoned within studies of society. (Which is not to say that we may not have to return to some of the questions asked in these debates.) All the imaginable comments which we might make about the male bias in collecting and interpreting evidence were made in the context of that nineteenth-century debate. The criticisms were often brought by men determined to 'prove' the historical primacy of matriarchy.

It is important to look at this struggle over patriarchy and matriarchy because although sexual relations appears to have been absolutely central (obsessively so), in fact, I would argue that sexual relations, in the sense that they are interrogated by contemporary feminism, were not the real subject of these debates. The real subject was that of the nature of political and social alliances. The real question asked of the data on sexual and familial organisations was what function they fulfilled in relation to wider social bonds. The importance attributed to the first form of sexual organisation, and its subsequent development was in order to understand the place which sexual organisation had in forming alliances between individuals and groups. In this book, I argue that the reason why sexual organisation became so crucial was because of social and political developments of the time. The theories which emerged then fed back into social and political decision-making.

In this debate as to the nature of alliances between groups, the real subject was the contest over how to theorise the relationship between instinctual and culturally determined behaviour. Sexual relations were crucial in this because they were taken as existing on the border between 'nature' and 'society'. On the one hand, sexual behaviour was taken as belonging to the individual; on the other hand, sexual regulation, such as marriage and the family, was seen as a social institution. Sexual relations therefore become the point of contestation as to the relation between nature and culture.

Looking back to these debates within the nineteenth century, the function which sexual relations fulfilled becomes very clear. The arguments about matriarchy were brought forward to challenge the 'patriarchal' theory, a theory which had dominated social and political sciences for some time. This theory was displaced because of a growing space given to the question of the 'natural', a realm which was largely in abeyance in the patriarchal theory. The patriarchal theory assumed that the first forms of society were in essence the same as their contemporary forms, based on the same forms of power. The obsessive interest in the possibility of mother-right societies, or primitive promiscuity, was to bring forward for consideration a new space, the natural, in which sexual relations became the privileged object of study.

The debates which ensued engaged virtually all the leading theorists of the time: political conservatives, feminists and sexologists alike. Violent divisions occurred as to whether sexual relations were always already regulated (cultural) or had ever found free expression (natural). But, as will be argued in chapter 3, there was much that was just assumed in these studies about sexuality. In all the violent divisions, even the positions which argued vehemently for a pre-social free sexuality, it was never questioned that men and women were radically different creatures with definite interests. In general, these interests were seen as arising from the exigen-cies of reproduction. Nowhere can there be found the sort of deconstruction of sexual identity and interests which characterises the drive of contemporary feminism.

What is more, not only was sexual relations not the real subject of these debates but many of the presumptions made were, in hindsight, decidedly wild. That these debates bore speculation about society in general produced some strange convolutions. So central was sexuality that it was made to bear speculation in some theories about every social institution in existence. Anything and everything could be explained by the state of warfare between the sexes, the knowledge of paternity, the form of descent of a particular group.

Such was the state of speculation, so extreme were the hypotheses, that there gradually emerged a reaction to it, a reaction which called for detailed empirical knowledge of other societies. This reaction was motivated by a very proper distrust of 'the armchair ethnologists', the lawyers and social theorists who read 'voyage literature' and pro-duced wild speculations about the universal history of humanity based on the changes undergone by sexual rela-tions. In chapter 4 of this book the reasons for this reaction are discussed. Many of the criticisms made by emergent anthropology are still relevant for our own attempt to understand the historical construction of sexual relations. They warn against the uncritical use of generalisations, against facile constructions of a unilinear history, against simple equations between the state of organisation of one social form with the relations between the sexes. Nevertheless, we will see how this very necessary reaction in fact jettisoned a series of general questions. These were questions about the basis of unequal power between the sexes; the ways in which kinship or family might operate to construct or maintain these inequalities; the role of kinship in structuring reproduction, etc. In addition, we will see the way in which sexuality was confirmed as belonging to the 'individual' and therefore 'natural' realm, through a suspension of certain forms of speculation on the family. The developments within anthropology are to some extent, therefore, taken as representative of general developments within social theories. We see the assumption of sex as individual and natural; we see the refusal of questions of determination of social relations; at the same time we see the acceptance of a diffuse causality, where some aspects of society are seen as determinant and others as determined. We begin to see in other words, why those people who have sought to explain the position of women by reference to general theories have been forced to use theories which remain marginal to social sciences, in particular marxism and psychoanalysis.

The final four chapters therefore examine marxism and psychoanalysis to see whether, indeed, these theories do escape some of the problems described. Both theories are important for understanding the position of women. Marxism insists on developing a theory of the inequalities between groups in a rigorously deterministic way. Psychoanalysis insists on deconstructing the 'naturalness' of 'sexed identity'. Yet it will be shown that both these theories used aspects of the debate outlined earlier. The patriarchal family was a crucial term for both and both participated in the debates already discussed. This is the reason why reclaiming them from a feminist perspective has seemed so appealing. However, the examination which follows will show how both theories in fact mobilised the notion of the family to fulfil other theoretical requirements internal to their own problematics. Ironically, within marxism, the fact that the family was both central and vital *and* was the point where women

were theorised meant that women, in fact, could be subsumed to other theoretical and political objectives.

With psychoanalysis, the commitment to the history of
the patriarchal family compromised the more radical aspects
of the theory and led orthodox psychoanalysis to posit a
real nuclear family as universally present behind all cultural
complexes. Psychoanalysis therefore placed itself in direct
opposition to the necessary criticism of universal hypotheses
described in chapter 4. For this reason, psychoanalysis has
been regarded with deep distrust by those social theories
which attempt to deal with specific cultures and not resort
to wild generalisations about the history of humanity.

The final chapter discusses the relationship between
psychoanalysis and anthropology as exemplary of the conflict between general explanations of sexual relations and
the 'culturalism' which came to dominate the social sciences,
in reaction to the earlier wild hypotheses. This conflict was
the inevitable outcome of the developments described in this
book. It is the same conflict with which this introduction
started, the conflict between explanations which claim universal validity and those which insist on historical and cultural
specificity. In this book it will be shown that this sterile
outcome was not necessary. It happened because sex and
sexual relations came to be thought of in very definite ways.
Once this had happened there was a certain amount of justification in the positions taken by either side. The one option
that was never taken, or never followed through, was that of
deconstruction the idea of the 'given-ness' of sexual identity.
Even psychoanalysis was forced, through internal theoretical
requirements, to insist on universal forms of the family.

The debates traced in this book show how we have come
to think about sexual relations. It shows how our understanding has been inhibited by a hopeless polarity between
forms of explanation – on the one hand, universal and
therefore essentialising claims, and on the other hand, a form
of culturalism which suspends any general investigation of
how and why sexual relations take the form they do. The
book will show how this polarity is sustained by a number of
theoretical assumptions. There is a theoretical division
between individual and society, in which sexuality is ascribed

to the individual and sexual relations to the social. There is an acceptance of a diffuse causality by which some social practices are considered determinant, some determined. Through this causality, any investigation which insists on analysing the specific dynamic of sexuality has been accused of not analysing the 'real material' causes, an accusation which has been made very virulently by marxists. Finally, there is a failure to deconstruct given assumptions about sexual identity, a failure which is marked by the way in which there has been little clarification of the various terms in play. Sex, sexuality, sexual identity, sexual divisions, and sexual relations are often simply run together as being the same phenomenon. This has added to the difficulty of producing accounts of transitions and functions of sexual forms in a non-essentialist way.

The aim of this book, then, is to clarify the history of how we think about sexual relations. It shows how many of our concerns are not new. The problems and limitations of some of these terms are still relevant. Uncovering the history of these debates has a purpose. It stands as a warning that, if any advances are to be made in understanding sexual relations in society, dominant ways of thinking about them have to be displaced. It is not a matter of supporting one form of explanation against another until everyone realises its advantages. The conceptualisation of sex, sexual relations and sexuality has been structured around some dominant presuppositions. The displacement of these would clearly have radical implications for our whole understanding of society.

1 The dissolution of the patriarchal theory

Introduction

Patriarchy has long been an important object of social and political theory. In the second half of the nineteenth century, however, discussions about patriarchy became particularly intense. In the 1860s the study of comparative law became the privileged object of social and political theory. It involved the comparative study of ancient law and the law of extant 'primitive' societies. This way of studying other societies and their implications for the history of Western society transformed existing political theories. It ushered in a highly controversial debate about the earliest forms of the family, their transformations and their functions in relation to other aspects of the social structure. In these debates, our sociological and anthropological notions of the family were formed. It was also here that crucial conceptions of the family and sexual relations were formed for marxism and psychoanalysis.

Henry Maine's *Ancient Law*, published in 1861, established the method of comparative law at the heart of studies of social and political organisation. Maine set out to demonstrate the historical variability of legal and therefore social practices, in particular, variability in property relations. The lynch-pin of his argument was, however, the family: the study of the changes in family forms would reveal the dynamic of all social development. From his study of the ancient law of the Romans, the Slavs and the northern Indians he deduced that the patriarchal family was the fundamental and universal unit of human society. The history of this 'original grouping' would reveal the history of wider social alliances and ultimately explain the emergence of the nation state. Typically, the family and its implications for the sexual ordering of society, was not the true subject of the debate started by Maine's claim. The family was the vehicle for speculation about the forms of, and determinants on, wider social relations.

Maine's *Ancient Law* was a critical moment for the social sciences. It marked the summation of ideas about the patriarchal family which had dominated political theory throughout the seventeenth and eighteenth centuries. But it also represented a methodological and theoretical approach which would ultimately overturn the last lingering traces of this political theory. For at the very moment when Maine advanced his ideas about the changes undergone by legal and property relations in the patriarchal family his own methods were applied to subvert his hypothesis. Theorists applied Maine's method to long-available data about societies which 'perversely' organised family and descent through women: so-called mother-right societies. This application challenged Maine's hypothesis about the original form of society. A new possibility had been opened. It became possible to think that the relations between the sexes characteristic of the patriarchal family had, in fact, undergone very drastic changes during the course of human history.

The systematisation of evidences against the universality and primacy of the patriarchal family provoked a series of violent debates. Controversy broke out over the original form of sexual and familial forms. In these debates an obsessive centrality was given to the organisation of sexual relations, and their interaction both with family forms and with other social alliances. This challenge to the patriarchal theory generated questions which dominated studies of society for many subsequent decades. The outcome of these divisions and debates has decided what terms are available to us in which to think about sexual relations, family or kinship relations and their interaction with other social practices. The social and political determinants on this debate will be examined in chapter 2. The remainder of this chapter will show the way in which mother-right societies became so crucial to social theory. It shows the way in which patriarchal theory was superseded by theories demanding to know the meaning of mother-right societies, and what light their existence shed on the history of social organisations.

Comparative jurisprudence and the patriarchal theory

Political theory had long been linked to accounts of other, non-European societies, usually culled from travellers' tales and cosmographies. It has even been suggested that the type of society encountered in expanding colonisation played an important part in the kind of social theory which emerged. Many seventeenth- and eighteenth-century writings displayed knowledge of social forms already 'discovered'. Some of these accounts were also primarily interested in the 'state of morals' of particular societies, that is, the position of women or marriage customs.[1] In general, however, most social theories which drew on early studies of other societies were primarily concerned with the origins of political sovereignty, the emergence of royal or political power and how it was exercised over subjects.

Maine's comparative law displayed a number of very different concerns from its predecessors, even from those which had made the patriarchal family central as source of social contract.[2] There were several reasons for Maine's shift of focus to the patriarchal family as the clue to the entire development of human history and different social organisations. One reason was that previous theories had operated with an idea that not only there had been a state of 'pre-social' mankind, but that some 'primitive' people still characterised that phase. But this proposition had, by the time of Maine, become virtually untenable. Excavations in France seemed to establish irrefutable evidence for a general stone age of humanity. Paleontologists officially accepted these findings in 1858, accepting the extraordinary antiquity of human society. Such conclusions could only destroy the probability that any group of people now extant still lived in a pre-social state. In addition, the possibility of a confident universally applicable theory as to the origins of all peoples from one group was dissolving under the evidence of the multiplicity of racial groups systematically recorded (and in some cases wiped out) by European imperialism. The previous century had seen the emergence of theoretical explanations of these differences in terms of geographical and climatic regions, and technical modes of production.[3] This form of theory made it possible to confront these differences *as* differences.

Perhaps, however, the most immediate condition for Maine's work was the consolidation of European rule over large areas of India. One of the first consequences of the declaration of formal rule was the discovery by the imperialist regime that the dominant civilisation was not only rigidly patriarchal but was also very ancient. Yet this observation was limited to a definite area, northern India, for resistance to European imperialism had been fiercest in the north. As a result, the societies of that part attracted more attention in the West, overshadowing the peaceful matrilineal societies of southern India.

The significance of the northern societies was that they gave new and seemingly vital evidence of the legal structures of human society. The study seemed to confirm that the patriarchal family was the fundamental unit of ancient society, a deduction fed by the legal similarities between the Romans, Hebrews, Slavs and Arabs. Now the ancient law of the Indians, 'seemed to justify the belief which had always remained popular in Europe, that the primitive state of man had been neither pre-social nor nasty and brutish at all; but in the best sense, "very good".'[4] Even at the time of writing, however, it was noticed that Maine's type of comparative study of law was confined to Indo-European groups.[5] Not only were the people of the same 'stock', but at the periods under consideration they had shared the same pastoral mode of subsistence.

Despite the local limitations of comparative law, at the time it was greeted enthusiastically. Its detailed attention to ancient law seemed to supply gaps in previous social and political theory. For it marked the consolidation of a historical method able to reach beyond what had been documented. Ultimately, it was this very method which was used to destroy the aims of the patriarchal theory. It was used to expose the fact that the patriarchal theory was only applicable to certain areas and certain modes of subsistence.

The patriarchal theory

The effect of the evidence derived from comparative law, wrote Maine,'is to establish the view of the primitive condition of the human race which is known as the Patriarchal Theory'.[6] The patriarchal family could now be proved to be the primitive social bond. Maine's investigation went far beyond previous speculation on the patriarchal family as a source of sovereignty in a society based on a contract between individuals. It constructed a general history of the origins of society.

The history which Maine outlined was based on 'the hints which are given us by legal antiquities'.[7]. These hints revealed to Maine that it was far from the case that the patriarchal family had always existed in a form identical to that which was known by his contemporaries. Instead, ancient law seemed to demonstrate that early society had been organised according to very different principles. In the ancient society of all the cultures studied, law specified 'status', the duties and obligations of the legal subjects. Modern law, on the contrary, specifies 'contracts' between 'free' individuals. The formulation of this difference was based on one 'discovery': that the basic unit of ancient law was the family and not the individual. The family was a legal subject. Rights and status were given within the family. This was the core of Maine's interest in the patriarchal family and the light it might shed on primitive history. His was not a defence of the naturalness of this family, but an interest in the complex, strange and 'artificial' system of legal statuses, defining rights, duties and inheritance.

In its simplest form, the *earlier* patriarchial theory had represented society simply as an enlargement of the primary family. The primary family, the father, mother and children under the authority and protection of the father gradually expanded as children married, extending the family group to include more distant relatives. While the first father lived, all such groups remained under his authority, but on his death, his descendants would naturally divide into as many families as he had sons and offspring. Each group would resemble the original group absolutely, as a collection of individuals connected by common descent, living under the authority of their common progenitor.

This theory was thought to offer an explanation of the development of wider social groupings — of society itself. First, it could explain the phenomenon of large tribes with overall allegiance to the first father and, over subsequent generations, the descendants of the first father might constitute many tribes and be the population of a large country. These tribes, being united by ties of blood, so the theory ran, would readily act together for common purposes. Gradually, as 'civilisation' advanced, they would come together to form some central government to facilitate action. In this way they would become a nation.

Maine saw no reason to challenge the naturalness of the patriarchal family in so far as he saw no reason to dispute the natural authority of the patriarch over the family. But he saw the realm of natural authority as separate from the household as legal entity. Early family organisation he claimed had been 'complex, artificial and strange'. The early family was based on the recognition of the household, held together by definite rules of descent. Maine suggested that this family was not based on the natural rights of first progenitor but on a cohesion based on the patriarch's power and authority.

The crucial term in the construction of such a group was the father's power, *patria potestas.* According to this, the bonds constituting family ties, that is, kinship, were arbitrary. The group 'is held to be related to him and to one another, not so much because of their being of his blood as because of their common subjection to his power'.[8] Thus 'the family would as readily include slaves and those adopted as it would exclude women who were blood relations'. This claim was based on his study of the form of descent operative in these ancient societies. This system of descent was called *agnation*; descent (i.e. who someone was deemed to be related to) and inheritance passed exclusively through men, excluding all women. Once a woman married, she came under the power of another patriarch and became a member of another patriarchal family.

Maine, then, was interested in demonstrating the arbitrary basis of kinship. He asserted that the family was not a biological unit, but a unit which created a fiction of biological unity. This could be proved by the existence of agnation, or patriarchal descent. The unit was held together by the dominance of one strong male, an undisputed fact, which would explain the form of descent. Commentators at the time[9] recognised the circularity of Maine's argument; the power of the father had to be assumed to explain the existence of agnation, but agnation is used to prove the previous and universal existence of patriarchal power.

Leaving aside this circularity for the moment, what is important to stress is that Maine was interested in the patriarchal family as a system of government and property holding. This view of the patriarchal family was logically coherent with his ideas on the functioning of a social group as subjects submitting to power. Society is seen as a series of concentric circles under the same power, sovereign patriarchal power. He has, however, added another element to this study of the patriarchal family. He concludes that kinship (that is, modes of reckoning relationships) is not based on blood, but is arbitrary and follows the formation of political groupings.

Maine's ideas on the patriarchal family and its clues as to the 'complex governmental' nature of early society were deduced from the discovery of the household as legal entity. It was this discovery, above all, which was followed up by numerous theorists of society. It generated a mass of work which has been crucial to the development of studies of kinship and the family. This is because Maine's comparative jurisprudence established a way of examining the interrelation between family forms and forms of property relations. It was the very movement which constructed the historical study of kinship which gave rise to the historical study of property relations and their possible variations.

Comparative law made it clear that laws on property had been completely different in earlier social organisations, and it was this difference which separated the ancient patriarchal family from our own.

This proposition was very different from the assumption to be found in both Locke and Hobbes that at the origins of society, the earth belonged to all. For in these earlier theories, the assumption had been that the absence of property relations is synonymous with a pre-social state. Locke had reacted against the idea that property had its origins either in the divine sovereignty of church, or the sovereignty of the conqueror. He had propounded a theory of individual work at the origin of all appropriation, and therefore property. Appropriation was the effect of the free exercise of individual creativity. Such theories had assumed certain transhistorical features in the form of holding property. Against this, comparative jurisprudence argued that the legal forms of holding property had undergone transformations in the course of the development of society. The study of kinship and household undertaken by comparative jurisprudence took a very particular form. For it appeared in the context of the consolidation of the imperative within social sciences to understand early history as a developmental process of technical stages to which correspond a series of 'superstructural' elements, like law, property, religion, morality, etc.

Maine's study of the patriarchal family was concerned as much with this historical study of property as with a simple defence of the universality of the patriarchal family. The patriarchal family was of such significance for Maine because it furnished an example of a form of collective possession.

Writers like Fustel de Coulanges, Frederick Le Play, Bogišić Lavalaye, and Kovalevsky all employed Maine's approach to history and ancient law.[10] It opened up new areas for historical and anthropological investigations, and the effects of these studies remain with us today, especially within sociological studies of the family. All, in various ways, wrote influential studies of the forms of property holding and household organisation in Indo-European history. Many were influential in the formation of policy towards the family.

All were fascinated by the 'discovery' of the European extended family with its forms of collective possession. The *zadruga* household of contemporary Yugoslavia was taken to be an extant example and became a particular favourite. Bogišić demonstrated how the early *zadruga* households were characterised by absolute dominance of patriarchal authority but collective possession by the household. No one member of the family could destroy the collective legal entity of the household.

Frederick Le Play uncovered similar legal forms of property holding in the French rural family. He used his findings to berate public policy which encouraged the modern small family and thereby undermined patriarchal authority and the stability of the household. The patriarchal authority of the 'stem-family', where the household remained the property of the family, was seen as ensuring peace, respect and obedience.

Bogišić and Le Play characterise the impact of comparative law within the social sciences; the object of attention was the 'household' and forms of property holding; its sustaining fantasy was the universal precedence of the patriarchal household, characterised by collective possession. But if the methodology of Maine was typical of social studies, his conclusions on the history of kinship came under violent attack. For Maine's ideas were based on several definite assumptions: the political dominance of one strong male; the complex 'governmental' nature of early society; and the stability of human nature. But in spite of this commitment to several universalising assumptions, Maine himself was slightly cautious about their universal applicability. 'The difficulty at the present stage of enquiry', he wrote, 'is to know where to stop to say of what races of men it is not allowable to lay down that the society in which they are united was originally organised in the patriarchal model.'[11]

The dispossession of the patriarchal theory

Maine's caution was indeed justified, for at the time of writing those words, the strongest challenges to the local limitations of the patriarchal theory were mounted. These challenges formulated an altogether different interpretation of familial relations which will be explored shortly.

Maine has often been characterised as having championed not only the primacy but also the naturalness of the patriarchal family. We have seen that, on the contrary, Maine actually described the patriarchal family as a complex and artificial unit with a governmental function. It was aspects of these *political* assumptions about social group which came under attack when non-patriarchal family organisations were scrutinised. What became problematic was the historical primacy of the patriarchal unit, and the primacy of the complex and governmental over the simple and 'organic'. The effect of this problematisation was to expose difficulties in the theorisation of the relation between familial forms and the political organisation of society.

If the dominance of the patriarchal theory for fifty years had owed its existence in part to the European imperial regime in northern India, the overthrow of this theory happened for at least some similar reasons. Superficially, it appeared to owe its decline to the expansion of the colonialising movement which marked the century from 1760 to 1860. This expansion involved the systematic recording of familial organisations which at first sight bore no real resemblance to the legal and statutory organisations of the patriarchal family. These were societies where descent was reckoned either exclusively or predominantly through the mother. A child took its name and kin allegiance either from his mother or her tribe. Moreover, in some of these societies, paternity was neither reckoned nor considered particularly significant.

It would be easy to demonstrate that knowledge of such societies had been available to Europeans for many years.[12] The availability of such information suggests the need to look elsewhere for the origins of the new interest in mother-right societies. Indeed, the stimulus to such studies clearly has correspondences with other theoretical and social preoccupations of the time which will become clear in subsequent chapters. These coincided with the impact of the expansion of colonialism. British administration had been extended over the non-Aryan south of India, and it was here that

British administration found itself confronted with types of societies which showed the profoundest disrespect for patriarchal family organisation.

This colonial 'problem' focused attention on a form of family organisation which was apparently common throughout south-east Asia:[13]

> Like the Lycians of Herodotus, these perverse people
> called themselves after their mother's names: they
> honoured their mother and neglected their father,
> in society and government, as well as in their homes;
> their administration, their law and their whole mode of
> life rested on the assumption that it was the women and
> not the men in whom reposed the continuity of the
> family and the authority to govern the state.

Later research suggests that this family organisation did not in fact correspond to a matriarchal inversion of patriarchal structures. But the attention drawn to these south-east Asian family forms led to the systematisation of reports of similar, non-patriarchal family forms, which had been proliferating over previous years. These south-east Asian families had been recorded since the days of Tavernier in Borneo (1676) and Laval in the Maldive Islands (1679).[14] There was also evidence that this type of family was not confined to one geographical area. Lafitau, in his highly influential book, *Les Moeurs de Sauvage Ameriquains comparées aux moeurs des Premiers temps*, had pointed to the prevalence of these forms amongst the Iroquois Indians. But it was Buchanan's account of the Nairs of the Malabar coast, written in 1807, which first attracted serious attention.[15] Here was a highly complex social form, of a highly sophisticated people in the very same country as the family organisation which had provided material for the patriarchal theory.

Buchanan's account was followed by a mass of similar evidence which came pouring in during the generation that followed, partly as a result of a systematic search through the accounts of the old travellers, but mainly through the exploitation of large areas of the world by European traders and colonists. Conspicuous amongst these was the 'rediscovery' of accounts of western and equatorial Africa, collected by Pinkerton in 1808.[16] This revival was accompanied by new material, mainly from southern Africa, which arrived in proportion to the increased activities of colonialists — bureaucrats, missionaries or explorers.[17] A mass of literature on America began to be written, most of which seemed to challenge the patriarchal theory.[18]

Significant too in the systematisation of attention to this data of 'primitive' peoples was the European colonisation of the Pacific peoples.[19] Here was a chance of studying humanity in truly 'primitive' conditions since the Pacific peoples, unlike the Americans, had not yet been 'spoilt' by their contact with Europeans. Australian family organisation also attracted attention; it was argued that there were some groups who observed neither paternal nor maternal obligations of kinship as they had been traditionally understood.

In the context of such evidence, it is not altogether surprising that almost simultaneous with the publication of Maine's *Ancient Law*, there appeared a spate of books arguing either against the patriarchal theory or in favour of serious attention to the meaning of what were designated 'mother-right' societies. Bachofen's *Das Mutter-recht* appeared in 1861, McLennan's *Primitive Marriage* in 1865, Lubbock's *Prehistoric Times* 1874, Tylor's *Primitive Culture* 1871, Post's *The Evolution of Human Marriage* 1875, and Morgan's *Ancient Society* 1877. To place these books in the context of imperial expansion and the systematisation of information on other populations and societies is not to reduce their appearance to the fact of increased information. For what *is* surprising is that evidence which had been available for some time acquired a new significance. The mode of systematising information and the kinds of objects of inquiry have forceful correspondences with other themes in discussion at that time and with political circumstances.

These books combined to usher in several decades of debate about the 'meaning' of marriage forms of different societies. They varied in their approach and conclusions. Some, like Morgan's *Ancient Society*, were informed by a close and detailed study of 'primitive' peoples. Others, like Bachofen's *Das Mutter-recht*, were more in the tradition of the study of classical myth and religion. Many were like

McLennan's *Primitive Marriage* and Lubbock's *Prehistoric Times*, that is, more or less philosophic speculation on the history of human societies, based on close study of ancient legal forms and 'voyager' evidence of primitive customs. They shared certain common features, however, enough for them to be recognised as the foundations of anthropology as a discipline.

These books are often grouped together under the blanket term of evolutionism — a concern with the way in which forms evolve from simple to complex. And indeed this period did see the diffusion of Darwin's conclusions for biology across a series of other areas of thought. Blistering attacks were delivered on Maine's theories precisely because the assumption of a primary, complex and artificial form of family at the origin of human society seemed to fly in the face of evolutionary notions.[20] Quite apart from the evidence of mother-right societies, Maine's complex family could only appear as a wild flight of fantasy from a Darwinian perspective:[21]

> the family held together by Power, with blood relationship recognised in it only to be ignored — no relationship at all through women acknowledged, no relationship through males acknowledged except in males subject to their father's Power and between those subject to that Power, a relationship equally close whether they are related by blood or not — the Power too, extending to life and death and sale, and grown up sons meekly submitting to it — propounded to us as the first form of the family, might as well be deemed — apart from the evidence — a mere fantastic imagination.

From the perspective of biological evolutionism, assumptions of legal forms and fictions, complex relations of power and subjection, political organisations at the origins of society, all seemed unthinkable. Nature seemed to insist that the complex emerged from the simple. 'Can anyone believe excepting for convincing reasons, that such a group as this was elementary and primordial?'[22] And with the proliferation of studies of non-patriarchal societies even evidence was now hard to obtain.

This attack on the artificial, complex and political nature of patriarchal theory spearheaded the attack on Maine's originary hypotheses. The coincidence of Darwinian theory; the culmination of the 'historisation' of early mankind; and the systematisation of evidence of non-patriarchal organisations all lent support to its overthrow. But the term 'evolutionism' is far too general to account adequately for this attack. It does not cover the very different forms of causality and explanation mobilised, and so cannot show what was at issue in the overthrow of the patriarchal theory.

In fact, various writers differed about the basis on which a society could be designated simple or complex. For example, was it a designation based on sexual morality or technical competence? They differed about how to make comparisons between different societies and what criteria were appropriate to make these comparisons, for example, race, psychological characteristics or technological developments. Finally, they offered very different arguments about *how* the complex evolves from the simple. However, at this stage most *did* share a general acceptance that some non-European societies could be taken as evidence of the early history of human society, and used the term 'primitive' to designate these societies in a way that was synonymous with 'simple'.

The identity between these writers is more correctly represented as a series of shared concerns, some of which differ from Maine only in conclusions. Foremost in these is an approach to history. Comparative jurisprudence had established that legal practices could explain something of society in its entirety — perhaps its history, perhaps its internal dynamic. The evolutionists insisted that all symbols — customs, rituals, language, etc. — expressed their history. From behind these practices it would be possible to bring to light the origins and history of certain institutions. It was for the philosopher or ethnologist to seek behind symbolism to theorise this history.

What became crucial in this reconsideration of history was the issue of mother-right, and the apparent sexual inversion at the origin of history. The debate over mother-right became the focus for a number of concerns. What was the nature of kinship, if not understood as Maine's artifical and complex legal bond? How was kinship determined? Did it involve relations of power between the sexes? How had sexual behaviour changed? Three writers, often recognised as the founding 'fathers' of contemporary anthropology, turned almost simultaneously to the same questions. Bachofen, McLennan and Morgan were all preoccupied with the evidence of kinship reckoned through the mother. All were convinced that this previously neglected data offered lessons of enormous consequence for the understanding of society.

Primitive matriarchy

Bachofen's *Das Mütter-recht* (*Mother-right*) differs from its predecessors not because it was an evolutionist text (Bachofen had, in fact, never read Darwin), but because it attributed an absolute centrality to transitions in forms of sexual and marriage regulations. The state of relations between the sexes were seen by Bachofen to determine all aspects of cultural life.

Bachofen combined a detailed scrutiny of the classics with evidence from so-called primitive societies to produce a hypothesis on early forms of sexual regulation which was in complete and utter contradiction to the patriarchal theory. From both these sources, Bachofen glimpsed signs of a hidden history, that of historical struggle between the sexes. First of all, there was evidence that there had once been a stage where women had occupied a position in society which men now occupy. This could be gleaned from 'historical' accounts in the classics — the ubiquitous Lycians and the Ancient Britons mentioned by Caesar. Secondly, Bachofen argued that classical literature and myth could be treated as a form of evidence, both because they were written within a historical context and therefore described actual customs and because texts could be interpreted as revealing certain hidden preoccupations.

From this perspective, Bachofen analysed Aeschylus' *Eumenides* as the record of a historic struggle between two orders, the older rule of mother-right versus the new rule of patriarchy. Orestes murders his mother Clytemnestra in revenge for her having killed his father Agamemnon.

31

over the right; that the moon took precedence over the sun. All are taken as evidence of an older order, an 'original mode of life', whose traces cannot be fully suppressed. Bachofen insists that all these traces in mythology 'are the necessary characteristics of a matriarchal age'. What is more, 'in view of the universal qualities of human nature, this cultural stage cannot be restricted to any particular ethnic family'.[23]

Bachofen deduces a universal phase of mother-right, prior to that of the patriarchal system. The principles represented by the matriarchal system were viciously suppressed by the paternal system. Bachofen suggests that these two forms of social organisation are radically different and their difference arises from the difference between maternal and paternal love. The maternal principle expresses the physical and material nature of women's capacity to give birth and love their offspring. It requires no intellectuality: 'the mother's connection with the child is based on material relation. It is accessible to sense perception and remains always a natural truth.'[24] The maternal principle is also religious and universalistic. It is religious because of women's natural concern with the supernatural and the miraculous, with the divine and irrational. It is universalistic as the mother's love is for all children; it partakes of 'the undifferentiated unity of the mass'.[25]

To specify a relationship with the mother does not need abstract reasoning. But a relationship with the father is of an entirely different order. It involves abstract reasoning to say, 'This child towards which I feel no sensuous connection, is mine.' The father, 'standing in no visible relation to the child' can never, 'even in the marital relation, cast off a certain fictive character'.[26] This leads Bachofen to suggest that recognition of paternity entails an advance in the capacity of thought. In place of sensual perception and lack of differentiation, there is the triumph of the spirit and the intellect. The triumph of paternity brings with it liberation of the spirit from the manifestations of nature, a triumph of human existence over the laws of material life. This 'triumph of paternity' gives to humanity its specific quality. The maternal principle is in operation for all animals. For mankind alone, there is the advance in spiritual and intellectual life based on

(Clytemnestra had lamented the sacrifice of their daughter and in Agamemnon's absence had taken a lover with whom she plotted the murder.) Orestes is pursued by the furies after his mother's murder, and Bachofen takes them to represent maternal rule. In the ensuing court case, Orestes is defended by Athene and Apollo and is eventually aquitted. Athene was the goddess born directly from Jupiter's head, and she therefore represents, for Bachofen, patriarchal rule. Orestes' acquittal is taken as a record of a historic triumph, that of patriarchy. Such traces, together with the general harshness of patriarchal rule, are evidence of a struggle for the overthrow of mother-right.

Bachofen finds his hypothesis confirmed by practices among contemporary 'primitives'. He examined the practice of the *couvade*, destined to become a point of obsessive interest in following debates. This practice involved the simulation by the father of certain features of pregnancy during the time of the mother giving birth. These ranged from lying-in, the father taking to his bed, to more extreme demonstrations of the pain of labour. Again Bachofen thought that these practices, were symbolic of a struggle which had taken place in human history, bearing witness to a transition from mother-right to father-right. He interpreted the *couvade* as the father taking symbolic possession of the offspring, a ritual act designed to deprive the mother of her former, absolute rights over the child.

All these practices were taken as manifestations of primitive thinking. They were survivals, more than spontaneous and impenetrable productions of strange people. Symbolic forms, myths, were to be analysed, to be penetrated, to find their real meaning. The problem was to uncover what had been suppressed, to follow the distortions of history and to trace the elements of primitive thought which could not be eradicated from mythology. The historical problem was to establish a causality for the present system.

Bachofen's reading of mythology pointed to one conclusion. There was incontrovertible evidence of a stage where societies had been governed by principles the exact opposite of our own. Thus evidence that ancient rites took place at night; that in former times the left hand took precedence the recognition of paternity. Recognition of paternity liberates mankind's higher aspirations, that is, spiritual or intellectual aspirations based on the possibility of differentiation and identity which overcomes the sensuous.

Thus Bachofen deduces a history of human development in utter contradiction to the patriarchal theory. This history, apparently so extraordinary, required explanation. There must have been something which gave women the advantage in early history for them to occupy so unnatural a role. To account for this, Bachofen suggests a phase of primitive promiscuity, what he calls hetaerism. If paternity was not recognised then, it must have been impossible to recognise it. Only the impossibility of knowing with certainty would have prevented men from establishing their 'rights' to their genetic offspring. In such a context, women would have sought to be elevated, not just because their relation to their offspring was 'natural truth', but because of women's religious natures. The emergence of mother-right then is seen as 'the origin of all culture, of every virtue of every nobler aspect of existence': 'Woman at this stage is the repository of all culture, of all benevolence of all devotion, of all concern for the living and grief for the dead.'[27] But this maternal love is only a beginning. It is loving based on the extension of physical connection.

The real triumph of humanity is when love can be based on intellectual appreciation, embodied in the love a father can have for his child. This is the prototype for the altruism at the basis of civilisation. It is the form of love which defines allegiance to family, to the state and to the nation.

Das Mütter-recht was based on unquestioned assumptions about different sexual characteristics, embodied in different parental feelings. Moreover, it assumed that evidence of different forms of symbolism was evidence of a culture based on sexual inversion and none other. It is not clear, for example, why different symbols might not arise from any social practice radically different from Bachofen's own culture. What is intriguing about his book is that it is the first systematic appearance of the insistence of the immense significance of transitions in sexual organisation for the history of humanity. Bachofen mobilises a tradition of romanticism where men and women are presumed to have radically different interests and where women represent nature.[28] He transforms these themes into an evolutionary account of the history of humanity. Literary though his work was, it typified the concentration on transformations in early sexual customs as the principle clue to the history of humanity.

'Survivals'

J. F. McLennan wrote at exactly the same time as Bachofen, though they were unaware of each other. He also aimed to destroy the argument which placed government by the father at the dawn of human history. He too suggested an evolutionary process whereby the patriarchal family was seen as the outcome of a long journey through many transitions of human sexual relations. McLennan's source of information was, like Maine's, that of legal codes and practices. He also added the study of contemporary customs, like the father giving away his daughter in marriage. From an evolutionary perspective, these practices could be related to those of 'primitive' cultures to form a picture of the earliest universal forms of marriage. 'We can trace everywhere, disguised under a variety of forms in the higher layers of civilisation, the rude modes of life and forms of law with which the examination of the lower cultures makes us familiar.'[29]

Typical of this period, the argument is that custom and law could be interpreted. They would reveal a hidden history; 'the symbolism of law in the light of knowledge of primitive life is the best key to unwritten history'.[30] These forms of representation were vehicles to be deciphered. Elsewhere, Tylor was calling them 'survivals',[31] revealing either a past event or past function which had survived into contemporary times.

For McLennan, one custom stood out as the key to the stages of progress in human civilisation. As with Bachofen, marriage and sexual relations furnish the key. 'There is no symbol more remarkable', wrote McLennan, 'than that of capture in marriage ceremonies.'[32] He included in this symbol not only the custom of mock capture of the bride by the bridegroom at a wedding, but also the payment of dowry, and indeed the contemporary custom of the bride being given away by the father. Perhaps most significantly, McLennan also included in this list, the almost general custom of prohibitions on marriage between close relatives and its concomitant practice of marrying outside your own group. He termed this practice of marrying outside the close kin group, 'exogamy' a term which has remained crucial in the development of anthropology. He thought all these customs added up to evidence for a time when women had been literally captured. This was his clue to the whole history of sexual and therefore social organisation.

From this evidence of a common past, presumptions about the state of early society could be elaborated. An extraordinary practice like capturing wives had to have some material cause. McLennan suggested that in early human groups the capture of women from other, perhaps inimical, groups was necessitated by the scarcity of women. He hypothesised, in order to support this, that the practice of female infanticide, of which there were a few extant reports, had been widely practised at the origins of human life.

To account for this practice, McLennan suggests that early society was characterised by a state of permanent warfare between neighbouring groups. Drawing on an unquestioned assumption about the weakness of women, he suggests that the presence of women would be a source of vulnerability so that in spite of their later usefulness, tribes might practice female infanticide. When the time came, the same tribe would be forced to capture wives from other tribes. McLennan does not feel the need to address the illogicality that the lack of women and the need to capture them from other tribes might prove a greater source of vulnerability and conflict than the tribe's own offspring. The improvidence of 'savages' is, after all, too well known to need explanation: 'we have only to bear in mind the multitude of facts which testify to the thoughtlessness and improvidence of men during the childish stage of the human mind.'[33] This lack of foresight would lead to the murder of female children which would cause an imbalance in numbers and enforce marriage by capture. Thus the 'strange' practices of 'primitives' or customary survivals such as incest-prohibition in our own culture could be explained as derivations from this early state of human society. Gradually, as more permanent alliances between groups were formed, the need for female infanticide and therefore marriage by capture disappeared, but the habit, so deeply ingrained, remained. The first development from marriage by capture was marriage by purchase where, with the growth of private property, it became possible to buy a wife rather than capture one. Second, exogamy was inscribed as a political practice as a means of alliance with other groups.

For McLennan, the clue furnished by these various marriage practices was a clue to the whole history of the development of sexual regulation, and hence, in a movement characteristic of all these writers, society in general. For the clue of marriage by capture was accompanied by other strange hints of early social forms: mother-right societies. Like Bachofen, McLennan focused on the scattered evidence of these societies as phenomena of immense significance in the history of human development. Unlike Bachofen, however, he did not presume that descent through the mother presupposed power invested in women as mothers. Joined with the hypotheses formed on evidence of marriage by capture they seemed to provide a complete account of the earliest forms of human organisation.

Descent reckoned through the mother could mean only one thing. It pointed to a stage of human existence where paternity was both unknown and unknowable. Such a form of reckoning descent would only be admitted if there was no other way of guaranteeing parenthood, that is paternity. Kinship reckoned through fathers would only become a system when paternity could be guaranteed. For what possible interest, so ran the argument, could fathers have in offspring which were not genetically their own stock? These factors pointed to the necessary deduction of a state of sexual and proprietorial communism. How could an offspring not know its father unless the practice of marriage relations was so loose that no certainty could be guaranteed? There were neither ideas of monogamy (the only state that could guarantee paternity) nor of individual property, (a state which would have lead to the taking of individual wives).

From this, McLellan deduces that kinship and family alliances were relatively late appearing on the scene. The first
social bonds were those of fraternity and common interests,
'ideas of kinship must have grown like all other ideas related
to matters primarily cognisable only by the senses.' Completely independent of Bachofen, we again encounter the
proposition of knowledge and thought as a crucial factor in
the 'advance' of human society. Bonds with the mother are
a sensual truth. If, then, a relation with the mother is know-
able through the senses, the deduction of consanguinity with
brothers and sisters could be thought to be a simple matter.
Hence early social bonds were fraternal.

For McLennan, these fraternal bonds, combined with
exogamy, would produce contradictions ultimately provok-
ing the emergence of the procreative family. For the capture
of women, combined with maternal descent, would introduce
'foreigners' into the tribe, foreigners even to the fathers. This
problem would not be resolved until, with the development
of wealth and private property, the men would necessarily
come to think of their wives as property. Only in such a
situation could rigid monogamy be enforced, but once it
was there would be sufficient a guarantee of paternity for
descent through the males to be established.

McLennan's writing marks a systematisation of a series of
preoccupations with the history of marriage institutions.
Transitions in marriage relations are taken as in some way
informative about the general state of social development
and the form of social alliances. It is an attempt to combine
theories of the transitions between familial institutions and
'political' institutions in order to demonstrate what was the
essential nature of these alliances and institutions. McLennan
makes definite propositions on this subject: basic social
bonds are fraternal, arising from comradely feelings based on
locality. Early society is a history of constant warfare whose
dynamic will set in motion the history of marriage customs.

Human sexual relations and technical stages

The theorists referred to thus far concentrated on human
marriage as the clue to all human development. The focus

of Lewis Henry Morgan is not so exclusive, yet sexual regulations and marriage are again central. Again, enormous claims are made for the significance of mother-right societies and the light they can shed on the nature of social alliances. Morgan addressed these questions through an extensive empirical knowledge of the American Indians. His work exercised an enormous influence on anthropology and social theory.

In *Ancient Society*, Morgan joins ethical transformations to a schema of technical and political transformations. Humanity has evolved, he argued, through various levels of social organisation passing from 'barbarism' to civilisation. He thought that the technical capacity of a given group to some extent determined its level of social organisation, and his aim was to examine the relation between technical stages and various social institutions, primarily private property, the family and the idea of government. These institutions are seen as being related particularly to technical advances. Private property for example, 'is closely connected with the increase in inventions and discoveries and with the improvement of social institutions which mark the several ethnic periods of human progress.'[34] The social institutions are not seen as reducible to technical developments. Transitions in technical capacities had already become a privileged explanation of social forms in the development of the social sciences. Morgan adds Darwinian theories of evolution to this, directing attention to natural selection. *Ancient Society* is unashamedly evolutionary, describing 'the progress of mankind from the bottom of the scale to the status of civilisation'. He studies the social, political and sexual organisation of the American Indian as evidence thrown up for geology like successive strata which have developed, or are developing at a different rate form our own.

Social and sexual organisation different from Western patriarchal society were taken as frozen or transitional forms of more primitive society. Matrilineal societies were either very primitive versions of our own or in the process of evolving. Morgan thought that much of the 'greatness' of the American Indians had been lost in the course of human development and he was a champion of Indian rights. He was nevertheless convinced that at the end of historical evolution stood the biological family, monogamous, property-owing and recognising the rights of the father.

Morgan does not conflate the growth of the idea of monogamy and the growth of private property. The scenario runs like this: under the influence of the unconscious workings of in-breeding, those groups which came to practise forms of prohibition survived more adequately than those which had unregulated mating. The earliest form of social organisation had been the gens, with descent through the mother's line. This was because a state of primitive promiscuity had prevailed, rendering the recognition of paternity impossible. The monogamous family, recognising the real progenitor, emerged only as the end product of ever-increasing prohibitions and alliances within the group. Meanwhile the idea of private property had been making headway, but could only become established when the 'principle of the inheritance of the property in the children of its owner was established'.[35] This resulted in the coincidence of strict monogamy with private property: the father took the most logical means at his disposal to guarantee that his property was inherited by his genetic offspring, and genetic offspring could only be verified through the strictest monogamy.

There is no primary cause in this history of the monogamous family and private property. Development is uneven and, although certain forms of social and sexual organisation are mutually dependent, their joint emergence is not the result of any necessary development. However, it is assumed that the enforcement of strict monogamy, the dominance of the father and the transmission of property through the biological father to his sons are mutually dependent forms of social organisation. It is assumed that once paternity *can* be guaranteed, this incontrovertible knowledge of who your children are will necessarily be accompanied by the desire to pass property and name on to these genetic offspring.

Morgan's history of the family is premised on the idea that no 'rational' society might organise descent, kinship and inheritance through the female line. A natural psychological instinct for, and interest in, paternity is assumed. A man would wish both to recognise his offspring and to transmit his property to these offspring. There is an idea at play of natural rights, embodied in the notion of the procreative family. What is produced by the hands, property, belongs to the body and genetic offspring are seen as extensions of the body. It is not surprising with such presuppositions that Morgan should have taken biological consanguinity to underly all systems of kinship.

Morgan's concern with the primacy of matrilineal descent, taken to be the necessary consequence of ignorance of pro-creation, is, however, primarily a concern with the foundations of social alliance in primitive society. It was for this reason that his work was of such importance for marxism. The patriarchal theory had proposed a relation between state and family as a homogenous relationship. Maine had assumed that both the early patriarchal family, and later 'political' society represented forms of government in which groups of individuals were subject to sovereign authority. Morgan's interest in the primacy of matrilinearity and the separate histories of family and the political level, was to demonstrate the qualitatively different nature of forms of social organisa-tion at different historical stages.

For Morgan, the term 'political' is not to be used for all societies regardless of their level of development and their relations of production. According to Morgan, political organisation only occurs in societies where a division of labour is in force, necessitated by the existence of private property. This form of organisation is to be distinguished from societies organised predominantly through relationships between persons. The basic unit of this organisation is the gens, that is, a body of consanguinei designated as descending from the same common ancestor — a group which share a gentile name. From his study of the Iroquois, Morgan sugges-ted that this initial grouping would, in becoming more complex, form 'phratries', 'tribes' and 'confederacies of tribes'. This organisation would be essentially democratic, where property is held in common by consanguinei.

Arising from different factors, there is the second basic form of government, political society: 'Political society is organised upon territorial areas and deals with property as well as persons through territorial relations.'[36]

The transition from one form of social organisation to another closely connected with the history of the family. We have already noticed Morgan's theory of the gradual emergence of various classifications by which biological in-breeding was removed as a possibility. This development involved first classification based on sex, then increasingly complicated categories of marriageability within the gens. The transition from mother-right to father-right had its own history within the history of the gens, and its own determinants. These determinants are a combination of psychologistic assumptions about paternal interests and a history of the accumulation of wealth with the development of agriculture and the concomitant emergence of private property:[37]

> With property accumulating in masses and assuming
> permanent forms, and with an increased proportion of
> it held by individual ownership, descent in the female
> line was certain of overthrow, and substitution of the
> male line equally assured. Such a change would leave
> inheritance in the gens as before, but it would place
> children in the gens of their father, and the father at
> the head of agnatic kindred.

Such a form of inheritance would begin to structure the possibility of transition from primitive communism, with its distribution of surplus between all members of gens, to inheritance of private property. Inheritance through the father would make possible accumulation of wealth by a strong male line. Thus the patrilineal monogamous family would emerge through the coincidence of the workings of unconscious natural selection with the development of the technical capacity of a given group.

The overwhelming evidence of mother-right societies

In 1880, Maxim Kovalevsky gave a series of lectures in Sweden summarising the state of the debate on the origin of the family and property.[38] Maine's patriarchal theory was dismissed as 'sustained by fantasy'[39] and this had been exposed by the contributions of Bachofen and McLennan. The initial lack in the new theory of mother-right of a 'minute description of the relations of kinship and the forms of marriage in the original epoch of human sociability'[40] had soon been rectified by detailed empirical studies.[41] All this work gave overwhelming evidence against Maine and suggested entirely new ways of thinking about the origins of society:[42]

> To the initiative of this intellectual elite, we are indebted for the most remarkable discovery effected in our times in sociological research. It shows that the individual family constituted in the way we now find it by marriage and consanguinity is never found at the origin of human sociability. In its place we establish the matriarchal family, recognising no other ties than those uniting the infant to its mother and its relatives on its mother's side.

It seemed it was no longer worth anyone's while to take seriously the patriarchal theory.

In 1883, Maine, himself everywhere refuted, once more turned his attention to the patriarchal theory. His defence shows clearly how the terms in which familial and social relations had been reconceptualised. He admitted that the evidence for mother-right societies seemed overwhelming; 'the group consisting of the descendants through women, of a single ancestress still survives, and its outline may still be marked out if it is worth anybody's while to trace it'.[43] But did this grudging admittance necessarily destroy the pertinence of the patriarchal theory? Did the existence of such societies really imply either the 'fact' of primitive promiscuity or the primacy of mother-right societies? By no means, answers Maine. Such hypotheses should be treated with extreme suspicion, since they seem to fly in the face of 'human nature'. The physiological family must surely always have existed in some form, and this would necessarily mean that paternity would, in some way, be recognised. After all, he declares, 'a human being can no more, physiologically, be the child of two fathers than of two mothers, and the children of the same man, no less than of the same woman, must always have something in their nature which distinguished them from every other group of human beings'.[44]

Ignoring these 'facts' reveals the glaring faults of the mother-right hypotheses; they put into abeyance notions of male power and sexual jealousy, that 'mightiest of all passions, a passion which man shares with all the higher animals, sexual jealousy'.[45]

If, as he assumed, these passions underlie the contemporary family, how came they to be put aside at the earliest stages of mankind's existence? If mother-right theories recognise that procreative fathers will claim their 'rights' as soon as paternity can be recognised, how can it be assumed that men will not feel these inclinations to dominate and possess from the earliest stage? Nothing, he asserts, could be more unsatisfactory in the writings of McLennan and Morgan than their account of the recognition of paternity. 'Morgan seems almost to suppose that it was introduced by popular vote. McLennan expressly suggests that it arose from a custom of putative fathers giving presents to putative children.'[46] But the truth is, he argues, that 'a great natural force must always have acted, and must still be acting on those aberrant forms of society, tending always to make the most powerful portion of each community arrange itself in groups which admit the recognition of fatherhood, and the indulgence of parental instincts.'[47]

Maine could count himself lucky that by and large his principal theoretical assumptions in the patriarchal theory had subsequently been corroborated by Darwin's work. After all, writing in the *Descent of Man*, Darwin had suggested that male dominance, sexual jealousy, and parental love could be found at the very origins of society. Thus if mother-right societies did exist, their explanation was quite simple: either they were the result of sexual imbalance caused by population factors, or, as Darwin had suggested, some societies, having advanced in intellectual powers were 'retrograded in their instincts'. Either way, the problem is not one of different family organisations and their meanings but a problem of knowledge. Mankind had lost the ability to recognise paternity. The structure of male power, sexual jealousy and parental love could never be far out of sight.

Maine opposed the ideas of an original state of mother-right because they had convoluted notions of how society developed. He insisted that there must be coherence between various social institutions. The state is organised along patriarchal principles, so it must have emerged from families with the same organisation. Why on earth should society start with the large horde, change into smaller groups, only to aggregate slowly back to the large group?

Conclusion

There is a theoretical distance between the patriarchal theory in *Ancient Law* in 1861, and Maine's defence of patriarchal precedence in 1883. It was the distance between a detailed comparative analysis of law, assuming the primacy of patriarchy, in order to speculate on political and legal history, and a defence of patriarchal primacy in terms of psychological and biological evidence. Maine remained preoccupied with questions of political theory. What, for example, was the relation between forms of dominance within the state and the family? Which social group takes precedence, the small or large group? Now, however, he defended his artificial and complex notion of the family in terms of its psychological and biological probability.

The distance between Maine's two reference points marks the emergence of a space in which a new configuration of concepts has been formed. Many of the questions addressed to the study of the family are unaltered, arising from considerations of political theory. But an additional series of concerns have emerged. These relate to the possible variability of the ways in which realtions between the sexes have been organised. In the space where this speculation is conducted, a concern with the natural and the instinctual emerges and becomes an overwhelming problem for conceptualisations of sexuality and sexual relations.

2 The meaning of mother-right

Introduction

The previous chapter traced the way in which the dissolution of 'the patriarchal theory' was none other than the dissolution of an assumed homogeneity between the forms of power in the state and the family. In this dissolution there emerged a new configuration of concerns, relating to the regulation of sexual relations. It became possible to produce a history of sexual relations as a form of social regulation before social institutions as such. In recognising the primacy of sociality but pushing back social rules, even as far back as the animal kingdom, the terrain was changed as to what constituted 'the social'. The social forms in which sexual reproduction was accomplished, its history and exigencies and prohibitions became possible sources of explanation of the nature of the social group itself. Forms of government could no longer be thought unproblematically to be the logical extension of natural forms.

Many of the questions remained the same as those asked by Maine: what is the relation between familial organisation, the forms of power exercised within the family, and the political organisation of society? But a series of additional concerns have emerged. The regulation of mating and reproduction, the rights of parenthood, the transmission of name, identity and goods, all came to be areas whose integration with the political level of society was by no means clear cut. Sexuality and the organisation of reproduction had become a point of speculation as to the transformation from animal to human, opening a whole new area of contestation. The supposed homogeneity between the form of power in the family and the state, proposed by Maine, was broken open, and in the ensuing study of sexual forms there appeared a space where the struggle to become human was played out. Could it possibly be, for example, that the monogamous family, recognising biological paternity, is the end product of a long history? Perhaps the first social groups had not recognised any sexual regulation? In this space questions can be asked as to how sexual regulation was achieved, what were its conditions, what were its relations to other social practices. What was the relation between procreation, the family and *other* social alliances? Lang, writing in *Social Origins*, asked a series of questions which encapsulated the political preoccupations of these debates:[1]

> Was marriage originally non-existent? Was promiscuity at first the rule, and if so what were the origins, motives, and methods of the most archaic prohibitions on primitive license? Did man live in 'hordes' and did he bisect each horde into exogamous and intermarrying moieties, and if he did, what was his motive? Are the groups and kindred commonly styled totemic earlier or later than the division into a pair of phratries? Do the totem kins represent the results of an early form of exogamous custom or are they additions to or consciously arranged sub-divisions of the two exogamous moieties? Is a phase of 'group marriage' proved by the terms for human relationships employed by many backward races and by survivals in manners and customs?

Given the significance of these considerations, it is not at all surprising to discover that the books of Bachofen, McLennan and Morgan ushered in a mass of literature orchestrated around the subject of patriarchy and mother-right. Debates stimulated by the foregrounding of mother-right societies extended over a period of approximately sixty years, stretching between the publication of Bachofen's *Das Mütter-recht* in 1861 until the appearance of what Malinowski called the swan-song of mother-right hypotheses, Robert Briffault's *The Mothers* in 1927.

The discipline which we now recognise as anthropology emerged in the context of these debates, but the meaning of mother-right was by no means only interesting for the study of societies for its own sake. Political philosophy, sociology, marxism, psychoanalysis and sex psychology were all involved in these debates. This is partly because the discourses were less rigidly separated at that time than now. Indeed, divisions between them emerged in the context of these debates. It is also because the history of the family and the organisation of sexual relations had become crucial for a number of reasons.

In the following two chapters it will be argued that this debate about sexual organisation was, in fact, the bearer of a number of preoccupations and questions about the organisation of society in general. Kinship, the family, sexuality and sexual relations were all merged to produce wider theories about society. In this chapter it will be argued that sexual relations and family organisation came to the centre of the stage at a particular theoretical and political conjuncture. It will then be shown how the debate was pre-occupied with the nature of social bonds; were they political, consanguineous, or instinctual? By the 1920s and 1930s this had become an explicitly political debate. In a later chapter it will be shown that the merger of kinship, family and sexual relations and their mutual service to other political and philosophical questions in fact meant that, ironically, sexual relations disappeared as an object of investigation.

The regulation of sexual relations

The new conceptual space in which sexual and familial relations came to be theorised was one characterised by the absolute centrality assumed by the regulation of sexual relations as the clue to social relations. Many have characterised the debate which preoccupied the social sciences in the second half of the nineteenth century as 'social evolutionism'. In particular, the treatment of sexual relations has been seen in this context. Various writers have remarked on the preoccupation with early sexual forms as the effect of Victorian moral prejudice.[2] 'There had to be some form of speculation about the earliest stages of this development but its general lines were clear since the terminal points were fixed – the female ape and the Victorian lady.'[3] The schema which was constructed by social evolution for marriage customs was based on an equation between 'primitive' and the 'opposite of Western civilisation'. It is virtually a platitude today to recognise a mode of evolutionary speculation in which the end-points were fixed: advanced industrial society based on the monogamous patriarchal family as the final outcome and, in all probability, its absolute inverse at the origins of society. It is also common to point to the overthrow of the patriarchal theory as coinciding with the tendency to treat 'simple' societies as primitive or original forms of society, through which all humanity had passed or would pass.

'Evolutionism' is, however, an insufficient characterisation of these debates. There was no simple homogeneous application of biological laws to social laws, nor any simple inversion of 'Victorian morality'. For one thing, biological categories were themselves contested: those which were accepted within the social sciences were as a result of other factors. This will be dealt with in the subsequent chapter. Nor does the idea of inversion adequately explain why it was *sexual* relations which were inverted. Such characterisations are misleading. They tell us little about the precise form which 'evolutionary' theories took within the study of the family. They tell us nothing about the divisions within the debates about terms, modes of explanation and different ideas about causality. Moreover, these characterisations obscure the fact that anti-evolutionary theorists were also involved from quite an early stage in these debates about familial forms. Summary characterisations drive too firm a wedge between the 'evolutionists' and the 'anti-evolutionists' and obscure the fact that many subsequent positions in different discourses were formed in these debates.

In fact, these debates about sexual regulation and its social meaning had very definite theoretical and political conditions of existence. One element was indeed evolutionary speculation. The effect of this was to establish an interest in different social forms as possible stages in a unilineal historical transition. Perhaps those societies which exhibited such peculiarities as matrilineal descent or non-monogamy were the earliest forms of social grouping, a form through which all humanity had once passed; 'in the main, the development of higher and better ideas as to marriage, relationships, law and religion etc. has followed in its earlier stages a very similar course in the most distinct races of man.'[4] Evolutionary theory, partially influenced by Darwinian ideas of the transition from animal to man, produced a form of attention to social institutions as possible stages on a unilinear history. It produced a different attention to 'origins'.

Yet 'evolutionary' theory was really only one element in a more general process of 'historisation' of studies of human society which had begun well before Darwin, at the beginning of the eighteenth century.[5] This involved the possibility of historicising the unwritten, through the simultaneous treatment of extant societies as 'primitive', and through a treatment of cultural practices and customs as expressing a history. What had begun to emerge was a 'diachronic' analysis of culture which involved treating representations and practices as effects of a history. Symbols, rituals, customs like marriage, began to be understood as expressing a hidden history, bearing in their contemporary forms the traces of bygone forms and practices. The aim of ethnology, from this perspective, would be to trace the history of a custom or symbolic practice to its origin; this would also be its explanation. It was in this context that Morgan's treatment of kinship terminology became so central. Even 'so small and apparently insignificant a feature as the classing of the sister-in-law with the sister has been found to lead back to a definite social condition arising out of the regulation of marriage and sexual relations'.[6] This ability to ask questions of the history of customs was simultaneously a question of determination. What explanations could there be for the particular forms which customs take? Once customs and representations were no longer seen as expressing their own inner essence, then the question of how they were determined needed to be answered. These elements, however, do not explain why it was *sexual* organisation, rather than any other kind of organisation, which assumed such importance in outlining this history of the human species.

Two factors were important here. On the one hand, there was the theoretical impulse from natural history. On the other, there was the impulse from social and political factors of that period, factors which had brought the consideration of sexual relations to the forefront of a number of social issues. The first impulse, that of natural history, will be dealt with in the following chapter. Here it suffices to remark on the impact of ideas from natural history which was far more specific than that of a nebulous impact producing social evolutionism. There was an apparent coincidence of objects studied — mating in natural history, marriage in the social sciences — which permitted the 'historisation' of sexual regulations. It became possible to speculate on forms of transition of sexual behaviour. And what was constructed here was a new area of theoretical contestation — the natural — in which animals are the natural and marriage regulations the human. In this apparent coincidence of objects it becomes possible to ask; is there continuity between the sexual behaviour of animals and humans? Finally, are these *the* significant differences between the animal and the human?

A second factor which impelled sexuality to the centre of the social debate relates to social and political forces in the nineteenth century. To account for these at all sufficiently would require a different account from that attempted in this book. But it should be noted that, contrary to the image of the nineteenth century as a period where sexuality was silenced, 'the debate about sexuality exploded'.[7] Jeffrey Weeks, in an important study of nineteenth century sexuality in Europe, has argued that even the silences about sexuality mark the way it became *the* secret, at the heart of a whole number of discourses, medicine, education, social statistics, etc. He writes:[8]

From the end of the eighteenth century with the debate over population and the hyperbreeding of the poor, sexuality pervades the social consciousness: from the widespread discussions of the birthrate, deathrate, life-expectancy, fertility in the statistical forays of the century to the urgent controversies over public health, housing, birth control and prostitution. The reports of the great Parliamentary commissions, which in the 1830's and 40's investigated working conditions in the factories and mines, were saturated with an obsessive concern with the sexuality of the working class, the social other, displacing in the end an acute social crisis from the area of exploitation and class conflict where it could not be coped with, into the framework of a more amenable and discussible area of 'morality'.

The explosion of the debate over sexuality was also an explosion of 'actions' towards the area of sexual behaviour. Culminating in a series of social policies in the 1880s, the second half of the nineteenth century had been witness to increasing state intervention in the organisation of the social field.[9] These political interventions provoked much violent controversy over the advantages or disadvantages of state invention, another political factor which was to prioritise the debate over the relation between state (political) regulation and familial organisation. Finally, the period covered by these debates was also the period where feminism began to emerge as an organised political force. Its effect was to produce violent controversy about the nature of sexual regulations and sexual behaviour, a factor which cannot have been coincidental in this becoming an important object of interrogation in the social sciences.

From mother-right to matrilineal descent

One of the most surprising elements in the dissolution of the patriarchal theory was that the hypotheses of those who had attacked it, were even more quickly dispensed with. Bachofen, McLennan and Morgan all to some extent saw an inversion of father-right societies at the dawn of human history. The inversion was sometimes theorised as absolute: not only was there primitive promiscuity but also power and descent were invested in the mothers rather than the fathers. The notion of mother-right which was initially advanced could be summarised as implying not only descent through the mother, but also residence in the mother's home and the political dominance of women. Very few writers, however, supported the idea of absolute sexual inversion. Virtually no one followed Bachofen's vision of all-powerful women, his Amazons, struggling to defend mother-right.

Instantaneously, writers were arguing against the likelihood that a state ever existed under the control of 'the weaker sex'. Surely, they argued, men dominate *as a sex* in patriarchal societies because they are the stronger sex? [10]

> communities in which women have exercised the supreme
> power are rare and exceptional, if indeed they ever
> existed. We do not find in history, as a matter of fact,
> that women do assert their rights and savage women
> would, I think, be peculiarly unlikely to uphold their
> dignity in the manner supposed.

Everywhere evidence could be produced that 'authority' in the sense of political or public power was, in fact, still held by the men, if not the biological father, at least the mother's brother: [11]

> The term 'matriarchal' was an improvement on earlier
> definitions, but takes too much for granted that women
> govern the family. It is true that in these communities
> women enjoy greater status than in barbaric patriarchal
> life, but the actual power is rather in the hands of their
> brothers and uncles on the mother's side. On the whole
> the terms 'maternal' and 'paternal' seem preferable.

When it came to the consideration of mother-right societies, power, domination and sovereignty began to be separated from descent and inheritance: [12]

> The famous matriarchal theory was as exaggerated in its
> early forms as was the patriarchal. It is now coming to
> be recognised that it is simply the tracing of descent
> through the mother and giving the children her name,
> though there were a few cases where inheritance of
> property has later come under the rule, some of these
> being due to sex.

The questioning of sexual inversion exposed how the notion
of 'rights' was thought of and it is significant that the term
mother-right gave way gradually to a series of differentiated
terms: matrilineal (taking the mother's name and group for
descent purposes), or matrifocal (residing in the home of
the mother's kin). Any suggestion that descent group and
lineage were equivalent to political rights and authority
began to be minimalised: [13]

> All then that can properly be meant by saying that a
> patriarchal tribe follows male and a matriarchal tribe
> follows female kinship is that their social arrangements,
> such as membership of family and clan, succession and
> inheritance are framed on one line rather than another.

Distaste for the possibility of an early stage of matriarchal
rule was motivated by several rather different tendencies,
not all reducible to Victorian horror at such a 'perverted'
state of affairs. After all, if the idea was so unacceptable,
how came it to enjoy such vogue in the first place?

The reaction was, in all probability, motivated by the
conjuncture of several strands of thought and research. They
reveal important factors both about the way empirical data
was classified and about how kinship relations and power
were conceptualised. The problem over the term mother-right
reveals the notion of rights which had previously been at
play. In the patriarchal theory, 'rights' had clearly meant not
only legal and political rights but also rights of possession and
control over property and family (wife and offspring). It was
this presumed coherence between the forms of authority
exercised by the state over its subjects and those exercised
by the patriarchs over their families which allowed the
hypothesis to be formed of the homogeneity between the
family, the state and the nation. Yet what is constantly
raised against the idea of mother-right societies is the fact
that nowhere, in the study of primitive society, was the
systematic exclusion of men from politics and government
equivalent to the exclusion of women in the West. Nor
could these investigators discover anywhere societies where
women governed the state as 'representatives' of the men in
the same way that middle-class men represented women in

nineteenth-century Western society. For these theorists and investigators, rights imply political rights, property rights and intersubjective capacities of authority and control. Therefore, women's widespread exclusion from political power and lack of capacities of intersubjective domination was taken to imply that the relationship between familial and political relations should be reconceptualised. Women nowhere seemed to have the same 'rights' as men. It is this which contributes to the disruption of the homogeneity assumed by Maine between different social units. Now, there begins to be an insistence that descent, inheritance and authority can be separated.

But the picture is not a clear one involving the discovery of exclusion of women from power, followed by a reconceptualisation of the family and political relations. The apparent universal exclusion of women from the political and governmental positions in society implies women's lack of social significance only if rights are conceptualised exclusively in terms typical of Western political theory. Women's exclusion from the political realm might mean other things in other cultures, where power is exercised in different forms. Then, as now, particular forms of classifying data, and colonial administration assumed that forms of power were the same as in Western Europe. It was the notion of 'rights' at play which determined how the evidence was treated. Rattray, describing his investigations among the matrilineal Ashanti, gives a poignant account of discovering the immense social significance of the 'Queen Mother': [14]

> I have asked the old men and old women why I did not know all this — I have spent many years among the Ashanti. The answer is always the same: 'The white man never asked us this; you have dealings with and recognise only the men; we supposed the European considered women of no account, and we know you do not recognise them as we have always done.'

The example indicates how both researchers and the colonial administration neglected and therefore undermined the ways in which women were significant in public life.

It should also be remembered that from the 1880s onwards

the effect of feminism in Europe had been initially to consolidate definitions (at least within the law) of women having radically different spheres of influence. The feminist campaigns against the exclusion of women from professions and franchise had been resisted by producing legal definitions of men and women which excluded women from the rights of citizenship: they were not persons.[15] Citizenship was for certain men; it entailed political and governmental influence. For women, there was to be governance of the domestic sphere. Western society, at the time of these arguments, was producing a definition of political rights based on sex as much as property, a notion of political rights of representation which coincided with the general social dominance of men. This model was by no means instantly applicable to other societies whose social and political structures did not correspond to our own. Yet this idea of rights as invested in a person, respecting property and familial relations, affected the way in which other societies were theorised. Representation at the political and governmental level was taken to be synonymous with intersubjective capacities of authority. In such a context, to point to women's exclusion from the political level was to declare them without social influence. It was the effect of this declaration which allowed the disruption of Maine's assumed homogeneity between political and familial forms. It now became possible to separate out the various strands of social organisations and suggest that they had different histories.

While the different strands of social organisation were separated by this reconceptualisation, it is interesting to notice what happened to the notion of power. Because the idea of societies inverted in all ways —sexual, and political — was rejected it became possible to talk of male supremacy in new ways. It ceased to be simply the assumed basis of political power and became a force theorised in psychologistic and biological terms, separated from the political forms of society. Nevertheless, these psychologistic and biological accounts drew on the notion of power from political theory, a notion implying intersubjective domination whose effect is the obedience of subjects.

The animal family

The theorisation of familial organisation in its specificity, permitted by the disruption of assumed coherence between political and familial relations, saw an increasing use of evidence drawn from natural history. In opening up consideration of sexual regulation, it was now possible to theorise the 'human', which was neither animal nor fully civilised, that is, politically regulated. The fact that animals too demonstrated a certain systematicity in the organisation of their familial life seemed to invite comparison between them and humans. If the bonds which constitute society could not be demonstrated as political, perhaps they could be understood by reference to the animal kingdom.

The 'evidence' drawn from natural history was at the forefront of the attack on theories of mother-right societies. Writers began to argue for the unchangeability of the 'natural' procreative unit. Highly influential in this argument was Edward Westermarck, who referred to the natural and unchanging unit, the family, applicable to animals and humans, as 'nothing else than a more or less durable connection between male and female, lasting beyond the mere act of propagation till after the birth of the offspring'.[16] Maine's idea of the artificial political family may have been thoroughly discredited but arguments about the natural basis of the family under patriarchal protection gained ascendency. Starke, in *The Primitive Family*,[17] Tylor, in *Anthropology*,[18] Lang and Atkinson, in *Social Origins and Primal Law*,[19] and Crawley, in *The Mystic Rose*,[20] all supported this position. As often as not, they appealed to an account of the life of the primates, and Darwin's account of patriarchal sexual jealousy among animals. They first disputed the primacy of unregulated mating at the origin of society, that is, theories of primitive promiscuity. Second, matriarchy could be rejected in favour of the primary family group under male protection. 'A reaction has set in', remarked Tylor, before which the theory of primitive promiscuity which had gained so much anthropological acceptance, 'is very likely to be transformed or pass away altogether.'[21]

Tylor argued for the basic animal-like family organisation

at the origin of social life. From this perspective, mother-right or a universal stage of the social and political dominance of women could be totally discounted; why should such an unlikely inversion occur at the moment of transition from ape to man? No, the meaning of mother-right or matrilineal societies had to be looked for elsewhere. That 'elsewhere' was in the function of descent and affiliation as social as well as biological institutions.

The social function of elements in kinship

The challenge to 'matriarchy', regardless of the perspective from which it was carried out, brought certain concerns to the heart of studies of kinship. Increasingly, considerations of kinship moved away from an idea of kinship as an artificial bond coherent with political power. The power of the patriarch could no longer be seen as the explanation of the cohesion of social groups. Kinship was to be broken down into parts: relations of power between groups, descent of name, descent of blood ties, sexual connections and the relations of all these to the procreative family.

When theories of matriarchy were rejected there were several effects. For the anti-evolutionists, it was one element contributing to the separation between objects of inquiry which had previously been run together. The assumption that lineage and descent necessarily entail power was gradually deconstructed. 'Descent need not necessarily entail "rights"; it could be seen as the series of social rules which regulate the social position of offspring according to that of its parents.'[22] There are different practices and institutions within society and each may entail different obligations:[23]

> in order to use the word descent in a definite sense it is always necessary to add what social group is meant. For it is possible that membership in the local group is determined by the father, membership of the phratry by the mother, and membership of the clan by neither of them. The facts of descent do not seem to play a very important role and are not suitable to be chosen as the

most important feature of kinship. The facts of inheritance also have not very much influence on kinship.

Even within speculative evolutionary anthropology, however, a similar trajectory was opened out. It had become necessary to specify various strands which made up kinship — the procreative family, descent, inheritance, social allegiance — and explain the interrelations between these various elements. The interrogation of simplistic inversions of the patriarchal theory was premised on definite theoretical assumptions. These involved a series of questions which studies of kinship were thought to answer: to what extent did the procreative family underlie social organisation; if it did not, what were kinship relations based on; what were the relative roles of 'biological' and social determinants? If the biological unit was disputed, what was the social function of kinship alliances? What were their relations with other social institutions and practices?

By opening out the question of sexual regulation as an area of speculation on the form of social bonds, the question of causality had become central. At issue was the relation between the various aspects of family and kinship if no necessary correspondence between political and familial organisation could be assumed. The question had become that of the social functions of the various aspects of the regulation of sexual relations.

For the evolutionists, the questions could be solved by asking what social determinants caused one family structure to change into another. Those who rejected the idea of unilineal transformation were left with similar questions. If one form, mother-right, had not evolved into another, there was still a problem of explaining different forms of social arrangement. Even if patrilineal and matrilineal familial arrangements simply existed as alternatives to one another, why should such different forms arise? The debates which followed the dissolution of the patriarchal theory thus tended to be dominated by a series of themes: the role of the procreative family; the problem of paternity; familial property; the function of sexual regulation. These themes reveal the concerns carried by studies of kinship.

The facts of procreation

The role of paternity and the procreative family were obsessive themes in the discussion of familial forms. The questions started with whether or not mother-right societies could be explained by primitive ignorance of the role of the father in the act of procreation. It was rare for any writer to take an extreme position, though the suggestion of a total state of ignorance among the 'primitives' was not absent: 'The history of mankind as far as we can trace it...exhibits the slow and gradual encroachments of knowledge on the confines of almost boundless ignorance.'[24] Even if theorists dismissed the suggestion of the infantile ignorance of the human race, virtually all interrogated, the relation between the 'facts' of paternity and the social arrangement of kinship.

It will be remembered that Bachofen had argued that the ability to understand the facts of procreation constituted an intellectual advance for humanity. This was because a social order (father-right) could be built on intellectual and altruistic love. Father-right represented the triumph of the intellectual or spiritual attributes (masculine) over the sensual and material attributes shared with the animals (feminine). Few writers took such a purely philosophical position as Bachofen, but aspects of his arguments recur with surprising frequency. Recognition of paternity, in these arguments is not an instinct but an intellectual appreciation 'a more accurate appreciation of (the) facts'.[25] As late as 1927, Robert Briffault, in *The Mothers*, extols a general advance in the intellectual capacities of humanity. Like Bachofen, he attributes this advance in intellectual capacity to masculine achievements even though he argues that it is female altruism at the basis of social achievement:[26]

> The process which has raised civilised humanity above savagery is fundamentally an intellectual process....
> Those achievements which constitute what...we term civilisation, have taken place in societies organised on patriarchal principles, they are for the most part, the work of men. Women have very little direct share in them.

Not many writers followed Bachofen in the division of history into the dominance of animal (maternal) and intellectual (male) capacities. There are, however, significant resonances across a whole series of developments to warrant attention, including that of psychoanalysis, as we see later.[27]

In general, speculation on the status of paternity in primitive society was not explicitly concerned with the advance of human knowledge but took the form of speculation on 'primitive' sexual mores. Perhaps ignorance of paternity and the facts of procreation should be seen as the product of a state where paternity could not be known rather than bearing witness to the extreme ignorance of primitives. For those who disputed the eternal nature of the procreative unit, this was indeed a favoured explanation. Early society must have been characterised by extreme moral laxity or complex forms of group marriage so that Schouten's pronouncement could be corroborated: 'Maternity is always certain, paternity always uncertain.'[28]

Indeed, only some such explanation could account for the transmission of group allegiance, name and property through the mother's line:[29]

> It is inconceivable that anything but the want of
> certainty on that point could have long prevented the
> acknowledgement of kinship through males, in such
> cases we shall be able to conclude that such certainty
> had formerly been wanting — that more or less promis-
> cuous intercourse between the sexes formerly prevailed.

That descent group would automatically be reckoned through the biological father if known is not in question. What possible advantage would there be reckoning descent through frail women?[30]

> But when reflection, which had previously established a
> system of kinship through the weaker parents, had shown
> that there was kinship through the stronger, we need
> not doubt that means would in general be found of
> ensuring the recognition of this kinship. And once recog-
> nised, it would almost as a matter of course, become
> forthwith the more important of the two.

This position is a stark version of one form of attention to paternity. Kinship had a biological referent. Where biological paternity was unknown, biological maternity would be all

61

important. A male would claim his rights to his genetic off-spring as soon as facts of procreation were known and monogamy could guarantee the child paternity.

But this stark proposition was also soon under attack. Day by day, more ethnographic data was becoming available which, unlike the earlier 'voyage' literature, asked certain questions of its data. These questions, predictably, were primarily about the nature of sexual regulation and descent groups. The turn of the century saw a startling increase in the number of ethnographic expeditions, and some of the most influential reports came back from ethnologists, dealing with matrilineal societies.[31] It was quickly being registered that not all matrilineal societies professed ignorance of the role of the father in procreation. Certain matrilineal societies seemed fully acquainted with the facts of procreation.

Confronted with these problems, other explanations for mother-right societies had to be sought; neither 'primitive ignorance' nor group marriage corresponded adequately with the forms of evidence. 'It follows that the uncertainty of paternity cannot be historically the reason for the reckoning of descent exclusively through the mother. Some other reason must be found.'[32] These 'other reasons' saw the emergence of concern with the social category of paternity, and with the relation between social categories and the facts of procreation. Even such a 'respected' anthropologist as Sir James Frazer remained preoccupied with the effect of ignorance of paternity on social structures. While he dismissed the necessary link between matrilinearity and ignorance of father-right, he remained convinced that totemism, the reverence of a particular object or animal by a group, was the product of primitive ignorance of paternity. Totemism, he suggested was the product of 'primitive theories of conception', where women become fixated on an object at the time of the first stirrings in their womb.

Against the idea of an intellectual advance of humanity, an alternative series of ideas emerged to explain sexual organisation around the so-called facts of procreation. The rejection of correspondence between states of sexual ignorance and mother-right societies resulted in the formulation of the quest for the 'social' function of kinship forms. A dominant consideration here was that of the role of the history of private property. A brief examination of this will again reveal both how kinship was the focus of problems on the nature of the social *and* how certain modes of explanation came to dominate.

Paternity and private property

While ethnographic evidence was making it difficult to hold on to any necessary connection between ignorance of paternity and mother-right societies, paternal rights were far from abandoned in accounts of the evolution of familial forms. Writers frequently returned to an idea partially explored by McLennan and Morgan, the idea of a sentimental and economic motive for the overthrow of mother-right. There are two related reasons for this. One is that there is a conflation between individual and paternal rights, and the other is that given this conflation, speculation on the emergence of paternal rights was taken as a source of speculation on the emergence of individual property rights.

In so far as an explanation was required by evolutionary theory for the transition from mother-right to father right, almost without exception it was agreed to be the effect of the accumulation of property.[33]

> The chief agency in effecting the transition from mother-kin to father-kin would appear to have been a general increase in material prosperity bringing with it a large accession of private property to individuals. For it is when a man has much to bequeath to his heirs that he becomes sensible of the natural inequity, as it now appears to him, of a system of kinship which obliged him to transmit all his goods to his sister's children and none to his own. Hence it is with the great development of private property that devices for shifting descent from the female to the male line most commonly originates.

What is assumed here is the natural authority of the male and the 'rights' connected with blood ties. Once property begins to be accumulated, authority will be undermined since property will pass into the hands of the mother's kin. Inheritance of name and descent group through the mother is no real challenge to this male authority compared with the terrible indignity which a man suffers seeing his property pass, not to his genetic offspring, but to his wife's family. *Primitive Paternity*, summarising various theories, agrees that there is no necessary connection between ignorance of paternity and mother-right. There was, however, a consistent motive for the overthrow of mother-right societies. This was the habit, deeply offensive to Western sensibilities, of inheritance through the mother's line. The woman as locus of transmission of property was totally suppressed; the all-important bond was that between the father and his biological offspring. Thus the awful prospect of a father deprived of the right to pass the fruits of his labour to the fruits of his loins, must constitute a 'sentimental and economic motive for the overthrow of mother-right'.[34]

A natural psychological drive of paternity to ensure inheritance of property by genetic offspring is assumed here. This became the predominant explanation for the development of patriarchy and the 'defeat of women', particularly in popularising accounts of anthropology. The ideas were formative for Havelock Ellis's account of human sexual development:[35]

> It was undoubtedly on the rock of property that the status of women and the organisation on which it rested [i.e. mother-right] usually split. At first property was distributed at death among the members of an ever-lessening circle of kindred. As a man's possessions became more extensive, and also as paternity tended to become more certain, it began to appear unreasonable that his children should be disinherited.

The psychologistic form of explanation, hidden in many of the writings becomes explicit in some accounts of the development of familial forms. Bertrand Russell mobilises it as one element in the development of human morality — the element which led to the enforcement of female virtue and morality:[36]

As soon as the physiological fact of paternity is recognised, a quite new element enters into paternal feeling, an element which has led almost everywhere to the creation of patriarchal societies. As soon as a father recognises that the child is, as the Bible says, his 'seed', his sentiment towards the child is reinforced by two factors, the love of power and the desire to survive death.

What was it, then, that was at stake in insisting on this motivation in evolutionary accounts of the family? Closer examination reveals that this motivation was a crucial element in both the theorisation of the earliest forms of property holding and in the violent divisions as to whether collective possession preceded individual possession.

There were almost as many theories on the first forms of property as there were writers on the subject. Some thought property arose from warfare and practices of conquest; others from a gradual but spontaneous growth of individualism by which the individual gradually differentiated himself (always himself) from the group. Where many of the writers agreed, however, was on the coincidence between transitions in family form and transitions in forms of property holding. For many the procreative family, with its requirements of inheritance by genetic offspring was synonymous with individual property interests. 'When the transition from a hunting state to a pastoral and agricultural state is finally accomplished, moveable property takes on a familial if not individual character.'[37]

It is this which explains why theories of paternal rights continued to be of crucial importance because the way in which procreative family forms came to be recognised was vital in the account of the history of property and social relations. The sentimental and economic motive for the overthrow of mother-right and the establishment of patriarchy was seen by some as the process by which the collectivity or clan gradually breaks down into individual, that is, procreative, units. It is the history of the triumph of individual interests over the collectivity:[38]

The moral direction of this slow transformation is evident, it proceeds from a communism more or less

extensive to individualism; from the clan, where all is
solidarity, to the family and the individual, having their
own interests, which are as distinct as possible from
those other families and other individuals. Each one has
endeavoured to get for himself as large a share as possible
of that which was formerly held in common; each man
has aimed at obtaining a more and more exclusive right
over property, wife and children. From these appetites,
more economic than ethereal have at length proceeded
the patriarchal family, monogamy, and familial property,
and later individual property.

What is interesting about such schemas is the extent to which
the organisation of patriarchal familial relations, 'exclusive
possession of wife and children' is related to ownership
of property. So much so is this the case that some of the
theories even include the individual appropriation of women
from out of the morass of 'sexual communism' as a vital and
formative element in the acquisition of individualistic appetites. Thus practices like wife capture and its supposed
modification, wife purchase, are seen as practices which
would instil a sense of private ownership. One writer[39]
insisted that patriarchy emerged as a result of practices which
subjected women and led to their being considered as forms
of movable property — rape and bride-capture. Female
'inferiority' could therefore be explained by marriage — an
institution designed by men to bring women into subjection.

The whole hypothesis of a state of 'sexual communism',
not just property in common, but wives in common too,
points to the extent to which family rights and property
rights were taken to be part of the same history; so much
so that, for the evolutionary schemas, property was *the*
privileged explanation of the forces which led to the dissolution of mother-right societies. Various factors may be
in play but it is the accumulation of private property which
was seen as the motor for recognition of paternity. This
paternity is not necessarily a biological fact, but a social
recognition through marriage. Paternal rights, then, were
taken to be synonymous with individual property 'rights',
that is, they involved a subject of possession with the

capacity to calculate and dispose of the labour power of others and to dispense with property to genetic offspring.

We can draw some conclusions from the centrality of paternity in these discussions. In so far as social explanations were sought for kinship, the explanations of the emergence of the paternal, that is, procreative, family were explanations for the emergence of individual property rights. These arguments about the emergence of individual property rights worked on certain conditions. First, individual interests were conflated with the procreative family with transmission from father to genetic offspring. Second, because of the theory of work as the origin of private property, it became possible to 'sex' property, assuming a natural division of labour between the sexes. Men created it, therefore property was masculine. Finally, there is an assumption of an essential male psychology which seeks power through genetic self-perpetuation. It is this which in many accounts is the motor for the break-up of former collective society into individual units.

The unchanging form of the procreative family; other explanations of mother-right

If a history of the emergence of the patriarchal family was the bearer of a number of considerations, what is there to be said of those proponents of the eternal nature of the procreative family, usually under paternal dominance? And what was the relation between the apparently antagonistic positions: the eternal procreative family, on the one hand, and the primacy of primitive promiscuity or mother-right, on the other?

The opponents of the theory of universal transition from mother-right to father-right, the supporters of the uninterrupted development of the procreative unit, were not exempt from problems raised by the issues of paternity. Just as the conflation of ignorance of paternity with mother-right was increasingly untenable for some groups, the evidence of some societies' neglect of paternity was also inescapable for the supporters of the natural procreative unit. But the solutions found to this problem were not entirely different from the solutions found by their opponents to their own problems. In both strands of thought we find a notion of kinship as a social function. And that social function is also predominantly theorised as an effect of economic considerations.

After an initial unwillingness to acknowledge the widespread evidence for the neglect of fatherhood in some societies, the upholders of the unchanging procreative family explained mother-right as a structural solution to contradictions within property and territorial relations.

Tylor was among the first to refute the significance of a state of ignorance of paternity. To the suggestion of ignorance of paternity, a zoologist, 'would probably reply that mutual recognition and kindness between male and female parents and their offspring appear too far down in the animal world for rudimentary ideas of paternity to be accounted a human discovery,[40] Tylor, defends the primacy of the patriarchal family unit specifying that he simply means by this, membership of family, clan succession and inheritance through the father's line. While Tylor hotly disputed that the matriarchal system might be a simple inversion of this family system, he also rejected the contention that the maternal family might be an effect of moral laxity or 'sexual communism'; *the matriarchal family system is one framed for order not disorder*' (my emphasis).[41] The maternal system is a practical solution to a practical problem, just as exogamy is: 'the two great regulations of early civilisation, matriarchy and exogamy, have nothing about them fantastic or outrageous, absurd, but are the practical outcome of the practical purposes of people like-minded with ourselves'.[42] The practical problem which the maternal family is said to solve is caused by a double movement. First there is the requirement for exogamy which according to Tylor has nothing to do with the prevention of incest for either sentimental or moral reasons, or for a practical reason like natural selection. For him, the reason for exogamy is entirely political; it is the regulation of relations between groups; 'the reason for exogamy is not moral but political...the purpose of systematic intermarriage between clans is to bind them together in peace and alliance'.[43] Second, however, the circumstances under which this form of political alliance takes place become more and more problematic as civilisation advances. Populations become more dense and settled, they develop more delimited property and territory: 'families and clans have more defined property and interests'.[44] The effect of these material circumstances is to raise most serious questions for the manner in which intermarriage takes place. In these circumstances the wife can either remain in her own home (matrifocal residence) or remove to her husband's (patrifocal residence). Of the first, Tylor can see the evident advantages. The bride's parents would not lose their daughter's assistance and they would likely benefit from additional helpers, their grandchildren.

From this perspective, there may be advantages to the maternal system, but there are also some very pressing reasons for preferring paternal over maternal family systems. For, going as it does against the 'natural' procreative unit, the maternal system would be under severe stress. The practice of bride-capture is taken as evidence of the husband's resistance to matrifocal residence, and the practice of payment to the bride's father is even more compelling evidence of the emergence of an amicable solution to the requirements of a paternal husband. They represent, 'the various modes of overcoming resistance of the family to being despoiled of their daughters'.[45]

There are several factors at play producing Tylor's explanation. A procreative referent is assumed underlying mankind's sexual behaviour. Exogamy is assumed to have a political function. Descent is seen as an effect of power in which power is associated with the ownership of property and persons. Kinship alliances are an expression not only of political alliances, but also of power, understood in terms of property rights. The biological tie is restored not because it is this which kinship expresses, but because it is the unit from which everything starts. Therefore, until it finds some way of expression, it will place other institutions under strain. The movement of civilisation is towards a satisfaction of this biological fact without abandoning the political and social advantages provided by wider methods of political alliance.

Tylor's is a clear statement of a position on the maternal

family which was to have wide currency and it ushered in a number of 'practical' explanations for mother-right once its universality and universal precedence had been dispensed with. Westermarck, the most systematic upholder of the fundamental nature of the procreative unit favoured the place of residence as an influence on systems of descent.

This might arise like the magical quality sometimes attributed to names by 'primitive' peoples. Thus the practice of recognising someone of the same name as a close relative (even though there may be no relationship) points to a power invested in names. Westermarck can therefore conclude that it is indeed the practice of matrifocal residence which would produce matrilineal inheritance but that this would be dictated not by preference of affections but because of the practice of taking the name of a residence group.

Across the various antagonistic interpretations of the history of the family, there are a number of common problems and common solutions. The problem is the disavowal of paternity[46] the explanations sought are those of what social interests might cause the repression of this 'fact'.

Paternity and political divisions

We have seen how the discussion of the recognition of paternity and the procreative family in fact condensed general pre-occupations about the nature of the sexual and social regulation of the early human group. The division between those who argued for the thoroughgoing transformation of the human family, from sexual communism to patriarchal monogamy, and those who argued for the unchanging nature of the paternal family in fact grew more vitriolic, transforming itself by the 1920s into a recognisable issue. Briffault, writing in the Frankfurt School's journal summarised the issues which had divided anthropology.[47] An enormous amount of discussion and controversy, he declared, had taken place with reference to the origin of the family as clue to the foundation of society. Briffault suggests that there is much more at stake than simply an argument over the extent of regulation of the first human groups that is, paternal monogamy versus primitive promiscuity. It is the interpretation of social history in its entirety. What elements are accepted as 'givens' in the development of civilisation? If certain elements like monogamy and acquisitiveness are accepted as 'givens', what does this mean about the possibility of change?[48]

> If it be supposed that the family in much the same form
> as it is now found in Christian European society, has
> existed from the first, or from a very early stage of social
> history, it must then be postulated that all the social
> phenomena, relations and institutions which are
> indissolubly connected with that form of social group are
> likewise coeval with social origins.

If existing social forms are taken as unchanging, then all extant social forms of political, economic and social power can be thought to be originary. If original social formations are seen as 'individualistic' groupings, consisting of heads of the family in which every male member has rights of property and authority to defend, then by virtue of the principle of patriarchal authority, society would be a collection of these units under the dominance of one or more patriarchs. Such a position rules out the possibility that the existing distribution of power and authority is the end product of a definite history and is therefore transitory:[49]

> The social historian who holds the view that paternal
> families existed from the first and constituted the foun-
> dation of human society will not have to enquire into the
> origin of the above principles. He will not be concerned
> with tracing the evolution of marriage institutions, of
> systems of sexual morality, of sentiments of pudicity,
> which are intended to safeguard them. It will be super-
> fluous for him to study the rise of individual economic
> power. He will have no difficulty in accounting for the
> authority of the state or its representatives. For all the
> elements of a fully individualistic economic society,
> similar in all essentials to those of Western civilisation
> will be by his hypothesis, present *aborigine*.

According to Briffault, the assumption of the unchanging nature of the paternal family is considerably more than simply an assertion of the inescapability of the procreative unit, it is a defence of the *status quo.*

It is interesting in this context to listen to Westermarck's bewilderment confonted with a very similar attack on his work.[50] Westermarck's ideas on the paternal family were attacked even in 1929 as a product of Victorian prejudice; in suggesting that monogamy prevailed amongst our earliest ancestors,[51]

> he was able to provide nineteenth century civilisation with an absolute that justified in perpetuity one of its main institutions. The family thus became an institution that radicals could no longer assail. No evolution in society could eradicate it. Neither could monogamy be attacked since it was rooted in man's primeval past, and was part of what Westermarck calls the 'monogamous instinct'. . . . His doctrines suppled a need of the time, a protection against...doctrines that threatened middle class supremacy in the field of ethics and economics... they became at once part of the cultural defense of the era.

Westermarck in response can only offer indignation; his 'scientific' approach surely cannot be accused of ideological bias?[52]

> Again, Dr. Briffault's and Mr. Calverton's allegations that I have attempted to support certain moral doctrines where I should have aimed at scientific truth alone, cannot be substantiated by a single line in my book. I drew my conclusions from the material which I had collected without any preconceived opinion, and when I had formed a provisional theory I endeavoured to take heed of every fact that seemed to contradict. The method I learned from Darwin's *Life and Letters.*

Clearly, by this stage in the debate, a great deal was at stake in these divergences; Briffault summed up the differences as a radical and incompatible division between conceptions of 'social history and the scope, principles and methods of social sciences'.[53] Those who uphold the original nature of the paternal family in fact view every phenomenon in the light of that original hypothesis. This struggle over the original nature of the human group became important in political theory.

The socialist tradition in general threw its weight behind the hypothesis of radical transformations in familial organisation — a commitment which will be explored more fully in Chapters 5 and 6. Socialist imagery of the period was full of democratic 'maternal' communism in opposition to individualistic patriarchal capitalism.[54] While positions on the originary form of society were not exclusively found with their corresponding political position, that they should have been adopted so ferociously indicates two interesting features. On the one hand, it confirms that kinship studies were still very much within the terms of reference of political theory. They were addressed often to solving problems of the interrelation of various instances of society and to making general statements about the forms of relations between humans in groups. That the family should have been such a central problem shows clearly that it had become a central and sensitive object of political concern. Second, it indicates how the *original* form which groups took had become crucial to saying something about their essential form. Even for those who argued fiercely for the transitoriness of familial relations, the aim was to establish that these relations *were* transitory.

Conclusion

Violent divisions between forms of explanation obsure common aspects in these early debates about kinship. They obscure, for example, the fact that both sides thought that the original form and subsequent development of kinship would reveal the nature of social and political alliances themselves. However much the significance of the procreative family was disputed, it was agreed that elements within kinship — as distinct from the procreative family — were explicable by their function for other social or political exigencies of a given human group.

In this agreement, an agreement which even the anti-evolutionists sometimes shared, there begins a period of systematic blindness to the specificity of sexual regulations. This blindness is paradoxical since these studies seem to treat not much else. But various hidden assumptions are made which resulted in dominant interpretations of kinship. First, there is an agreement that alliances made through kinship, for example marriage, have only *one* function. This function will be the same within and across all cultures. It is as if marriage had an essence which could be abstracted from all cultures; divisions simply concerned what the history or function of that practice was. Second, because of this assumption, sexual regulation becomes one of 'the determined' aspects of social forms. It becomes an element of the 'cultural' level of society, here referring to systems of beliefs, language, artistic practice, religion etc. It is separated conceptually from the real 'material' elements of society — the economy, property relations, the division of labour, and in many instances becomes reducible to these aspects. It is in this context that property relations became a privileged moment of explanations of kinship relations.

The aim of characterising these debates thus is not to suggest that kinship relations are perhaps determinant social forms (as did various theorists reacting to early forms of reductionism).[55] Here the aim is simply to draw attention to how a dominant form of theorisation emerged which in fact evaded dealing with the specificity of its own subject.

In the following chapter an account will be offered of how and why this non-theorisation of the specificity of a 'cultural' level was a problem. For it will demonstrate how sexual relations at the heart of kinship studies were hegemonised by definitions drawn from other disciplines. These definitions inscribed a notion of the natural which has compromised attempts to theorise the specific form of cultural relations.

3 Sexual antagonism: theories of sex in the social sciences

Introduction

The previous chapter traced how discussions revolved around a study of kinship as a social practice. It is a practice which is assumed to be based on the regulation of sexual reproduction. It is clear that in so far as these theories deal with sex, it is as an element in reproduction; either an element which instinctively belongs to the function of reproduction or which has to be forced towards it. A major determinant on this emphasis was the influence of theories from 'natural history' though not in the ways usually assumed.

The theorisation of reproduction owed much to biological arguments, even in those writers who did not explicitly espouse 'the man among the other animals'[1] argument. But simply to point to the centrality of explanations from natural history obscures what were the particular definitions of sex and sexed reproduction, how they were contested, and the differential effects of these definitions depending on their coincidence with other aspects of ethnological and social theory. A very distinctive configuration of elements did come to dominate in explanations of sexed reproduction in relation to human culture and its institutions. The major impact was the influence of the Darwinian notion of sexual selection rather than natural selection. This entered into combination with a rigid conception of the absolute quality of sexual division and with a particular notion of social determination already present within the social sciences. The result has been a notion of sexual reproduction which has long dominated the social sciences, and which was not fully displaced even in the critique of evolutionary theory.

Natural selection and sexual selection

In Darwin's theory of natural selection, there is little of the teleological character imprinted on evolutionist theories by such writers as Herbert Spencer. Natural selection, according to Darwin, involves the formation and variation of the species in relation to their environment: 'This preservation of favourable individual differences and variations, and the destruction of those which are injurious I have called Natural selection, or the Survival of the Fittest.'[2] There is, however, no necessity to the form or course which evolution will take as a result of this variability: 'Several writers have misapprehended or objected to the term Natural Selection. Some have even imagined that natural selection induces variability, whereas it implies only the preservation of such variations as arise and are beneficial to the beings under its conditions of life.'[3] It should be recognised that what is proposed here is not a theory of the necessity of evolution along any given direction. It is simply the method by which species and sub-species multiply and undergo mutations in relation to their environment. Indeed, the lack of teleology has occasionally worried commentators:[4]

> many critics have held that this is not scientific because the expression 'survival of the fittest' makes no predictions except 'what survives is fit', and so is tautologous, or an empty repetition of words. For example, if we ask, 'which are the fittest?' one answer might be 'those that survive' so that 'survival of the fittest' means only 'survival of the survivors'.

The purpose of Darwin's theories was not to propose a science based on predictability, but rather to displace notions of species as immutable entities.

While there is nothing in the theory of natural selection to justify a teleological theory of evolution, and hence no real theoretical basis for Darwin's appropriation by ethnocentric social evolutionists, this does not mean that the theory is without substance. It involves certain very distinctive and mutually dependent propositions, which can be summarised as follows. All organisms must reproduce. All organisms exhibit hereditary variations. Hereditary variations differ in their effect on reproduction. Therefore, variations with favourable effects on reproduction will succeed, those with unfavourable effects will fail, and organisms will change.

In all these propositions, one element is crucial. This is reproduction as the means of variation of the species. Moreover, it is *sexed* reproduction which, in the 'higher' organisms, is the mechanism of variation. Darwin assumes sexual *division* as the necessary element by which sexed reproduction takes place. 'Sexual selection' is, in fact, named as a principal motor of selection within species, entailing as it does, competition between individuals of the same species in order to kill a rival or attract the opposite sex. Hence it is the principal motor for the survival of the fittest, 'This form of selection depends, not on a struggle for existence in relation to other organic beings or to external conditions, but on a struggle between the individuals of one sex, generally the males for the possession of the other sex.'[5] The great variation between the colour and the structure of the sexes within a species can be accounted for as the effect of sexual selection. It involves the exaggerated growth of secondary sexual characteristics, such as plumage, etc., which are used to attract the opposite sex during courtship displays:[6]

when the male and female of any animal have the same
general habits of life, but differ in structure, colour and
ornament, such differences have been mainly caused by
sexual selection: that is, by individual males having had,
in successive generations, some advantages over other
males in their weapons, means of defense or charms, which
they have transmitted to their male offspring alone. Yet I
would not wish to attribute all sexual differences to this
agency: for we see in domestic animals peculiarities arising
and becoming attached to the male sex, which apparently
have not been augmented through selection by man.

77

Sexual selection is not, however, the only source of variation as far as Darwin is concerned. A species varies by the modification of the offspring in relation to its parents, but this variation is sometimes connected with modifications in relation to environment, sometimes with the nature of the organism and not as a result of variation through sexed reproduction.[7]

> Some naturalists have maintained that all variations are connected with the act of sexual reproduction; but this is certainly an error; for I have given in another work a long list of... plants which have suddenly produced a single bud with a new and sometimes widely different character from that of the other buds on the same plant ...we clearly see that the nature of the conditions is of subordinate importance in comparison with the nature of the organism in determining each particular form of variation.

But while the *form* of variation to a large extent is given by the constitution of the organism, the primary motor for adaptation to environment, is through sexed reproduction by which mutation is made possible.

Making this mechanism crucial, Darwin assumed sexual division, an assumption which fuelled debate among his contemporaries for a variety of reasons. Why, argued one, should the female take the place of the environment as she appears to do in the case of sexual selection.[8] Another critic objected to the free choice which sexual selection seemed to attribute to 'female aesthetic sensibilities'.[9] No, the dullness of the female should be attributed to the need for inconspicuousness during incubation, whereas male splendour is 'due to the general laws of growth and development', it being 'unnecessary to call to our aid so hypothetical a cause as the cumulative action of female preference'.[10]

This constitutional account argues that exaggerated sexual differences are not the result of struggling against rivals, rather 'something within the animal determines that the male should lead and the female follow in the evolution of new breeds'.[11] There must be something distinctive about the male and female cells; the female cell ensures the constancy of the species whereas the male reproductive cell has acquired a peculiar and distinctive capacity for mutation. What all these theories were concerned with was an *explanation* for the origin of sexual division and difference, which is simply assumed in Darwin's theories as an absolute, natural, distinction with a particular function in relation to a general structure of natural selection.

Geddes and Thompson, in *The Evolution of Sex*, explicitly raise the problem of the origin of sexual division. Apart from evolutionist biology being in its infancy, they isolate a very real suppression of this question, a suppression motivated perhaps by an unscientific acceptance of the 'delights' of extreme sexual difference:[12]

> Darwin was, indeed, himself characteristically silent in
> regard to the origin of sex, as well as many other 'big
> lifts' in the organic series. Many however, have from time
> to time pointed out that the existence of male and female
> was a good thing. Thus Weismann finds in sexual repro-
> duction the chief if not the sole source of progressive
> change. Be that as it may at present, it is evident that
> a certain preoccupation may somewhat obscure the
> question of how male and female have in reality come
> to be.

These debates point to the fact that Darwin's notion of sexual characteristics and their function did not go undisputed. 'Biological' explanations were not fixed, immutable categories with definite content; they were contested, even within the biological sciences.

However, as 'biological' theories of sex appeared in theories of kinship, they often appeared as ultimate explanations, beyond the realm of contestation and not subject to internal criticism. Thus in considerations of marriage and kinship, the *assumed* quality of sexual division constantly reappears. Sexual reproduction was premised on absolute sexual division and taken to be the activity on which other social structures operated. This can be seen more clearly by a consideration of the two related aspects of Darwinian theory — natural selection and sexual selection. The impact of these theories and the form which they took in studies of kinship can be seen to be dependent on their coincidence with other aspects of social theory.

Natural selection; the prohibition of incest

A cursory glance at debates on kinship at the turn of the century might reveal an overwhelming interest in the structures governing whom one may or may not marry. Furthermore, one might be forgiven for thinking that it was as a solution to this question about the prohibition of incest that Darwinian theories were primarily brought to bear. But a closer study of the theories of incest-avoidance serves to demonstrate that Darwinian notions of natural selection did not affect kinship debates in any unilateral way. There were too many other elements at play in these debates for them to be hegemonised by one particular version of Darwin — elements corresponding to other discourses within and outside ethnology itself. Moreover, where Darwinian theories were taken up, it was by no means in a homogeneous fashion. It will be remembered that Morgan talked of natural selection, entailing the survival of those peoples who practised incest-avoidance whose brain-capacity was thereby greatly increased. Others accepted this solution; exogamy was adopted to avoid the observed ill-effects of inbreeding. Arguments about the ill-effects of inbreeding, however, were met with an immediate barrage of criticism. In 1875, A. H. Huth had written in *The Marriage of Near Kin*[13] that avoidance of incest was nothing to do with conscious or unconscious knowledge of the ill-effects of in-breeding. This was primarily because there were no such effects: 'the statistics on which so much reliance has been placed, as a proof of the harmfulness of consanguineous marriage, are, when not absolutely false, miserably misleading and defective.'[14] No evidence from animals, which as species were in-breeding groups, nor humans, of whom many practised cross-cousin marriage, suggested any direct connection between degeneracy and in-breeding. In fact, Huth is more concerned to prove the disastrous effects of marriage *outside* the racial group, giving 'evidence' of sterility and degeneracy amongst the 'mulattos'.

Various ethnologists supported the dismissal of the

degeneracy/incest equation. In 1927, Briffault was still having to argue that 'attempts to substantiate the belief that inbreeding is harmful have resulted in complete failure'.[15] Lord Raglan, too in *Jocasta's Crime* (1929) also contested these ideas, arguing that none of the tribes which practise consanguineous marriage could be proved to be less healthy or mentally advanced than those which practised a rigorous taboo in both lines of descent.

The positions from which natural selection was taken as a valid explanation for marriage prohibition were varied. Westermarck suggested an instinctual aversion to incest, in the service of a bastard imitation of science. This was attacked by many, including Frazer who berated Westermarck for an unadulterated application of Darwin without considering the things which make men men.[16] Yet having argued that an instinctual aversion would, in fact, be witness to the instinct having once been very strong, Frazer himself then goes on to agree in an extraordinarily patronising fashion that exogamy may well correspond to an unconscious mimicry of science:[17]

> The end which it accomplished was wise though the thoughts of the men who invented it were foolish. In acting as they did, these poor savages blindly obeyed the impulse of the great evolutionary forces which in the physical world are constantly educing higher out of lower forms of existence and in the moral world civilisation out of savagery.

What is interesting about this preoccupation is that it combines a biological account with what has subsequently been designated a functional account. Marriage prohibitions are in the service of some other force, in this case the force which accidently prevents biological in-breeding. In terms of *how* marriage is theorised, the form of explanation is not so very different from that which saw marriage regulations as having a political function, that of consolidating relations between groups. The point was that sexual reproduction premised on absolute sexual division and expressed in marriage was unquestioned as the axis by which these structures could work.

Side by side with this combination of Darwinian theory and functional explanations, there existed another rather different interpretation of incest-avoidance, that characterised by Durkheim.[18] Here incest-avoidance was related to primitive modes of thought in particular religious thought, which itself arose from social structures. For Durkheim, the clue to incest-avoidance lay in another taboo practised by some savages, the isolation of menstrual women. Both are to be understood as a prohibition against spilling and therefore seeing the blood of your own totem group. This would amount to an act of cannibalism. In England, *Jocasta's Crime* was written from a broadly similar perspective. What irritated Lord Raglan as much as theories of natural selection underlying exogamy, was the functionalism which this often accompanied. Functional explanations of religion which assumed either a residual or historical expressivity, or the mystification of other social practices were hopeless. They assumed criteria of thought and action totally alien to our own society. First, why should rituals arise as a commemoration of a real historical event:[19] 'It would be impossible to find in England a sane man or even mad man who would plunge an arrow into his eye in order to commemorate the Battle of Hastings, yet this is the kind of thing which the savage is supposed to spend his life doing.' Second, there is no reason why religious practices and superstitions should arise from political and economic functions. Are we to believe that,[20]

> If the law as to dog licenses continues in force, people will come to believe that to take out a dog license is an infallible means of securing the favour of the Deity or defeating the machinations of the evil one, and that a dog for which there is no license in force will inevitably die of distemper.

The whole system of explanation of incest-probition combining natural selection and functionalism offended Raglan. Why should certain practices and beliefs, like marriage and religion, always be explained by reference to some other, 'material' function:[21]

The chief tenet held by the followers of this system and one which makes the scientific study of social origins and developments impossible, is that any one who can invent a plausible excuse for a silly custom has not only justified but completely explained that custom.

Raglan's solution to incest-avoidance is not similar to Durkheim's. He claims that it is motivated by religious superstition which dictates that it is harmful to have sexual intercourse with anyone who lives on the same side of the stream as yourself. This apparently 'irrational' conclusion is premised on Raglan's insistence that religious forms of thought and superstitions do themselves construct social practices and are not necessarily the effect of other material social practices. It was motivated by a rigorous rejection of 'rationalist' explanations which are, in fact, simply an imposition of Western rationality.

Differences in theories of incest-avoidance serve to demonstrate that there was no simple way in which Darwinian notions became the dominant form of explanation of these practices. Themes of incest-avoidance touched on, and contributed to, many other discourses and considerations outside social sciences; explanations did not go uncontested. For the same reason, where Darwinian ideas of natural selection were mobilised as explanations, they were by no means simply mobilised to bolster reactionary political arguments about primitive and advanced races.

At one level, stressing hereditary and species, the theory of natural selection fuelled growing racialist doctrines which took races to be subdivisions of the human species, some being designated as more advanced than others. But the application of the theory of natural selection to the phenomena of incest-avoidance created a whole series of contradictions. There was, for example, a contradiction between that interpretation which stressed the necessity for groups (e.g. an exogamous tribe) to marry outside themselves, and racialist arguments which stressed the imperative for the race to remain pure. The racialist tendency was further complicated with the consolidation of eugenicist arguments which stressed the damaging effects of heridatory, and in many cases argued that only the 'healthy' should breed.[22] As with racialist arguments, the eugenicists tended to see breeding outside the group more damaging than a healthy, vigorous in-breeding stock. What is interesting about these contradictions are the confusions over the terms of family, social group and race. Morgan took the crudely ethnocentric view that Western society is advanced because the taboo on incest which is operated there exercises the most effective bar on in-breeding. For the theorists who were more subtle, the problem of defining where an exogamous social group ended and a species began proved to be rather difficult.

The extent to which eugenicist arguments were present in political debates of this period is only just beginning to be fully appreciated. It is clear, however, that intervention in family practices and sexuality was considered a highly important object of social regulation and this applies both for the left and the right. Not surprisingly, then theories of the effects of breeding and hereditary were not to pass in any uncontested way into usage in social sciences.

Not only were eugenicist and racialist arguments crucially interested in, and contributory to, debates as to the marriage regulations of cultural groups, but the question of incest-avoidance was one which was also at the centre of some violent social controversies of that period. Problems of extreme poverty and urban overcrowding finally began to assert themselves in the latter half of the nineteenth century. The image which seems to have haunted the literature on housing reform and provoked extreme horror in the middle classes was the spectre of incest among the working classes. It is interesting to see that the terms in which various reports on the immorality entailed in overcrowding have distinct resonances with some of the debates referred to in these chapters. Reports referred to 'promiscuous herding'[23] 'relapses to the wild man',[24] 'the promiscuous ways in which families herd together',[25] and 'families styed together in the promiscuous intimacy of cattle'.[26] The horror of this 'moral degradation' was a strong element both in the development of social policy on housing and on the development of philanthropic activities.

Finally, the same period was also witness to a struggle over the redefinition of incest laws. Historically, incest had been 'an ecclesiastical not a criminal offence'.[27] Incest, in other words, was a sin, and the church prohibited sexual intercourse between persons related either by blood or by marriage (affinity). Since the Reformation, marriage with a deceased wife's sister or with a deceased husband's brother had been illegal. An act of Queen Mary's had legalised marriage with the deceased husband's brother but not with a deceased wife's sister. In 1835, a bill had been brought in the House of Lords to legalise this form of marriage and for the next seventy years this was a hotly contended issue. Jeffrey Weeks has suggested that this debate bore witness to tensions between residual kinship forms and the construction of new domestic relations throughout the nineteenth century:[28]

> there was in force in England from the Restoration to the early twentieth century a system of marriage that approved cousin marriage and discouraged marriage to affines (that is, inter alia, the deceased wife's sister). The established system conceived of marriage as an act of incorporation which maintained social status, it kept the family name from being lost and the family property from being distributed. The other system stressed that alliances could be maintained by remarriage and could be used to improve social standing. Inevitable conflicts developed. The law upheld the first system as long as the aristocracy were supreme. The ban against marriage to a deceased wife's sister was rescinded in 1907, another sign that the middle class had come into their own.

The debate on the subject stimulated violent controversies; innumerable tracts appeared and even an association called the Marriage Law Defence Union came into existence to prevent the law from being passed. When the law was finally passed in 1907, it was followed the next year by the Punishment of Incest Act, a law changing the status of incest from that of a sin to that of a crime. A study of the process of the creation of this law[29] has suggested that the primary influences in this change were concern over 'working-class morality', the offensive of the social purity movement, and the protection of minors — not, as has sometimes been thought, the influence of eugenic arguments. The centrality of theories of incest-avoidance had clear correspondences with several important contemporary issues. Such correspondences should alert us to the unlikelihood of any crude interpretation of natural selection passing unquestioned into the discourses of social sciences.

This caution is further confirmed when we see that notions of natural selection and heredity were sometimes taken up in the cause of progressive arguments, especially in the case of relations between the sexes. Charlotte Gilman Perkins, the American feminist, was by no means alone when she mobilised theories of natural selection to argue for the liberation of women. She argues that the two elements of Darwin's theory are distinct; natural selection develops race characteristics, sexual selection develops sexual characteristics. Sexual selection is the means by which reproduction, and therefore variation, occurs. But women, she argues, have been cut off from the real environment, the economic world of work, and have been forced to develop sexual characteristics alone. Because of the enforced dependency of women on men, man becomes the economic environment of women. The only characteristic that women are able to develop is sexual differences which they have done to 'morbid excess': [30]

> it can be shown that sex distinction in the human race is
> so excessive as not only to offend injuriously its own
> purpose but to check and pervert the progress of the
> race, it becomes a matter for most serious consideration.
> Nothing could be more inevitable however, under our socio-
> economic relations. By the economic dependence of the
> human female upon the male, the balance of forces is
> altered.

Yet despite the necessary caution for approaching the effect of Darwinian theory on theories of kinship, Charlotte Gilman's ideas do confirm that his idea did enter social sciences in one relatively uncontested way. Despite the divergences over the applicability of theories of natural selection to specifically human institutions, there was formed a distinctive configuration where functionalism was combined with a selective appropriation of Darwinian concepts. This occurred through the way in which marriage sometimes came to be treated as a means of variation of the species and thereby came to be synonymous with sex. In this merger, which involved a slide between notions of mating and marriage, a definite notion of marriage was formed. Marriage was sometimes taken as the point at which societies without political organisation adapted to their environment. Environment, here, consisted not only of geographical elements, but of the various economic social institutions which mark a given culture.

Sex determination

One strand was particularly strong in effecting an elision between marriage and mating. This was the theme of population, which had acquired enormous currency, both politically and intellectually under the impulse of what has been called the development of neo-Malthusianism. Many of the problems raised by 'the conditions of the poor' debate, the urban overcrowding, unemployment and the terrible conditions under which many working-class people lived, were seen in certain quarters to be soluble through limitation of the population. Increasingly, this became the eugenicist strand in British politics, advocating not just limitation of the population, but also selective limitation which sought to deny the possibility of reproduction to 'degenerates'.[31] Population exigencies appeared as widely accepted explanations of the function of marriage. They appeared to advance an idea that mating and marriage functioned to replenish the population numerically to the equilibrium which could be supported by a given environment. Again and again marriage was theorised as having the aim of uniting sexually divided creatures for the purpose of reproduction, not just of themselves but of the equilibrium of a given population, 'sex...by being the means of variation of organic life, enables the organism to withstand changed environmental conditions.'[32]

Sex antagonism

The function of marriage thus appeared within speculative

ethnology in a quite distinctive way. Sexual division was absolute. It generated a whole series of antagonistic interests and activities. Darwin's quite limited propositions are here far exceeded. No longer is sexed reproduction simply a mechanism of variation. It becomes a principle entailing different functions, activities and interests of the sexes. It becomes, under the impulsion of the romantic influence, a theory of different spheres of influence, different principles in the formation of culture. Sexual division is transformed from an assumed but arbitrary category into a meaningful and symbolic division, pregnant with cultural antithesis. The mode in which the sexes are theorised as interest groups varies considerably within different theories, but there is virtually no writer of this period who systematically challenges the very idea. It appears explicitly in the idea of sex antagonism as a motor of history, implicitly in the contest over descent groups for control of reproduction in evolutionary theories, and finally as an effect of theorisation of division of labour along sexual lines.

In particular, the theorisation of the accumulation of private property as a primary cause in the emergence of patriarchal families had the effect of constructing the sexes as antagonistic interest groups. Where the accumulation of private property is given as the motive for the transition from one exclusive line of descent to another, the motive rests not just on the deduction of the deprivation of the father under mother-right, but on an idea of a necessary antagonism between the sexes. This is a consequence of positing a necessary transition from one stage to another which is premised on a struggle for control of reproduction through control of descent group. This was, indeed, one of the points of attack which the anti-evolutionists brought to bear against general theories of transition: 'It is not easy to see why a traditionally sanctioned inheritance rule should suddenly rouse antagonism since a man is as likely to benefit as suffer by inheriting from a maternal uncle rather than from his father.'[33] Ranging from Bachofen's Amazons, defending their right to control descent groups, through to Engels arguing for the relation between the patriarchal family and private property, the transition to father-right was a transition theorised as resulting from an antagonism of interest groups. It arose from the desire of the fathers to perpetuate their identity through descent of name and property.

In some writing this implicit assumption of sex antagonism became an explicit theory. In *The Mystic Rose* [34] a fundamental antagonism between the sexes is taken to be a constitutive factor in social organisations. The marriage ceremony is a public working-through of the dangers which each sex presents to the other. The public expression of harmony is a mode of neutralising antagonism by an expression of a contrary intention: 'women cling together at marriage till the last moment. These phenomena also show how marriage ceremonies have inherent in them, as binding the pair together, or neutralising each other's dangerous influence, the intention and power to make their life harmonious and sympathetic.' [35] This assumption of the sexes as interest groups is by no means uncommon. It has two principle forms of expression; that which attributed to the sexes biological or reproductive interests, and that which theorised interests as arising out of the division of labour. The first was consolidated under the impulsion from Darwinian accounts of man amongst the other animals.

I have already shown the way in which Darwinian arguments were used to place sexual division as absolute, serving procreation, and the means by which the species effected variations in relation to the environment. In some hugely influential discussions no distinction was drawn between the function of marriage and mating; Westermarck, for example, transforms Darwinian sexual selection into an account of the different characteristics of the human male and female and their different interests in the process of mating and reproduction. He is slightly hesitant in his use of terms male and female but, in general, dominant definitions from contemporary biology can be unproblematically accepted: male is active, female is passive. The interest of the male is to disseminate his seed widely; the interest of the female is to secure care and protection for her young. [36]

Speaking of the male and female reproductive cells of

plants, Professor Sachs remarks that, wherever we are able
to observe an external difference between the two, the
male cell behaves actively in the union, the female
passively. . . .
The rule holds good for the human race, the man
generally playing the more active, the woman the more
passive part in courtship.

Marriage customs can be interpreted in terms of their ser-
vices for sexual selection. All behaviour should be understood
as having an instinctual basis, instincts rooted in sexual
behaviour always in the service of reproduction. Typical
beauty, for example, by which partners are selected, should
be understood in terms of the exaggeration of secondary
sexual characteristics, things like body hair on men. These
are the exaggerated sexual attributes by which animals make
their sexual display to attract the opposite sex. Equally,
incest-avoidance has its roots in instinctual aversion, an aversion springing from the lack of interest created by familiarity
and the stimulation pertaining to strangeness and difference.
Not many accounts of human marriage regulations were
so rigorously 'zoological' as Westermarck's. However, the
absolute division between the functions of the sexes both
biologically and within culture was quite the opposite. Again
and again we find references to the different functions of the
sexes determined by their role in the act of sexual reproduction. It is these different functions which generate mutual
antagonism:[37]

Social evolution, which has its origin in the association
and co-operation of the sexes, has accentuated the fundamental opposition between their respective aims and
interests. That antagonism is rooted in the profound
biological differences between the function of the
reproductive instinct in each — periodic rearing of
offspring in one sex; maximum dissemination of the
breed in the other.

The theme of sexual antagonism and sexual interests is
rarely absent in these philosophical speculations on the early
stages of human organisation. Occasionally, the implicit

assumptions of the debates erupt on the surface in what might be called 'hysterical' texts, like Walter Heape's *Sex Antagonism* (1913) and *The Dominant Sex* by Mathias and Mathilde Vaerting (1923). Hysterical, because these texts are not exactly representative of the mainstream of the debate, but they nevertheless take up the various preoccupations of these debates. Both start from the assumption that the history of social institutions is an effect of the violent struggle between the sexes. Both have their origins in political considerations, and therefore show up quite clearly how the themes of sexual antagonism and conflict were fuelled by the political climate of feminism and the reaction to it.

Heape's book attempts this history across the evidence and debates within anthropology, discussing totemism, exogamy, ignorance of paternity and the function of marriage. What the study of these factors can illuminate is 'the discontent in one form or another which is rife among us'.[38] Daily,'it becomes more evident that...what has for long smoldered as a grievance cannot any longer be restrained from bursting out into active antagonism'.[39] What can the sources to this discontent be? There are three, say Heape, 'Racial antagonism, Class antagonism and Sex Antagonism'. The first is unavoidable 'because of our great possessions'.[40] The second, class antagonism,[41]

> has ever been common with us as it has been with all
> civilised peoples:...although drastic change in the
> relation of class to class seems once more immanent,
> changes of this kind are no new thing, and we may have
> confidence that so long as the people of the country are
> patriotic, class readjustment is not necessarily a national
> evil but rather a sign of the vigour of the people'

But the third, sex antagonism, is the most fateful and spells doom for the human race: 'Sex antagonism is a family war and as family strife leads to the most bitter of all quarrels, so this war threatens to lead to enmity which may last for many years and work untold evil on the nation.'[42] It is the tactics of the suffragists which have caused this dread. They have confronted society with, 'strife as selfish, as brutal, as bitter and as unrestrained as that shown in any class

91

war between men alone'.[43] As a result of this confrontation 'man's opinion of woman has definitely been modified'. His attitude towards her 'as an integral part of society can never be the same again'.[44] Women of the contemporary women's movement have shown themselves to be reverting to a 'primitive condition', closely in accord with savage women.

This primitive condition, Heape argues can be seen in the institutions of savage society, totemism and exogamy, and these, like everything in Heape's schema, 'can be accounted for by biology'.[45] The essential aspect of biology as it is understood here is the irreducibility of the difference between the sexes, whose different biological instincts, 'reducible to their sexuality' can explain everything. Armed with this understanding, Heape can supplement the analysis of social institutions such as advanced by Frazer. Totemism and exogamy, it should be quite apparent, are the product of the male and female mind. Totemism is the product of 'the sick fantasies of pregnant women'[46] and represents the suppression of the male role in procreation. Exogamy, however, has all the characteristics of male supremacy; 'the scarcity of women, their capture, the religious sentiment regarding menstruous blood, and the instinctive aversion to sexual intercourse with those who have lived close together from youth; all are based on the idea of the male supremacy,[47] This supremacy is rooted in the idea of the male getting for himself as many and as varied women as possible. Exogamy is conceived of as a structure of power by which men achieve this, an achievement corresponding with the need to disseminate their seed as widely as possible. As a primitive male habit, exogamy with its emphasis on sensual stimulation, 'would certainly itself precede any superstitious, fanciful ideas evolved by the female'.[48] Exogamy, therefore, precedes totemism as a form of social organisation, since totemism is simply the product of pregnant women's sick fantasies. But the coexistence of totemism and exogamy point to a compromise having been formed between the sexes. Totemism eagerly seizes on the habit of exogamy to evolve laws which would consolidate the interests of the family, that is, women.[49]

it cannot be denied that while sexual passions and sexual gratification are of far more moment to the Male, the idea of the family in its turn [is] an essentially female sentiment. The former incalculates and stimulates roving freedom which is the characteristic of the Male, the latter consolidates the family and for the first time establishes the female as an essential part of the social structure.

Whereas sex struggles in the past were fought in the interests of the family and reproduction, the contemporary sex struggle is waged only by a minority and against the family, hence its terrible danger for society. The contemporary women's movement is a war waged by a minority, spinsters, 'the waste products of our female population'.[50] The reason why they are waste products is that they have forgone the only contribution which women make to society, that is, their function as reproducers, 'for on no matter wholly divorced from maternity and the rearing of children has the woman ever succeeded in establishing herself permanently as of essential, of irreplaceable, value to society'.[51] Moreover, human beings so completely dominated by their biological functions are geared to those biological functions. Women, according to Heape, absorb nourishment in a way which is geared towards reproduction. To neglect reproductive functions and to pursue mental stimulation is a fateful path for women to tread. It can only result in degeneracy and the pathological condition so typical of the suffragettes: 'degeneration in its turn is associated with disuse; the risks run by elderly spinsters who consistently indulge in violent and unrestrained excitement is a real one'.[52] It is an attribute of just how pervasive these ideas were that a book like this was not just laughed aside. Instead, it was actually given serious consideration by some influential conservative ethnologists. Sir James Frazer even acknowledges Heape as having suggested the relation between totemism and women's 'sick fantasies'.[53]

In much less extreme texts than *Sex Antagonism* the supposition of women as an interest group constantly reappears. We have already seen how this is partly accounted for by biological explanations, the function of the sexes in the act of reproduction. But the supposition of interest groups was no less prevalent where interests are theorised as the effect of work, in particular the division of labour. Within this context, endless texts mentioned the different roles which the sexes played in the various modes of production, and the effect of this on the relative position of the sexes. 'This separation of the sexes within the limits of the tribe, necessary in the interests of morality, was upheld and promoted by a differentiation of pursuits and by property.'[54] If the possibility of matriarchy had disappeared, the debate on the relative positions of the sexes gained new impetus mainly under the pressure of the theorisation of the division of labour. Where some argued, like Marx and Lafargue, that 'property in its origin was confined to a single sex', others suggested that women had invented agriculture while the men spent their days in animal-like warfare and hunting. Women's predominance in these areas might then explain their apparently high status in other societies. Endless books were written on the situation of women in primitive societies; a concern which preceded the particular configuration of kinship studies which I am now discussing. What was at stake now was the need to establish a certain homology between the technical mode of production, forms of property and the position of women. The disagreements on the subject were violent and irreconcilable.

At one extreme there was Herbert Spencer's assessment of 'the abject condition of women' among the savages who exhibit an 'entire absence of the higher sentiment that accompanies the relations between the sexes'.[55] But even liberals like Hobhouse, Wheeler and Ginsberg,[56] who made no such ethnocentric judgment about the morality of 'savages', saw no problem with taking 'the status of women' debate as a starting point for a statistical assessment of the correspondence between technical modes of production and social institutions. These writers refuse to deduce any necessary history or development from the existence of a particular institution. Different institutions of marriage may exist, but their causality is hidden. What is proposed is a cautious process of deducing the history of civilisation by a statistical method. This will establish patterns of correspondence between material institutions and social practices, for example between hunting or agricultural societies and the morals, law, religion and 'the position of women'. To this end a table is proposed whereby various practices are attributed certain scores. For marriage by capture for example, there is a negative score of −1!

In a rare instance, we are confronted with a book, *The Dominant Sex* by Mathias and Mathilde Vaerting, which starts from the assumption of the absolute division between the sexes but begins to deconstruct the terrain of the debate. History, they argue, is indeed the product of the struggle between the sexes. The course of history has been traced by the swinging of a pendulum between 'men's state dominance' and 'women's state dominance'. But the characteristic of these states is that not only will the dominant sex rigorously oppress its opposite but it will also attempt to obliterate any evidence of the other sex's former dominance. Such is the motive behind the ethnologists' systematic suppression of the data of mother-right societies, a suppression of 'the accounts of matters which fail to harmonise with current views concerning sex discrimination'.[57]

Even a progressive like Morgan was impelled by a systematic blindness, characteristic of his own age. This led to his defence of a uniform evolutionary pattern of society advancing towards monogamy and paternal dominance. For the Vaertings, this is an impossible combination of features. If a society is under paternal dominance, it can never have genuine monogamy but only 'duplex morality' or double standards. A genuinely monogamous society could only be premised on equality between the sexes.

The Dominant Sex starts from the political problem of how this genuine equality can be achieved. One of the first steps towards this is seen as the exposure of the ways in which male bias influences ways of thinking about masculinity and femininity especially in anthropological literature: 'The psychical trends that appear both in men and in women when one sex dominates the other, are universally human and not specifically masculine or feminine.'[58] Writers who assume the 'givenness' of the interests of sexed groups have been misled by the ideology of men's state dominance. For under male dominance, women are forced by the division of labour into a subordinate and inferior position:[59]

> We regard it as incontestable that the first division of labour was that between a dominant sex and a subordinate sex. Herein is perhaps to be found the origin of all division of labour. . . . The division of labour between the sexes originates in this way that the dominant sex tries to stabilise its power and to secure greater freedom for itself by providing food for the subordinate sex.

Thus so-called sexual characteristics have nothing to do with innateness. Either sex can acquire the characteristics of the weaker sex, including physique. Fattyness, for example, will always be a sign of the oppressed sex, as it is a characteristic associated with domestic labour. 'The cause of this difference between the sexes in the matter of bodily form when mono-sexual dominance prevails is unquestionably to be found in the sexual division of labour. The tendency to fatty deposits always affects the subordinate sex.'[60] What is more, sexual domination takes certain forms. It involves, for example, taking the subordinate sex as predominantly sexual beings. In this respect the Vaertings, themselves marxists, criticise the marxist tradition which too readily assumes a natural sexual division of labour instituted by the function of reproduction. It is quite wrong to assume that the first division of labour was between man and women for the procreation of children. There is nothing innate to the positions of subordination and domination and the physical and mental characteristics which accompany these states.

The Dominant Sex, is formulated on precisely the same terrain as *Sex Antagonism*, but asking questions of the material which begin to deconstruct the terrain itself. It argues that the struggle between the sexes has characterised human history, yet it also argues that there is nothing necessary about those sexual characteristics or the interests of the sexes. There are simply the interests of the dominant group. Yet the latter half of the proposition leaves no room for the former; if the sexes as such do not exist then how can they constitute themselves as a dominant sex? The book is strange and contradictory because it fails to see its own impossible position. It is also hugely revealing. It shows clearly the way in which the theorisation of the relation between the sexes entered accounts of social institutions; it attempts to expose the problems of these accounts, but in accepting the original premise of a historic conflict, it remains unable to deconstruct the naturalness of 'the sexes'.

Conclusion

This chapter has begun to argue that distinctive theories of sexual reproduction were dominant in these debates on the family. Partly, this was an effect of ideas from natural history. However, it was partly determined by other notions of sexual division and social determination already prevalent within the social sciences. The study of sexual regulation increasingly looked like the study of the regulation of sexual reproduction by social exigencies. As a result, the old problem of philosophy, that of nature versus culture, begins to be viewed in a distinctive way.

Sexual relations were taken to be based on sexual instincts shared with the animals. Animals mated and produced offspring. Yet institutions of marriage appeared to reveal fundamental differences. Everywhere there was evidence of order, regulation, the mobilisation of sexual relations for specific social functions — adaptation to the environment, formation of political alliances, consolidation of property, or whatever. It is in this context that the fascination with 'classificatory' relations of kinship must be understood. Decidedly human, requiring instinctual renunciation, the object on which they function is mating, an instinct shared with the animals. Marriage relations begin to be theorised as the critical moment between nature and culture.[61]

> Society is founded not on the union of the sexes but on what is a widely different thing, its prohibition, its limitation. The herd says to primitive man not 'thou shalt marry', but, save under the strictest limitations for the common good, 'thou shalt *not* marry'.

That marriage relations should be situated as the moment

between nature and culture left their status ambiguous, and, therefore, their theorisation open to contesting definitions. On the one hand, the apparent coincidence of mating and marriage seemed to excuse the use of explanations from the natural sciences. If mating followed certain exigencies within the animal kingdom, perhaps mankind's complex laws were simply a human variation of this. On the other hand, as distinctly human attributes involving prohibitions and systems quite unlike anything found among the animals, they seemed to invite explanation in purely social terms. What specifically human function did they fulfil — the formation of political alliances, the consolidation of property arrangements, the governance and stability of certain groups? If explanations purely in zoological or biological terms missed what was specifically human, explanations in purely social terms ironically affirmed a space of 'naturalness'. This was the instinctual attraction of the opposite sexes for the purpose of procreation — on which society operates its more 'complex' relations. Increasingly, culturalist explanations affirm a space for the theorisation of the 'instinctual'; increasingly biological arguments leave a space for the theorisation of culture. Each potentially can be compromised by the modes of explanation offered by the other.

What these developments bear witness to is, in fact, an affirmation of human sexual relations as distinctively cultural, perhaps *the* specifically human cultural relation. Simultaneously, however, this distinctiveness is theorised in such a way that its distinctiveness is assumed rather than explored. The sexual instinct is relatively unproblematic for these studies of marriage; it is an instinct mobilised by society for social reasons. Hence the explanation of marriage relations is increasingly in terms of their function for other social relations, those relations which have assumed the significant place in the account of social development — technology, the economy, property relations.

In the account of the theories of sex in sexual regulations, it is clear that sex has very distinctive meanings. It means a rigid notion of sexual division and a rigid notion of the instinct of reproduction. The notion of sexuality on which these theories turned is a rigid notion of sexual division in which the sexes have quite different activities and charac-teristics. In this respect, the theories corresponded to an ideological work characteristic of the period under con-sideration. For this period saw the construction of very definite categories of masculinity and femininity, partly arising from state intervention to produce a household in which women could be responsible for the domestic, while men would participate in the public arena.[62] Even though ideas of rigid sexual division had been contested within biology itself and within emergent psychology, they passed unquestioned into studies of familial relations. This fact shows clearly how the implicit agreement to treat marriage relations, initiating family and kinship, as cultural relations resulted in a systematic blindness to the implications of studies of sexuality from other areas.

4 The impasse on kinship

Introduction

In the previous three chapters, it has been shown how debates about the family and kinship were the bearers of a multitude of preoccupations about social relations. Where they did deal with sexual relations in their specificity, accounts were hegemonised by explanations starting from the primacy of the heterosexual reproductive instinct, and the absolute difference between male and female sexual interests. In general, however, the discussion of kinship and the family was dominated by the desire to produce a unilinear account of a universal human history. The study of kinship was therefore weighed down by a number of theoretical considerations; what, for example, was the essential difference between animal and human bonds; what were the earliest forms of alliance between groups; what was the first form of 'political' alliance? The work was cut out for the critics of evolutionary theory to deconstruct the tangle of assumptions and wild hypotheses which had come to surround the study of kinship and the family.

Some anthropologists like to present the emergence of criticisms of unilinear accounts of human history as the voices of reason emerging from the mists of 'speculative error'. And indeed it is true that this period saw a very necessary criticism of some of the wild flights of fancy indulged in by 'the armchair anthropologists'. Unilinear histories of the human race, based on speculation about

family forms, were criticised for ripping one or two practices out of their contexts and basing a whole history of
the human race on how this practice had been transformed.
But these vital, and still relevant, criticisms of evolutionary
hypotheses gained momentum neither as an outright rejection of the terms of evolutionary anthropology nor as
discourses which bore no relation to them. Rather, the
criticisms were formed in the very space where evolutionary
theory began to deconstruct itself. Because of this, many of
the assumptions and blindnesses of early anthropology were
carried through into the more cautious comparative study
of 'non-Western' societies. Moreover, in the reaction against
the excesses of evolutionary theories, some of the general
investigations of sexual relations disappeared altogether.

It might, perhaps, be asked why those arguments which
have so far been traced necessarily began to deconstruct
themselves. The reasons can be summarised in the following
way: comparative data assumed an increasing importance;
from the moment of the disruption of the patriarchal theory,
studies of the family turned around a wealth of comparative
data on forms of marriage and sexual relationships. Both
from the perspective of constructing a unilinear history and
from the perspective of assessing the social function of kinship relations the emphasis is on the differences between
forms of organising what is assumed to be essentially the
same institution, that is, the institution of sexual reproduction. Were there only differences or was there some identity
between the multiplicity of rules discovered? For the evolutionists, the aim was to find this identity in a unilinear
history or function of the institution of sexual reproduction.
Yet, at the same time, dominant explanations of determination made it difficult to specify what this assumed central
institution was. For, as we have seen, there was an insistence
that sexual regulation was specifically cultural, perhaps *the*
element on which culture was based, yet this regulation was
increasingly to be explained by reference to other social
practices. Sexual regulation, though claimed as a distinct
cultural practice, was theorised as fulfilling a function for
other social relations.

The double requirement of the distinctness of human

society, distinctive through its regulation of sexuality, and a simultaneous emphasis on comparative data, placed evolutionary theory under strain. It was difficult to maintain a speculative philosophy concerned with the distinctiveness of mankind in opposition to the animals, but increasingly founding itself on minutely detailed empirical knowledge. Its reliance on 'empirical' data opened all its postulates to contradiction. For every example of one practice, its exact opposite could be found. It became a philosophy which argued for the distinctiveness of human culture, but always sought to explain 'culture' by other aspects of the social. Certain elements of the social formation had assumed the position of determinants, for example technical developments, the distribution of labour, and property relations; other aspects, such as rituals, symbols, language, and now sexual regulation, were to be explained by reference to these determinants.

As the ensuing chapter will show, some aspects of the discipline which we know as anthropology emerged in the space of this internal deconstruction. Some theorists found a temporary solution to this double requirement of empiricism and the distinctiveness of human culture in the idea of each society as an expressive totality. The amalgam of all social practices express through their function the equilibrium of any given society. Paradoxically, the refusal of general accounts of the specific functioning of the cultural level laid anthropology open to explanations from other discourses. The notion of expressive totality lays itself open to precisely the question of the determination of that expressive totality, a question answered by appeal to those other refused disciplines, biology, demography, marxism and psychology.

This chapter concentrates on one moment in the formation of modern anthropology. It is an important moment because it illustrates how certain terms and approaches arose which still inflect our discussions of sexual relations. In the first place, the thorough criticisms of the ideas underlying evolutionary speculation on kinship and the family are still relevant. The criticisms of wild theories of 'patriarchy' or 'matriarchy', based on one practice taken out of its context, are criticisms which still hold good today. So, too, does the deconstruction of assumptions about the relation between the position of women and the role of property or technology in determining this position. Moreover, a note of caution was raised as to how far kinship is based on sexual regulation and how far universal theories of this are possible. Again, this is relevant to our contemporary investigation of sexual relations.

However, these criticisms of the excesses of earlier theories also exemplify certain very problematic developments within the social sciences. Many of the earlier assumptions about the nature of the sexual instinct were, in fact, retained. What is more, the possibility of conceiving of the 'instinct' as separate from 'society' was reinforced. A theoretical division between individual and society was reinforced. This division was established in the re-conceptualisation of the family. In addition, there was a hidden hierarchy of determinations which meant that the specific treatment of sexual relations could be evaded; sexual relations tended to be split between sexual relations (social forms) and sexual instinct (individual behaviour). It is around this division that some of the more sterile divisions between discourses have come to be orchestrated. These divisions are major barriers against contemporary theorisation of sexual relations. The solutions outlined in this chapter show how some of the questions now pursued by feminism dropped out of theoretical investigation.

The false problems from anthropological tradition

In 1930, writing in *Man*, Malinowski turned his attention to what he called 'the impasse on kinship'.[1] The article marked the culmination of a growing critique of the general speculation which had so far dominated the discussion of kinship. The criticisms had been accompanied by the emergence of anthropology as a distinctive discipline[2] and the widespread acceptance of empirical field-work as the dominant means by which 'primitive' societies were to be discussed.

Malinowski declared that 'kinship is the most difficult subject of social anthropology'.[3] Its study, however, had now reached an impasse because, 'it has been approached in a fundamentally wrong way'.[4] In opposition, Malinowski praised a new tendency[5] with its 'full recognition of the importance of the family', and 'the application of what is now called the functional method of anthropology — a method which consists above all in the analysis of primitive institutions as they work at present rather than in the reconstruction of a hypothetical past'.[6]

For Malinowski, the impasse in studies of kinship was self-evident: it 'is really due to the inheritance of false problems from anthropological tradition'.[7] On the one hand, there was the sterile debate as to whether kinship had 'collective' or 'individual' origins, that is, whether kinship was based on the clan or the family. On the other hand, there was 'the obsession' with classificatory systems of kinship. Both these debates failed to grasp the full complexity of the social group, and the way in which statuses and relationships are distributed within a given group.

These problems he argued, had emerged because of a dominant preoccupation with providing a monocausal account of the history, and therefore the origin, of kinship. On the contrary, kinship should be approached from the standpoint of the present: what do these kinship systems do *now*? The inadequacy of the earlier approach is demonstrated by the study of kinship terminology where these terms were frequently taken as 'survivals' of past forms, an effect of looking only at the history of kinship relations. Instead, the anthropologist should consider what kinship means to the natives now and through this understand how it functions in any given society. Only then can a picture be built of the relations between the family, the clan and the tribe, not as isolated, but as interrelated institutions.

Malinowski's arguments drew on elements in a mounting critique of earlier studies of kinship. To the forefront was a deconstruction of simple, unilinear, evolutionist accounts of human history. It produced a growing scepticism over the possibility of any single 'history' of the family or any single explanation of what determines familial forms. The deconstruction was fuelled partly by the contestation over the applicability of evolutionary theory to human societies, and partly by a political reconsideration of notions of primitivity. There was also a consolidation of field-work, carried out under the dominance of an ethic of comparative studies and accompanied by an increasing insistence on the 'truthfulness' of empirical data. Finally, the deconstruction of unilinear histories of an institution like the family was partly an effect of the retreat from general accounts of 'cultural' forms.

Contesting causalities: the critique of evolutionary theories

The critique of evolutionist and unilinear histories of kinship had several aspects. It was spearheaded by a growing distrust for theories of 'a unique form of cultural beginnings',[8] and an emphasis on cultural differences and complexities. The criticism of evolutionist explanations for social institutions was partly fuelled by a general criticism of the way in which evolutionary ideas were being used in political philosophy and the social sciences. There was a growing discontent with the way in which Darwin had been appropriated for a defence of political conservatism, absorbing 'the survival of the fittest' as an apology for unregulated economic competition and restriction of the franchise.[9] Some recognised that contemporary society was not the zenith of progress, but riven with contradiction and conflict.

The main reservation about simple transpositions of evolutionary accounts to human society, however, was their failure to consider the nature of the social: the complex of culture, art and language by which a society transmits its history and traditions to the ensuing generations. To suggest that one generation simply transmits physiological and biological characteristics is clearly problematic when it comes to the transmission of specifically cultural rules and traditions. For some, it was precisely the capacity of 'social inheritance' which gives mankind its great advantage over the animals.

If the neglect of these aspects was problematic within political and social theory, it was even more so for anthropological studies of 'primitive' societies. If nothing else, the emphasis on complicated systems of kinship arrangement undermined the possibility that any extant cultures were really 'primitive'. The drift of the work was towards a rather nebulous notion of culture as a structure made up of complex, interacting and mutually dependent parts.

Representational practices and sexual regulation had become the two great pillars of that totality designated culture; crucial, but always theorised by reference to other social practices. However undertheorised, all writers stressed this distinct realm, a distinction which rendered problematic the accounts drawn from the animal kingdom. Notions of hereditary and transmission drawn from evolutionary accounts had no room for a notion of transmission adequate to this conception of culture. Simplistic appropriations of evolutionary theory could therefore be dismissed as 'pseudo-scientific dogmatism'.[10]

Even amongst those peoples thought to be the most 'primitive', such as the Australian aborigines, a complex system of marriage regulations seemed to emphasise the insurmountable difference between mankind and the animals, whereby 'intellectuality' rendered mankind subject to tradition and culture. Any theory, then, which assumed that the primitive past of mankind was self-evident from contemporary 'primitives' was clearly blind to the evidence. Such an assumption must be attributed to the contemporary intellectual prejudices.

One major effect of this critique of unilinear histories of the family and the emphasis on differences between cultures was a widespread agreement that existing notions of causality would have to be revised. The expansion of field-work and the emphasis on cultural difference undermined the assumption that like phenomena could be assumed to have like causes. Indeed, there was a growing sense that general explanations of any kind would have to be abandoned.[11]

In the context of this attack on monocausal explanations of kinship and the insistence on different circumstances, there was a revival of explanations such as 'diffusionism'. This suggested that similar practices arose only through the interaction of cultures, not because they have the same origin or history. Whatever explanation was adopted, what was general was a crisis in the notion of causality; for some there was a general crisis of monocausal explanations; for others, it involved a reconsideration of various contesting explanations.

The critique of unilinear histories had several aspects, by no means reducible to anthropology's fantasy of itself as scientificity triumphing over the intellectual prejudices of a past era. There were the problems of the applicability of evolutionary doctrines to 'cultural forms'; there was the emphasis on complexity, and difference, backed up by extensive and detailed field-work; and there was the theoretical concomitant of this, the challenge to the causality presupposed by evolutionary doctrines, that is, the causality of a necessary teleology by which all human beings unfold the same characteristics and forms of social behaviour. This challenge to the causality that was ultimately presupposed by a unilinear history of culture was also characterised by a general suspension of any hypothesis of ultimate determination. This suspension of theories of ultimate determination and concentration on difference and complexity in fact concealed a nebulous but widespread adherence to the hierarchy by which some practices are thought to determine others. Nevertheless, the suspension of explicit theories of ultimate determination left the way open for anthropological studies to be constantly 'claimed' by those theories which held more rigorous notions of determination: marxism, psychology and biology.

If a simplistic characterisation of the critique of unilinear histories of kinship as the effect of contemporary intellectual prejudices is rejected, the terms in which the attack was carried out on the 'speculative errors' generated by the assumption of a unified history of the development of human society must be examined closely. There were three principal areas in which this clearing of the ground took place: the debate over the position of women; the question of property; and the study of kinship.

The status of women

Chapter 3 indicated how debates over the status of women in society formed a central part of hypotheses of the evolution of society. Even if commentators disagreed as to what constituted the 'highest' position of women, for a long time aspects concerning women's role and behaviour in society had been thought to be indicative of aspects of that society in general. There were a number of preconceptions to be cleared away by the serious student of 'primitive societies'. These preconceptions had passed into popular versions of primitive society. On the one hand, conservative philosophers took the position of women in early society to be little better than a slave or beast of burden, condemned to hard labour, bought as a commodity with no redress against her husband's brutality. Only Western civilisation had managed to elevate women to their proper place, outside production and politics. For socialists, evidence of matrilineal societies tended to be interpreted as evidence that primitive women were undisputed mistresses both of the family and society in general. The dominance of maternal principles was taken as synonymous with communism. Both conceptions, 'fall ludicrously wide of the mark', for as Lowie and the critics of evolutionary speculation point out, 'there is so much variability in the relations of woman to society that any general statement must be taken with caution'.[12] The notes of caution to be sounded are various but amount to a serious challenge to the assumption of any necessary connection between the mode of production of any given society and the status of women.

We have already noted the deconstruction of the assumption that descent reckoned through women implies their higher status. Following this, there was a note of caution related to the whole problem of how to talk about status, since status is ascribed in any given society in a number of different ways; 'the treatment of woman is one thing, her legal status another, her opportunities for public activity still another, while the character and extent of her labours belong again to a distinct category'.[13] Only confusion can result from mixing what might be empirical coincidence between these theoretically distinct realms. Commentators on the status of women should be warned against taking any of these levels singly as sufficient evidence of the status of women in any given society.

Lowie insists on the theoretical separability of these aspects of the position of women, although his grounds for

doing so are no less androcentric than some of his predecessors in so far as he poses the problem as one of how
men 'treat' women:[14]

> The harem beauty is not compelled to perform the
> drudgery of a menial, yet her position is not consistent
> with our ideals of human dignity, and the same applies
> in only slightly lesser degree to the European lady of
> quality in the age of chivalry. In a very different
> environment the Toda women, while well-treated,
> rank as inferior and are excluded from the ritualistic
> observances that occupy the foremost place in Toda
> culture. . . . On the other hand, the Andaman Island
> woman is virtually on a plane of equality with her
> husband, though a somewhat larger share of the work
> may fall upon her shoulders.

Further, the reassessment of the assumptions of unilinear
histories challenges the schema by which women's status
was attributed to economic factors. Lowie noted the 'exaggerated part' which economic factors had come to play in
interpretations of the position of women in primitive societies. There appeared to be fundamental problems, however,
with any simple equation of the status of women with the
technical mode of production, for example: 'the Amur
River fishermen, the Chinese agriculturalists, the Turkic
horsemen and cattle-breeders, and the Ostyak reindeer
nomads, all share essentially the same conception of the
female sex.'[15]

Lowie's reservations are twofold. On the one hand, there
is the likelihood that certain practices are diffused and
retained through conservatism rather than necessarily corresponding to the technical mode of production. Moreover,
there are many examples contradicting the correlation:
among the 'Hottentot', pastoral life goes amicably hand in
hand with sexual equality, while among the neighbouring
Bantu, where the women till the soil, they occupy a lower
position. These facts are 'certainly favourable neither to the
doctrine that economic activity automatically raises women's
status, nor to the theory that pastoral life as such prejudices

her status'.[16] A consideration of economic data fails to establish a particularly close correlation between them and
women's position: Lowie concluded that no real conclusion
can be drawn as to the correspondence between the status
of women and the mode of production — too many variations occur which seem to have their roots in 'customary
law', religion and forms of the division of labour. Concluding,
but still in androcentric terms, he confidently asserts that
so-called primitive societies do not consistently 'treat' their
women badly.

Primitive property

If evolutionary speculation had produced untenable hypotheses as to what the social position of women might tell
about the state of social organisation, it had produced no
less unsubstantiated hypotheses on the role of property in
primitive society. It was the duty of the anthropologist to
demystify some of these 'demonstrably false'[17] assumptions.
Detailed studies demonstrated the difficulty of assuming
any *necessary* correlation between technical modes of production and forms of property.

Lowie isolates several aspects which point to the need to
reconceptualise property relations and primitive society.
First of all, he argues, both communally held property and
individual rights over certain goods, etc., can be found co-
existing in societies like that of the American Indians. The
existence of forms of communal ownership cannot be
assumed to imply communism, for example the clan or
'sib' studied by Morgan as groups with collective ownership
in fact are themselves structured around rights of access
and inheritance. These are often sex-specific and the exclusion of certain groups from access and control of property
according to ideological functions serves as a warning against
any simplistic designation of communal property.

There are also different kinds of property, not all entailing
the same rights and statuses. There are differences between
movable and immovable property; differences between these
and chattels, human and otherwise; there are forms of incor-
poreal property, such as copyright and control of sacred or

religious paraphernalia; and there are often differences between hereditary and acquired property. All these forms, can be held differently even within the same society. Land tenure, for example, might be between a fraternal clan, but movable goods might descend through one particular descent group; an individual might be entitled to goods which she/he has acquired. Only one sex might inherit one form of goods, or, within collectively held land, there might be definite forms of individual possession, given by customary rights or springing from individual acquisition.

Certain assumed correspondences fall away. First, there is no clear correspondence between technical forms of social organisation, such as hunting, and forms of property holding. Individual rights and statuses are often determined by customary law which may vary greatly between cultures. Second, the role played by any particular group in production does not necessarily determine what their rights will be to hold property. For example, that women take an active role in production does not rule out the possibility that they may themselves appear in marriage law as chattels. Finally, political democracy cannot be confused with economic communism. Morgan was wrong to assume that the political democracy of Indian clan organisation is built on economic communism. The close examination of the Indian tribes reveals that collective and individualistic rights of possession are coexistent, yet the tribe structure is characterised by an advanced political democracy.

None of these clarifications was intended to belittle the crucial importance which forms of holding property play in the construction of social organisations. Nevertheless, this critique destroyed the possibility of constructing an evolutionary account of forms of holding property which itself would account for the development of kinship relations. It points to the fact that kin groupings themselves form part of the customary law by which property rights are often decided. This emphasis on the comparative nature of property relations and the emphasis on different forms, particularly within any given society, neglected the question of what relation these forms of property holding have to power and control. It was an account which neglected questions of the process of production, the forms in which it is initiated and controlled and the effect of this on social statuses and rights. It nevertheless points to speculative errors which were the legacy of evolutionary theory.

Kinship

The end product of the consolidation of critiques of unilinear histories was that kinship studies were hegemonised by a particular mode of explanation. In its initial moment, however, the reconsideration represented itself simply as a long overdue clarification of a state of theoretical confusion.

One of the favourites to disappear first was speculation over which form of descent had universal precedence, mother- or father-right. Such speculation is 'now gracing the refuse heaps of anthropological theory'.[18] Every one of the basic points in an argument for the unilinear development of kinship could be dismissed as contrary to ethnological evidence. Not only was monogamy common among the so-called rudest tribes, but even in the cases where this was not so, nothing is proved of the necessity for matrilineal descent; 'Biological paternity is one thing, sociological fatherhood another.'[19] Briffault's *The Mothers*, was the swan-song of theories which still maintained the evolution from unregulated mating. Malinowski closed the case on it as a work of 'brilliantly speculative erroneousness'.[20]

While there may be some correlation between rules of inheritance and rules of descent, this is by no means a necessary correlation. In general, it may be true that in a matrilineal society there will be matrilineal inheritance (that is, to the mother's brother's family) and in a patrilineal society inheritance will pass from father to sons, but there were too many exceptions to be ignored:[21]

There are matronymic tribes like the Crow and Hidatsa where some kinds of property are transmitted matrilineally others patrilineally; there are patronymic tribes like Warrumunga among whom the legacy goes to the maternal uncles and daughters, husbands of the deceased, that is to his mother's moiety not his own.

Finally, the necessity that patrilineal descent should be established as soon as property begins to be accumulated is proved to be totally fallacious:[22]

> A number of historically known cases show there is no automatic necessity. For example, the Navaho of Northern Arizona profited by the introduction of sheep into the South-West some time in the seventeenth century so as to develop into a prosperous pastoral people, yet in spite of their thriving flocks tended by the men, they have remained obstinately matrilineal.

Nothing other than the arbitrary imposition of an evolutionary schema of history on to this evidence could produce a necessary relation between the accumulation of property and father-right societies. This schema would be able to account for these societies as being in a state of transition but it would be imposing a schema which did not start from the facts.

Kinship — heterogeneous elements

The rethinking of kinship, and in particular the rethinking of work on the classificatory systems of kinship, took place in the context of an emphasis on 'kinship' as a series of heterogeneous relationships with distinct social functions. Kinship was broken down into a series of discrete functions, a move spearheaded by the attack on the idea that classificatory systems of kinship have procreative referents. Attention to the social functions of kinship led to a dismissal of the 'monstrous' mistakes which characterised Morgan's interpretation of the classificatory system as the petrified remains of a previous social organisation. Evidence of common words 'does not teach us that the mother's brother is called father but that both mother's brother and father are designated by a *common term* not strictly corresponding to any in our language'.[23] The critics of evolutionary accounts concluded that: 'There is no reason for assuming that the natives ever meant to imply more than a social status when applying kinship terms.'[24]

This separation of kinship terminology and kinship

relations from any necessary procreative referent was fundamentally premised on the insistence that any institution or
practice which exists now must have a place and function
within the entire extant social system. Various areas could
not be separated out as having distinct and isolated histories,
they had to be understood as having an immediate function.
Social forms which had previously been treated in isolation —
the clan, the procreative family, affiliation and inheritance —
had to be approached now as interrelated and having an
immediate function. All these elements could sometimes be
seen at play in the same society as part of 'an organically
connected whole'.[25]

This is a social structure made of a number of interrelated
entities. What had been treated previously as atomised units
at various stages of development could now be seen as units
functioning together to create an overall unity: 'while the
family exists in many societies alone, the clan never replaces
it, but is found as an additional institution.'[26] The problem
for anthropology then becomes one of finding out how the
various institutions are related to one another, and how they
function in relation to any given society as a totality: 'The
real problem is to find out how they are related to one
another, and how they *function*, that is, what part they play
respectively within the society, what social needs they satisfy
and what influence they exert.'[27]

From diachrony to synchrony; complex relations and the elementary family

The shift from considering institutions in isolation to considering them as part of an immediate and functioning
structure established a synchronic rather than diachronic
approach to the social structure. The shift meant that the
quest for a unilineal relationship between procreative family
and complex kinship relations would be abandoned once and
for all. But for some, the procreative family was in fact reinstated with a new importance.

Wild speculation about the history of the family and
kinship arrangements was suspended; the aim of anthropology was increasingly to study social institutions and

114

practices as elements interacting in a structure; increasingly, its object was minutely detailed accounts of distinct social units. These developments amount to a rigorous separation of strands which had often been run together.

First of all, kinship and descent should be distinguished. Kinship implies a series of statuses and their interrelationship according to a variety of rules and principles; it distinguishes groups of kin from those defined as non-kin. Descent should be taken as the formation of a unit, designated as consanguinary related kin. Not all kin are included in a descent group. Moreover, descent and inheritance do not necessarily follow the same lines. Authority, descent and inheritance are by no means confined to the same group. Recognition of a descent group or shared lineage does not imply anything about the state of obligations between an individual and a social group. Finally the existence of the procreative family does not necessarily tell us anything about the complex of social statuses decreed by other practices, including kinship relations.[28]

> Biologically every community must rest on the family — the grouping comprising a married couple and their children. But biological and social necessity need not coincide. It does not follow that the biological family must exist as a unit differentiated from the rest of the society aggregate of which it forms part. The matter is not one for a priori argument but of empirical fact.

In this context, a clarification of certain terms takes place. Relations of affiliation and obligation, which in general had been run together, were now conceptually separated. As early as 1912, Malinowski had been insistent that kinship should be recognised as a series of heterogeneous modes of constructing relationships - between various individuals. Relations of consanguinity, descent and inheritance should be conceptually separated. In each culture ideas of kinship can be quite different and are socially recognised in a variety of ways.

Beyond parental kinship, there are, according to Malinowski, a whole series of other ideas connected with kinship, given by 'the legal, moral and customary ideas by which a society

exercises its normative power in reference to the said relation'.[29] These legal, moral and customary ideas can be
broken down further into relations of descent and inheritance
within kinship. The question had become one of how to
specify the various practices operating on the individual to
define his/her social place. A series of practices, it was
argued, would define the position any individual would
occupy. There would be allegiances arising from the procreative unit, allegiances arising from descent group, from
marriage; indeed, a whole series of obligations according to
generation, sex and status would have to be acknowledged
as important in determining the social relations of any given
individual in any given society.

The insistence on the multiple obligations in which an
individual is caught was accompanied by a simultaneous
challenge to some of the previous assumptions as to the
relation between the clan and political society. Lowie, in
The Origin of the State, moves against Morgan's suggestion
that kinship-based societies and political societies (that is,
with state apparatuses) are radically different. Instead, he
insists that even in societies where clan affiliation is to the
forefront, there is often evidence of territorial organisation
existing simultaneously with clan organisation.

Thus the challenge to the conception of isolated and
mutually exclusive nature of social institutions is replaced
by a notion of society made up of complex, interacting
elements. A segment cut through an extant society would
reveal not its successive geological strata, as Tylor had
suggested, but a network of dependencies in which all elements are mutually interdependent and vital. No practice
can be understood except by reference to its relation to the
sum total of all other social practices.

Two features are striking in this theoretical development.
One is the move towards society as an expressive totality.
Societies can only be treated in their specificity yet an
account of all practices in their interaction adds up to 'the
social', and each aspect of the social expresses something of
that society as a totality. The second feature is that in this
initial move against unilineal accounts of kinship structure,
the procreative family in fact occupied a significant conceptual

116

role, and to some extent gave a specific colouring to the development of structural functionalism.

The reduction of the significance of the procreative family and the reconsideration of the interrelation between social and political practices provided the conditions by which social institutions could be conceptualised as elements interacting in a structure. It was no longer necessary to pre-suppose a coherent function or history for kinship and procreative family. The biological family had to be taken for granted in order that wild speculation about the history of the family could be suspended. Procreation and parental care exist — this does not exhaust what can be said about the numerous and complex ways in which social position and identity is constructed.

In the writers under investigation the apparent suspension of speculation on the procreative family did not mean that it disappeared as an object of investigation. These writers are not presented as typifying the anthropological trajectory. However, their treatment of the procreative family and the effect of this treatment on the conceptualisation of sexuality is representative of general tendencies within the social sciences. They demonstrate how the procreative family was assumed through the theoretical division between indi-vidual and society. This also reveals how sexuality was ascribed to the side of the individual, an ascription which has affirmed essentialist theories of sex.

The initial situation

The family, wrote Brenda Seligmann, never exists in isolation but always appears crossed by other social units, such as the clan or territorial groupings. However, that the 'facts' of procreation could be presupposed does not mean that the concept had no further place in the study of social relations. Allegiances and structures found in this 'primitive family' (Seligmann), or 'initial situation' (Malinowski) or 'elementary family' (Radcliffe-Brown) could sometimes be taken as a model for other social relations.

'The initial situation of kinship', writes Malinowski, 'is a compound of biological and cultural elements, or rather

...it consists of the facts of individual procreation culturally re-interpreted.'[30] While much of the wild speculation on the history of the family had been abandoned, it was accepted that the obligations, emotions and structures found within the procreative unit were theoretically separable from relations formed at a wider social level: 'every human being starts his sociological career within the small family group ...and whatever kinship might become later on in life it is always individual kinship at first'.[31] The initial situation is, however, always deeply modified by the particular cultural configuration in which it arises. There are only ever the broad outlines of the initial situation; from the outset it is 'deeply modified by such elements as maternal or paternal counting of kinship, matrilocal and patrilocal residence, the relative position of the husband and wife in a community, length of lactation, types of seclusion and taboos'.[32]

For Malinowski, the interrelation between the initial situation, in its broadest outlines, and the wider social relations which inflect it, express the two fundamental functions of kinship in society — the 'individual' and the 'communal' function. The wider or 'communal' functions can either be a consolidation or a distortion of the relationships found in 'individual kinship' (that is, the initial situation). The communal aspect is a function of allegiances within the group as a totality; sometimes it distorts relations of the initial situation with its complex series of relationships and obligations. The particular way in which an individual comes to enter the culture is through the internalisation of the collective representations by which the wider group represents itself — an 'interpretation of facts by the collective mind',[33] a collective psychological interpretation.

This insistence on the mode in which the wider relationships are internalised points to the importance with which the basic family is being invested. In spite of the insistence on cultural differences, it is the initial situation which is taken as the moment through which cultural relations are internalised. Thus the study of the initial situation, far from being trite and insignificant, is seen as a rich field of sociological investigation, and a field on which the anthropologist and the modern psychologist meet in common interest. This position is particularly revealing in the context of this book. It shows how one effect of the rigid insistence on a synchronic analysis — the analysis of the mutually interdependent elements and functions of a social structure — was to leave the way open to psychologistic, sometimes biological explanation of the causality of social structures.

When Malinowski makes the claim that: 'Parenthood is the starting point for most other sociological relationships',[34] he lays the way open to accounts about what constitutes the essential relationship of parenthood, however much he may say that this initial situation is already prestructured. In particular, it inscribes a division between the individual and the social. The individual is theorised as the 'given', the characteristics of the human, which are theorised as presocial and essential; this is exactly a dominant division within psychology, which is a mode of explanation favoured by Malinowski. This tolerance for 'psychological' explanations is characteristic of the space left open by the particular form which structural functionalism developed. There is the suggestion, for example, that the basically 'human' is a substantive realm, made up of emotions, sentiments and behavioural responses which can be accounted for an abstracted from the social relations in which they appear.

There is a division between individual and society which was formed critically around the division between 'intitial situation' (that is, basic family) and social regulations. In other words, a slippage between individual and 'basic family' took place, and 'individual' was increasingly assigned to the realm of psychology. This designation of an individual and initial situation, given in the procreative family, entailed a series of conceptual slippages around the notion of sexuality. Sexual regulation came to be thought as something internalised in the initial situation — thus the initial situation was constructed as an exchange between the instinctual and the social, constructing sexuality on the side of the individual, rather than as a social form with its own history.

In this way, the minimum common features of marriage relations — degrees of prohibited and preferential marriage (incest-taboo and exogamy) come to be thought as the definite area of regulation of the instinctual. Yet the determination of these instinctual regulations is thought to pertain to accounts of the 'instinctual', 'individual', 'human', etc. Within accounts of the structures and functions of social relations, these elementary structures can only be noted — their explanation can be taken care of by other disciplines:[35]

> It is not the function of the ethnologist but of the biologist and psychologist to explain why man has so deep-rooted a horror of incest, though personally I accept Hobhouse's view that the sentiment is instinctive. The student of society merely has to reckon with the fact that the dread of incest limits the biologically possible number of unions. He must further register the different ways in which different communities conceive the incest rule. For while parents and child, brother and sister, are universally barred from mating many tribes favour and all but pre-scribe marriage between certain more remote kindred. This is to say, while the aversion to marriage within the group of the closest relatives may be instinctive, the extension of the sentiment beyond the restricted circle is conventional, some tribes drawing the line far more rigorously than others. For example the Blackfoot of Montana not only discountenance the marriage of cousins but look askance at any union within the local band because there is always the suspicion that some close blood relationship may have been overlooked.

Here, the suspension of general accounts of sexual regulation leaves the way open, as Lowie correctly notes, for accounts to be drawn from elsewhere — biology and psychology. Almost imperceptibly, 'sexuality' has become the realm of the instinctual and individual outside the social whereas marriage is firmly entrenched in the social — it is a means by which groups make alliances with each other.

Anthropology here suspends consideration of the sexual — either as instinct or historical form. It concerns itself only with the effects of sexual regulation, and leaves a space — the instinctual — which is theorised as qualitatively different but the proper subject of investigation for other disciplines. Thus a theoretical division within the social sciences is in-scribed in the heart of these tendencies within anthropology, a division between the individual — instinctual, emotional, behavioural — and the collective — social, economic, political. The family, understood as the early life of the individual, becomes theoretically distinguishable from so-called wider social relations like the clan.

It is partly an effect of the way in which the family is treated that reinforces this hopeless dilemma in the heart of the social sciences. The dilemma is still difficult to overcome; accounts of social relations are constantly confronted with substantive accounts of the individual, theorised as if this initial situation could be abstracted from the social relations in which it occurs.

The extent of the problem can perhaps be grasped by just considering the effects in these studies of the social even at this early stage. Brenda Seligmann, for example, suggests that clan and tribe relations took their specific form from the model of the relations within the primitive family. She gives the example that relations of super- and subordination between generations in wider social relations can be attributed to infantile dependency and parental authority.

The circularity of the argument should be apparent. Why should it be assumed that generational divisions entailing domination by the elders is the effect of 'natural' relations of domination between parents and children? The domination of a dependent group is by no means a given of all human relations. Indeed, such domination, where it occurs, could well be argued to arise from other forms of domination in society at large. Yet Seligmann assumes that parental relations can be abstracted from the society in which they occur and then applied to that society as an 'explanation' of relations between social groups. Thus, far from leaving a neutral space within an account of the social structure, the effect of such arguments is in the first place to construct an artificial division by the construction of conceptual differences; second, to draw on disciplines whose account of the 'initial' situation has been developed again by abstracting a hypothesised state, outside social regulations. This example is extreme; it nevertheless attempts to outline some of the problems accruing to the conceptual separation of 'initial' family situation and 'wider social relations'. Even if this separation is made and nothing is said about this initial situation, the positing of its existence as a conceptually separate space, constructs a space for 'the instinctual', the given, the individual response as being somehow outside society.

The notion of social structure which is beginning to emerge is quite distinctive; certain questions were either suspended or it was thought to find their explanation elsewhere. There was the insistence on approaching culture as a horizontal segment, in which all parts are assumed to have a complex but necessary interrelation. There was a cautious suspension of the necessity of deducing any sequence between procreative unit and wider social groupings. Yet this suspension was also an affirmation. It constructed the procreative unit as a conceptually different space from society, hence other disciplines could be asked for causal explanations for the relationships found there. Moreover, the procreative unit, or parental family, could be theorised as the means by which 'wider' social relations are internalised. While anthropology itself need not be asked to comment on the individual of the initial situation, it could usefully listen to these explanations of instinctual or sentimental attachments. These, in turn, could provide the explanation for other social relations; kinship, for example, might be seen as an extension of the relations and functions of the initial situation: 'kinship presents several facets corresponding to the various phases or stages of its development within the life history of the individual...kinship could be studied as a biographical approach'.[36]

A critical problem with this theoretical division is that it affirmed essentialist notions of sexuality. This happened, in two ways. On the one hand, the confinement of sex to the realm of the individual meant that it would be theorised by those disciplines which are founded on forms of essentialising arguments, for example biology or psychology. Moreover, the acceptance of the idea of instinct was also acceptance of this instinct as the hererosexual reproduction instinct. On the other hand, the social sciences guarded themselves against radical criticisms of the notion of the individual, such as were implicit in psychoanalytic theory, thereby favouring theorisation of the individual in terms of instincts, behaviour, fundamental character, or whatever.

Expressive totalities

Having isolated the way in which a theoretical division between individual and society was confirmed, it is now necessary to look at what is the overall conception of society. These accounts suggest that individual parts of society cannot be understood in isolation but must be understood as having an integral and functional relationship to one another. No understanding of one aspect of society can be produced without looking at all other aspects. All the aspects add up to the totality of that particular society, and each part taken in isolation expresses something of that totality. Such theoretical developments have added to the difficulty of theorising sexuality, kinship and social relations.

The claim is that it is theoretically possible to designate a social totality. The means by which the totality can be ascertained is by a detailed comparative study with other societies. The aim of that theoretical investigation is to demonstrate the *function* of social practices, understood as an effect of their relation to all other elements in that totality. The total social structure is understood as 'an arrangement of persons in relations institutionally defined and regulated';[37] in other words, social structure is theorised as a series of relationships between human agents. The point of regulation of the places ascribed to these human individuals is to ensure the continuance and stability of that society as a totality. Thus kinship is often seen as a social structure whose function is determined by its relation to all other elements of the social structure. It is the means by which the individual is ascribed places within society by which the continuance and stability of that society are guaranteed.

The problem with this is the notion of expressive totality. The implication is that at any point a segment could be drawn through society and everything which is seen there will express something essential about that particular society. It assumes, therefore, that there are general principles by which the society is articulated. Each aspect of the society will, in itself, express something of the overall interrelations which make up the social totality. This is going a good deal further than saying that any social practice or institution has definite social conditions of existence. Such a theory does not exclude the possibility of social changes occurring but it implies that these changes would consist in transitions from one general principle to another. (In these accounts the articulating principle is rarely specified since, general theories of the determination of the social formation are refused.) Thus the conception would largely entail the idea of transition from one state of stability to another; the function of the interrelating social elements would then be to reproduce the state of stability.

This notion of an expressive totality does not conceive of practices constructing agents in contradictory and antagonistic positions. Nor does it allow for the fact that practices, although arising in determinate social conditions, need not express an essential general principle of the social structure.[38] In theories of expressive totality, kinship was seen primarily as a mechanism by which places are ascribed to human agents in a functioning social structure. It becomes an agency of reproduction of the general principle of the social totality. In general, the possibility that kinship itself might be a practice by which antagonistic statuses and sexual relations are constructed was not pursued. Kinship relations clearly do produce men and women, and different generations, in differential, deferential and often antagonistic relations. In these theories, however, this suggestion is marginalised in order to emphasise an underlying social order which is expressed through kinship relations.

A second limitation is the suggestion that a structure is an arrangement of persons institutionally defined. This says much more than society is made up of individuals. It is the effect of a definite theoretical position: society is primarily human relations. It marginalises the suggestion made by marxism that relations between humanly constructed institutions may not be relations between human agents, but rather that the relationship between institutions may well determine the available positions for individuals within a given society. The definition of society as institutionally defined relations between persons is a particular problem in that it allows the theoretical distinction individual/society to run rife. The individual, as I have already remarked, can be abstracted from the society and theorised as a substantive unit of emotions, instincts and sentiments, even if many anthropologists did not pursue this explicitly. It leaves open the possibility that social structures might ultimately be explained by primary emotions or behaviour.

This theoretical space combined with another aspect of the structural functionalist trajectory to produce a social science which was for a while peculiarly unsuited to make any general analysis of cultural forms yet left itself open to explanations from other disciplines. On the one hand was the theoretical division between individual/society; on the other was a rigorous refusal of any explicit general theory of the determination of social relations. Whereas marxist theory might claim determination of cultural forms by the relations of production, the initial criticism of evolutionary theory was vehement in its rejection of any such generalised claim.

While many of the criticisms of the thoughtless equations produced by general theories of determination may still be considered valid, the refusal of any explicit general theory of social relations has resulted in very real problems, many of which anthropology itself soon recognised. Not least in these problems is that determination is, in fact, rarely refused; it is simply implicit. Psychological and biological explanations for sexual behaviour are evidence of a hidden causality. In the context of the refusal of general theories of the determination of such forms, spontaneous notions of power and domination and the distribution of inequalities frequently arise. Inequalities and the distribution of status are attributed to different forms of 'customary law', and differences between societies can only be recorded, never explained. This is clearly to be a problem for anthropology's relation to political theory. Whereas comparative data from other societies had had an honourable tradition in political sciences, which had employed it to indicate the determination of different customary forms by different factors of material life, the rigorous insistence on difference was to leave the way open to a hopeless spontaneity of difference. While not exactly recognised as a political problem, reservations about the apparent suspension of causal explanations were articulated quite early even within anthropology.

Comparative sterility

Kroeber, reviewing Lowie's *Primitive Society* in 1920,[39] takes the opportunity to review the current state of the discipline of anthropology. The method of *Primitive Society* 'is the ethnographic one. That is, it is descriptive instead of primarily interpretative. It is historical in the sense that it insists on first depicting things as they are then inferring generalisation, secondarily if at all, instead of plunging at once into a search for principles.'[40]

The approach is one that describes; it does not interpret. It takes each unique event, stressing difference and not 'the common likeness that may seem to run through events'.[41] The work creates a double impression. First, there is the 'endless diversity of institutions', and second, 'the uniformity of human motives'.[42] The end result is a sense of the immense multiplicity of cultural phenomena, and more than a suggestion that nothing can be done to interpret these phenomena.

Kroeber recognises the necessary demystification of the wild speculations of evolutionary theory. After all, he writes, 'honesty is the primary virtue and Lowie's soberness is a long advance on Morgan's brilliant illusions'.[43] But there are some serious reservations to be raised about the direction taken by this work. There are no causal explanations advanced and the end product is what Kroeber felicitously refers to as 'comparative sterility'. Here the theoretical shift which has taken place in the formation of anthropology becomes apparent. First, there is agreement that the only justifiable study of other cultures will be the detailed and exhaustive study of all aspects of that culture; second, it is agreed that anthropology is about human relations and that the 'human' should be explained by substantive accounts drawn from the 'sciences' of the body and the mind. Finally, no a priori causal explanations can be offered.[44]

It may be nothing but the result of a sane scientific method in a historical field. But it seems important that

ethnologists should recognise the situation. As long as
we continue offering the world only reconstructions of
specific detail, and consistently show a negativistic attitude
towards broader conclusions the world will find very little
profit in ethnology. People do want to know why.

There is an uncanny resemblance between Kroeber's reservations and those expressed by critics of contemporary attempts
to deconstruct general theories.[45] It does point to a still unresolved antagonism between the requirement for general,
usually 'materialist', explanations of human culture to which
comparative studies of cultures have been frequently suscept-
ible, and a discipline which refused any explicit adherence to
a theory of determination.

Kroeber's account of the state of the discipline is, however, also a mythology; it is the representation which this
trajectory also sought to give itself. For as the already-
discussed tendency towards psychologism and biologism
shows (a tendency which becomes explicit in the development of the culture and personality school of anthropology),
it is not causality in general which is being suspended, but
rather particular forms of causality. What is refused is the
unilinear history of any social institution and in particular
theories of determination by the economy. Yet, ironically,
the aggressive form taken by this rejection conceals the
fact that these arguments retained the nebulous hierarchy
of determination discussed earlier. In this, certain practices
occupy the role of determining, others the role of being
determined.

The peculiar combination of the apparent suspension of
general theories of determination, combined with very
definite propositions as to the structural relation between
elements in a social totality, produces a very distinctive
theoretical configuration. On the one side is an insistence
that societies express in all their parts the general principles by which the totality is articulated as a totality; on
the other side is an insistence that all societies exist as radically distinct from one another and that general theories
of social determination should be suspended.

There is an interesting paradox in this development. It

127

takes for granted that its specific object of investigation is a culture, yet those elements which have been described as the cultural level — beliefs, representations, sexual regulations, etc. — are rarely studied as specific and systematic activities. These studies are left to be dealt with by other disciplines, those dealing with the individual, where these practices are properly thought to belong.

Conclusion

This chapter has focused on one form of response to the debates covered in the previous chapters. This response has been favoured because it illuminates what criticisms can be made of earlier premises, criticisms which remain pertinent. Yet this chapter has also argued that these criticisms are typical of a development within the social sciences which has hindered the production of non-essentialising theories of sexuality.

The form taken by cultural relativism and the insistence on empiricism rendered these arguments problematic for studying sex in anything other than essentialist terms. This is because sex was divided up into sexual relations (marriage, household, etc.) and sexual instinct (individual behaviour). Sex, therefore, fell under a theoretical division between individual and society. In this, those practices which are deemed to come under the individual — that is, behaviour, sexual behaviour, instincts, needs — are excluded from systematic study within the social sciences. Yet a distinctive space is left for them to be theorised as a substantive and essential realm which will be illuminated by biology or psychology. The effect of the individual/society division and the particular model of social structure which was evolved had definite consequences. Social divisions, antagonisms and change disappeared as objects of inquiry. Where relations of power and domination were considered, they were often thought of in the same term as previously, that is, as relations of intersubjective domination. Because they are thought to arise spontaneously, from the individual as it were, they evade theorisation. The possibility of studying sexual relations as constructed, with definite histories producing divisions and conflicts, virtually disappears.

The second part of this book will examine two theories which now have the greatest claim on our attention for providing an account of sexual relations in society: marxism and psychoanalysis. These theories are important for two reasons. On the one hand, marxism confronts the problem of the social construction of division and conflict while psychoanalysis attempts to elaborate a non-essentialist account of sexuality. Yet both these theories can be demonstrated to be inadequate when an account of sexuality in forms of domination between men and women is required. It will be argued that this inadequacy is partly dependent on the fact that both disciplines relied heavily on the terms outlined in the earlier chapters. It is also partly dependent on the internal exigencies of each discipline.

5 The concept of the family in marxist theory

Introduction

In the previous chapter it was argued that in the rejection of evolutionist doctrines and some of their theoretical premises, some forms of interrogation of the family and the position of women became virtually impossible. The form taken by cultural relativism in these critiques rendered them problematic for developing general theories about the social position of women. Social divisions, antagonisms and change disappeared as objects of inquiry in the development of ideas of social structure. Yet where relations of domination were considered, they were often thought of in the same terms as previously, that is, as relations of intersubjective domination. Because these were thought to arise spontaneously or naturally, they were, to some extent, exempt from theorisation.

Surely such criticism could never be levelled at marxist thought, a factor which would appear to constitute its appeal?

Unlike those theories considered in the previous chapter, marxist theories have attempted to deliver a rigorously deterministic account of social relations and divisions. According to marxist thought, divisions and antagonisms within the social structure do not just arise spontaneously; they have definite historical conditions of existence and can therefore be overcome.

This is one of the reasons why marxism has had a constant engagement with feminism. Not only has equality between the sexes been an integral aspect of the formal beliefs of socialism, but within the theoretical works there has been a commitment to understanding the origins and forms of subordination between the sexes. This understanding has been very firmly tied to an investigation of the family which was crucial in the development of marxist political theory at the turn of the century. It provided an account of the relationship between 'civil society' and the state in a class-divided society.

This chapter will trace the two dominant influences on the theorisation of the family, that is, German idealist philosophy and the enthographic debates already discussed in this book. Ethnographic data allowed marxism to push back its account of the emergence of the state in order to assess the state's relation to class division. The outcome of these two influences was a history of the family accounting for how the 'mass' was gradually individualised with the development of private property. The account replaced previous economic histories characterised by the myth of the acquisitive individual who initiated production and was the natural possessor of private property. Instead, marxism produced the family as economic agent of the bourgeoisie. The history of the family, therefore, explained the relation between private property and the state. Yet, as we will see, the concept of the family in fact allowed marxism to retain a notion of agency of possession theorised in human terms.

The history of the family, then, was seen as crucial because it allowed the unification of a number of concepts: property, possession, class and the state. It was also used as a model for the interaction of these forces; the relations between the sexes in the family were sometimes taken as a model for other relations of domination, theorised as relations of intersubjective domination.

We will see in the following two chapters that it was precisely the weight which the family came to bear in marxism which has prevented adequate understanding of the relations between the sexes. Those theorists and practitioners most concerned with feminism or the woman question were those who drew most extensively on the theoretical writings on the family. Ironically, because the notion of the family was so crucially linked to other theoretical objectives, sexual division could never be adequately understood.

The family and the social totality

The centrality of the concept of the family can be demonstrated by considering the enormous impact of Engels's *The Origins of the Family, Private Property and the State*[1] on the first generation of marxist politicians. In a lecture delivered in 1919, Lenin asked the following questions, fundamental, he claimed, for developing a communist strategy: 'what is the state, how did it arise and what fundamentally should be the attitude to the state of the party of the working class, which is fighting for the complete overthrow of capitalism – the Communist Party?'[2] To answer these questions, he recommended that students should 'turn for help to Engels' book, *The Origin of the Family, Private Property and the State*':[3]

> This book says that every state in which private ownership of the land and means of production exists in which capital dominates, however democratic it may be, is a capitalist state, a machine used by the capitalists to keep the working class and the poor peasants in subjection; while universal suffrage, a Constituent Assembly, parliament are merely a form, a sort of promissory note, which does not alter the essence of the matter.[4]

The quotation demonstrates the immense political significance attributed to Engels's book which overtly focuses on the history of the family. Lenin relies upon Engels's claim that the history of the family has revealed the relationship between the state and private property. Lenin argues that for as long as private property exists, the state has arisen precisely in order to regulate the interests of private property.

This is a marxist political position which is frequently encountered. The questions which it raises are: what is this 'private property'? What is the agency which possesses it? How is the agency of possession related to the state that the state should necessarily represent its interest? These questions are answered in *The Origins*, Lenin asserts; such an assertion demonstrated clearly how the family was a concept by which the interaction between various elements of the social formation was theorised. More than just dealing with the position of women in society, Engels's text was frequently taken as a general statement of marxist philosophy by which political priorities could be formulated.

The study of the family assumed such an importance within marxism because it was developed by Engels in one of the texts where a more general account of the workings of the social formation was formulated. The early works of Marx himself had been concerned with developing a political and social theory, but these works were not widely known to the first generation of marxist intellectuals and activities. Their main inspiration was Marx's political economy, *Das Kapital*.[5] Many marxists, however, sought to supplement the analysis offered in *Das Kapital* with wider, more directly political analyses of the interrelation between all aspects of the social formation. Thus the dominant influences on early marxist political thought were simultaneously Marx's *Das Kapital*, on the one hand, and, on the other, the more 'sociological' works of Engels – *The Anti-Dühring* (1878), *The Origins* (1884) and *Ludwig Feuerbach* (1888).

That Marx's political economy seemed to lack an overall philosophical and social theory was a fact often bewailed, and it was generally claimed that Engels's writings, with their broader concerns, provided the basis of marxist social and political theory. Ryazanov noted how the younger generation which began its activity during the second half of the seventies learned what was scientific socialism, what were its philosophical principles, what was its method mainly through Engels. 'For the dissemination of Marxism as a special method and a special system, no book except *Capital* itself has done as much as *Anti-Dühring*. All the young Marxists who entered the public arena during the eighties – Bernstein, Karl Kautsky, Plekhanov – were brought up on this book.'[6] In 1920, Max Adler remarked that this work by Engels contained that general philosophical theory the absence of which had been so frequently lamented in the writings of Marx.

The peculiar significance of Engels for the development and formation of marxism, lies[7]

> in the way in which he liberated Marx's sociological work from the special economic form in which it first appeared and placed it in the larger framework of a general conception of society, enlarging Marxist thought . . . into a world-view by his prodigious development of its method, and his effort to relate it to the modern natural sciences.

Engels's interest in general histories of human societies existed in the context of interest in explanations of origins and functions of a whole series of disparate social elements. Evolutionism was but one account of the way in which social institutions and beliefs could be demonstrated to have a unified history or functions. It was this *unifying* feature which was significant for the development of marxist political theory. It suggested a way in which society as a totality could be conceptualised. Hence, it offered a way of specifying political priorities in order to transform that social totality.

What is especially interesting about these wider accounts is the extent to which the family is frequently the central object of interrogation. Both Cunow and Kautsky, leading politicians in the German social democratic movement, actively participated in the debates outlined in the first three chapters. They argued over the historical primacy of mother-right or father-right; Kautsky's article 'The Origins of Marriage and the Family' argued, before Engels, for the historical primacy of mother-right and its importance for theories of communism, suggesting the integral link between patriarchy and private property.[8] Cunow made detailed studies of ethnographic literature, contributing to studies of the family.[9] Both later took issue with Engels's outline in *The Origins*, disputing the 'naturalness' which Engels assumed to underlie sexual division of labour.[10] Marx, Engels, and Bebel were all deeply influenced by the ethnographic debates on the history of the family. For these writers, the literature on the family was seen as vital for understanding the workings of society, and hence for formulating a political position.

Given what has been said in earlier chapters, it is hardly surprising to find marxist theory implicated in these debates.

Studies of the history of the family were the bearers of speculation on the nature and form of alliances between groups. The family was frequently taken as the key elements which would explain the history and the function of the interrelation between social institutions. Perhaps this centrality would also explain a factor which has often puzzled commentators on the history of marxism. For these commentators have often been worried by the fact that some of the early marxists were involved in population politics and eugenics programmes. It seems insufficient to attribute this to a climate of political concerns. Rather, it would seem that the importance which the family had assumed in all social theories, including marxism, made it an important, perhaps *the* important, object of intervention. Given the fact that the family was frequently taken as the lynch-pin of social relations, it should be hardly surprising that social theorists should have considered that changes in family structures would be solutions to wider social problems.

Yet this centrality within marxist thought also requires explanation. For at another level marxist theory, particularly embodied in the later economic writings of Marx himself, challenges any theories which negate the overriding importance of the *economic* contradictions of bourgeois society. These later writings are geared towards accounts of bourgeois social relations. They stress the overarching importance of the structural economic contradictions between classes and the determination by economic structures on the form taken by social relations.

Basing itself on these later writings, there is a tradition within marxism which insists that the marxism which concerns itself with histories of the family and with the family as an agency of possession are based on an early 'humanist' theoretical position which was subsequently disclaimed even by Marx himself.[11] A marxist account of the capitalist mode of production, they argue, does not require that the agency of possession should be personified; an account of the capitalist mode of production should be of its relations of production, that is, with the economic relations of exchange, circulation and distribution.

The status of agency of possession does not seem to have

one consistent theoretical interpretation within marxism. Marxist scholars will doubtless continue to pit one reading against the other, since both cases can be made with equal validity. However, the contestation between the 'humanist' and 'the anti-humanist' readings of Marx evades the issues which these two chapters attempt to raise. I am trying to argue that there was a tradition within Marxist thought in which the family was crucially important to an overall theorisation of social relations. This was of especially importance for those who attempted to develop a feminist perspective within marxism. The tradition where the family was a crucial concept was also the tradition where feminist issues were given some importance, for example within the early stages of European social democratic parties. What is of interest is how this concept of the family arose, what functions it fulfilled in relation to overall marxist theory, and what its limitations were, given that an examination of sexual division was, hegemonised by the theoretical interpretation of the family.

It is for this reason that the remainder of this chapter traces a genealogy in the marxist treatment of the family which could perhaps be disrupted by the anti-humanist readings of Marx. The genealogy is traced here to indicate how the concept of the family functioned in relation to other concepts within marxist theory when it was brought forward as a crucial explanatory concept. It is hoped also that this genealogy will demonstrate that the concept of the family has been much more important than has previously been recognised, particularly in the formulation of political priorities, and that this is a major reason why feminist issues have not been properly raised.

The family, civil society and the state

The family was central in Marx's early criticisms of the idealism of German philosophy, as embodied particularly in Hegel's *Philosophy of Right*,[12] Marx agreed with Hegel's argument that the modern state was riven with contradictions and that the state appears as abstract and separate from civil society. Contrary to Hegel, however, Marx was anxious to explain this by reference to the material history of the state.

What was at stake for Marx in this dispute with idealism was to argue that although the state *was* indeed a higher or abstract level of society, this was not an effect of advances in the Idea. Instead, he argued that it was the form by which a conflict-ridden society is regulated. The state, according to Marx, has its origins in the real material history of the family and of civil society which is a history of conflicting interests, and social divisions. For Marx, the crucial term in these divisions is class conflict, premised on the division of labour.

The antagonism which Hegel described was, in fact, the conflict between wealth and private property but he failed to start from an analysis of the empirical family and civil society. Had he done so, argued Marx, he would have discovered the emergence of the state as a direct consequence of the division of labour and differential access to social wealth, He would have discovered that society starts with the family as 'simple social relations' and gradually becomes a complex society riven by the division of labour and different access to the means of production. The state arises as the space where the interests of private property are inscribed in the abstract against the contradictions and antagonisms, the potential chaos, of a society governed by individual property interests.

The only way a society fragmented into competing private interests can achieve community is by the abstraction from, or dissociation from, contending private interests:[13]

> One obtains man as an equal of other men, man as a
> member of his species and of the human community only
> by ignoring him as a member of an ethereal community.
> One obtains the citizen only by abstracting from the
> bourgeoisie.

Marx makes his argument by reference to primogeniture, the custom of inheritance through the eldest son. This proves the abstract regulatory function of the state, creating a community based on private property rather than individual interests. Such a society, requiring abstract regulation, rendered the possibility of a 'true family life' meaningless. Equally loved children do not share in a father's wealth. It is automatically entailed to the eldest son and demonstrates how it is property interests, not individuals, which are recognised by the state. Hegel was therefore wrong, Marx concludes, to assume that the family recognised by the state is a true family, meaning a unit based on love. Instead, it represents 'the barbarism of private property as opposed to family life'.[14]

In this contestation with Hegel around the notions of state and family, Marx was anxious to establish class contradiction at the basis of the antagonisms of 'modern society'. The family is central because Marx sought to indicate that what starts with the 'natural' family, based on love, slowly emerges into a complex society with competing private interests. It is this alone which requires the state to regulate the interests of private property at an abstract level. 'The political state cannot exist without the natural basis of the family and the artificial basis of civil society.'[15] Marx insisted that the concepts of family, civil society and the state should be separated. They should be seen in a chain, as a history, the one emerging from the other as a result of the increasing contradictions of private property. It is not a question of the inevitability of these forms but of their material history.

The contest between Marx and Hegel over the family is a contest over the relation between classes and the state. The study of the family was seen as crucial for understanding the material history of how society developed a state which regulated the interests of 'the family'. The works of Marx and Engels continued to develop these arguments. They attacked the 'German ideology' of the family which saw the family as the natural and eternal basis of society. It is in the family that social divisions arise; the history of the family reveals the accumulation of wealth and the division of labour which gradually transforms the 'sole simple' relations of the family group.[16]

The *German Ideology* and then sections of the *Grundrisse* began to deal with that vertical account of the development of contemporary capitalist social relations and thereby to deconstruct the forms in which capitalism appears. While Marx, in the *Grundrisse* and *Capital*, increasingly devoted his time to a detailed analysis of the economic operations of contemporary capitalist society, the necessity for a historical account of the emergence of these forms is never lost. It remained, however, for Engels to rework the earlier philosophical manuscripts under the influence of ethnological debates, into a general sociological treatise on an outline of human history.

Increasingly, the writings of Marx come to be concerned with a detailed description of the workings of the specifically capitalist mode of production: the structures entailed by exchange, capital accumulation and commodity production. In *Grundrisse* and *Capital* the division of labour is theorised as giving rise to an antagonism resulting from the contradiction between control of, and separation from the means of production. Separation involves the separation of the workers from the means of production, usually by means of legal property and effective possession through the agency of ownership. Effective possession is the agency with the capacity to control the means of production, that is to set them in motion, to finance enterprises and to control decision-making bodies. These two structures are, however, combined in a distinctive mode. The worker is always combined with the means of production through the wage form in which labour power is converted into a commodity. In addition, possession is not only the capacity to control and to exclude others from its use. The means of production are also possessed in the forms of commodities. Labour power is purchased in the form of wages and the production process takes the form of the production of commodities by means of other commodities, that is by the means of production and labour power. It is the division of labour within this schema which constitutes the class relations of capitalism.

It has been argued that it is the description of these abstract structures of capitalist relations of production which became all-important for the development of marxist thought.[17] It would be difficult, however, to ignore the fact that the early preoccupations with the history and the function of the family did not just disappear in the later writings. For one thing, the family continues to function as an implicit concept in Marx's *Das Kapital*; on the one hand, he refers to the wage being set by the cost of reproduction of the labourer and his family; on the other, he discusses the increase of female labour as destroying this reproductive unit, bringing more labourers into the labour process and thereby facilitating the increase in the production of surplus value. Thus, although Marx often appears to talk about the abstract nature of relations of production, his actual analysis often requires concepts of ideological social relations. Moreover, there was an explicit continuance of marxist concern with the family especially as a solution to the question of the social position of women.

During 1879–82, Marx himself carried out extensive research on the ethnographic writings on the family; his object was to research different modes of production and he concentrated on the debates generated by comparative jurisprudence over different forms of property holding. He was particularly concerned with studies of the so-called peasant collectives, studies of the *zadruga* household, and Morgan's accounts of the primitive gens. It was on Marx's ethnological research that Engels drew heavily in writing *The Origins of the Family, Private Property and the State*. Both Marx's research and Engels's development of this research show how the theme of transitions in the family is crucially linked to other theoretical objectives in marxist thought. Both these writings show that the interest in the family of Marx's early philosophical writings, although changed by the encounter with ethnography, remained fundamentally similar. The following study of *The Origins* attempts to outline a particular theoretical configuration around the concept of the family which developed within marxism. It is outlined because it was this configuration which tended to dominate both debates and politics addressed to the woman question. Thus the discussion will demonstrate the conditions which rendered marxism paradoxically weak in dealing with the specificity of sexual division.

The Origins of the Family, Private Property and the State

Published in 1884, Engels's *The Origins* offered itself modestly as simply fulfilling the bequest of Marx. It was simply an ordering of the ideas reached by Marx in his extensive reading of ethnographic material; it was 'a meagre substitute for what my departed friend no longer had time to do'.[18]

Yet, as I have already suggested, the impact of the book was of far wider significance than these modest claims would suggest. On the one hand, it was a systematisation of Marx's previous thought on the relation between the state, the family and private property. As such, it was received as an easy and comprehensible summary of the marxist philosophy of the state and private property. On the other hand, it did also specifically address the question of the position of women in society, and from a socialist standpoint. Together with Bebel's *Woman under Socialism* it was important in articulating a position on 'the woman question' which transformed the question from one entailing individualist solutions to one necessitating socialist solutions. Clara Zetkin, Alexandra Kollontai and numerous other socialist women recorded the profound influence which Engels's text had on their own formulation of the woman question. As such Engels's text deserves detailed consideration for it reveals above all, the political theory by which the woman question became such a problematic area in marxism while at the same time being absolutely central to it.

The Origins offers to supplement Marx's materialist account of history with Morgan's account of the prehistory of the human species. There are two questions to be asked of Marx and Engels's adherence to Morgan's historical schema. The first is what tenets of *Ancient History* were taken as demonstrating the fundamental historical materialist method? The second is what elements of Morgan's schema caused Engels's partisan support of Morgan's as against all other versions of prehistory?

The first can be dealt with briefly, since it is also well covered in commentaries on Engels's text. Morgan is taken to be arguing in support of 'the materialist conception' that 'the determining factor in history is, in the final instance, the production and reproduction of immediate life'.[19] Against the primacy of the idea and consciousness, labour and the processes by which the human species reproduces itself are foregrounded. Two points can be made in passing. First, although this statement is often claimed to be a statement of the historical materialist methodology, its blandness in fact evades any precise specification of the relations of causality and determination between social elements in 'historical materialism'. Second, it refers to reproduction as a purely procreative function. There is not the slightest hint in the following quotation of the idea of reproduction as the reproduction of the social totality. The production and reproduction of immediate life.[20]

> is of a two-fold character: on the one side, the production of the means of existence, of food, clothing and shelter and the tools necessary for that production; on the other side, the production of human beings themselves, the propagation of the species. The social organisation under which the people of a particular historical epoch and a particular country live is determined by both kinds of production: by the stage of development of labour on the one hand and the family on the other.

Some[21] have taken this statement as opening the way to a separate materialist history of the family, though, as any examination of *The Origins* will reveal, the history of the family proposed there has little to offer a feminist perspective. More generally, it can be said of both these propositions that at best they offer a bland statement that history delivers a record of the production and reproduction of human life. However, this tells us little of the particularity of the forms of determination and causality proposed by those theories.

Because of the vagueness of this statement as to what is entailed in the historical materialist method and the way in which Morgan is said to uphold it, I would argue that of much more interest is the second question: why the partisan championing of Morgan? It is this which reveals the theoretical function of the family for Engels.

The matriarchal gens

The peculiar significance of Morgan for Engels lies in this claim of the universal and historical primacy of the matriarchal gens:[22]

> The rediscovery of the primitive matriarchal gens as the earlier stage of the patriarchal gens of civilised peoples has the same importance for anthropology as Darwin's theory of evolution has for biology and Marx's theory of surplus

value for political economy. It enabled Morgan to outline for the first time a history of the family in which for the present so far as the material now available permits at least the classic stages of development in their main outline are now determined. That this opens a new epoch in the treatment of primitive history must be clear to everyone. The matriarchal gens has become the pivot on which the whole science turns; since its discovery we know where to look and what to look for in our research, and how to arrange our results.

Why is it that the hypothesis of the matriarchal gens should show 'where to look and what to look for in our research and how to arrange the results'? Why should such a hypothesis be so important for an account of society which was to influence the development of marxist political theory?

The matriarchal gens is a significant hypothesis because it is an account of a society based neither on the supposed supra-individual abstract regulation which characterises the state and the political level, nor on the supposed 'individualism' of the family. It is thus an account of social relations before the emergence of class society, where the primacy of the regulated collectivity is stressed over individualism or unregulated promiscuity. The account of the dissolution of first the matriarchal gens, then the patriarchal gens is a complex one. In Engels's hands, it entails not only the history of the monogamous family but also the transformation of modes of production and the history of the division of labour. These histories are given a necessary interrelation which is absent in Morgan. In the construction of a rigorous theory of causality, 'the family' comes to bear a great deal of weight.

The significance of stressing the primacy of the maternal collectivity becomes clear in Engels's dismissal of theories of an initial stage of unregulated promiscuity.[23] Engels insists on group marriage at the origins of human life. It shows the absence of any feeling of jealousy which 'develops relatively late'[24] and the absence of the morality which later becomes customary, such as the prohibition of incest. Prohibition of incest can be considered as 'a very valuable' invention;[25] It is a response to the unconsciously discerned advantages resulting from natural selection.

143

The first social form, then, for Engels, is the collective household practising group marriage, premised on absence of jealousy and primitive communism. Husbands and wives are possessed collectively and the only form of sexual prohibition is that between generations. While collective possession to some extent remains in force, gradually more extensive forms of incest-prohibition begin to be practised. A prohibition which emerges between siblings with the same mother is gradually extended to all collateral brothers and sisters. Siblings become organised into separate sexed groupings, each group being united by their claim of a female ancestor. Female lineage is seen as inevitable since fatherhood is unknowable. This is the matriarchal gens, a group recognising common ancestry but not differentiated into the individual or pairing family.[26] It is significant because it reveals a social bond without individualised possession, providing us 'with an unsuspected wealth of information about the fundamental features of social constitution in primitive times, before the introduction of the state.'[27] If this is the fundamental arrangement of the social constitution, how then did individual possession arise; how did the pairing marriage emerge; and why did the state arise if none of these forms is fundamental to society itself? To unravel the strands in the history of these relations is offered as an understanding of their contemporary function and a demonstration of their transitoriness.

The emergence of the pairing family

Initially pairing marriage arises partly as a result of ever-increasing marriage restrictions contingent on the workings of natural selection, partly as a result of the action of women who seek to raise themselves from the degraded position in group marriage. With growing populations, group marriage became more oppressive for women who, unlike the men, became motivated to press for more restricted marriages. In order for this change to become widespread, however, new *social* forces had to emerge and these were the effect of transitions in the mode of production. Formerly food had to be won afresh every day. But with the domestication of animals and the development of agriculture, long-term supplies, even possibly a surplus of provision could be created.

At this stage, wealth belongs to the gens but it instantly begins to transform social relationships. Slavery, for example, becomes a viable form of social relation. Whereas conquered tribes previously were either killed or incorporated, now the existence of slaves is seen as a source of increased production. This is because the family did not increase as quickly as the cattle; thus more people were required to look after them. Here arises the possibility of the 'individual' family: the possibility that an 'individual' family may be able to acquire adequate labour outside its relation to the gens. Marx, registering the significance of slavery in the emergence of the individual family, had written in his ethnological notebooks, 'In fact the monogamous family rests everywhere, in order to have an independent isolated existence, upon a domestic class which originally was direct slaves.'[28] The slavery inherent in the family is thus expressed in the acquisition of direct slaves.

These two factors deal the death blow to the matriarchal gens, and the overthrow of matriarchal principles which Engels called 'the world historical defeat of women'. On the one hand, the pairing family introduces the certainty of paternity. On the other hand, the accumulation of wealth, and in particular the form in which it is acquired, leads to the men seeking to transmit *their* property to their own genetic offspring. This is because the sexual division of labour is such that property in the form of the domestication of animals is in the hands of men; as a consequence it is *their* property. It is this which lies behind the emergence of the patriarchal family, the absolute control vested in the hands of one patriarch, and the establishment of the patriarchal gens. At this stage, the patriarchal family retains vestiges of the former collectivity of society. The conception of the patriarchal household taken from comparative jurisprudence furnishes evidence of collective possession; it is a collective economic unit in which absolute control is vested in the hands of the patriarch. From this stage, it is a small step to the monogamous family, which is 'based on the supremacy of the man, the express purpose to produce children of undisputed paternity'.[29]

Engels's account is steeped in the errors of speculative anthropology which assume that a general and universal history of the family was possible. Further, it assumes a natural social division of labour in which men as the creators of property are also the owners of property.[30] Presuppositions are also made about the functioning and interests of the sexes. Women will abhor promiscuity; men, on the other hand, will pursue their promiscuous interest wherever possible. Men will inevitably seek to establish their genetic rights over 'their' offspring. Not only is it assumed that what is created is owned but also that the acts of creation and ownership will be accompanied by the desire to transmit property exclusively to genetic offspring.

Engels's argument finally rests on a curious circularity resulting from the presupposition that pairing marriage is the unification of man and women for the purpose of pro-creation with a definite economic and legal relation. The collectivity – primitive communism – is 'proved' by the apparent prevalence of group marriage which apparently proves the absence of property rights. What is presupposed is that pairing or monogamous marriage in and of itself entails a form of possession in the sense of possession of commodities. The exclusivity of sexual relations is therefore assumed to be a contract in which one human subject becomes the possession of another – in general, the husband acquires the right to use the labour power of the woman and her offspring. Lineage thus becomes a sign of the capacity to dispose of the labour power of others – and this, as we will see later on, is Engels's model for the first form of private property. But in order to prove that the original social forms did not entail private property, Engels has to presume that monogamous marriage always expresses possession when the aim of *The Origins* is to demonstrate the particular history by which this, in fact, emerges. The absence of pairing marriage can then be taken as a sign of the absence of individualisation and private property. All share equal rights in marriage, they must therefore share equal rights to the product and control of labour. The 'authority' of the patriarch, put to use to guarantee a particular form of accumulation becomes the model of ownership. It entails the capacity to dispose of others' labour power. The relation of marriage, however, is a contract which permits this first form of private ownership. In this account, then, the individual family is both an effect of a mode of production and a social relation which makes a mode of production workable.

Engels's history is, however, also integrated to the transformation of the 'governance' of the gens and the transformations in the mode of production. The history of the family is inseparable from the history of the state. It is the individualised family which is a precondition for the emergence of the state and to which the state addresses itself.

The dissolution of the gens and the emergence of the state

Engels saw the gens as a distinct social group with distinct forms of social organisation which is not yet individualised. At first the gens is democratically organised; it elects representatives to wider confederacies, that is, the phratries and the tribes. Yet this social structure was doomed, despite its 'moral greatness'. There was a lack of regulation between tribes which led to a state of constant warfare. The organisation was premised on an undeveloped state of production and an extremely sparse population: 'However impressive the people of this epoch appear to us, they *are completely undifferentiated from one another*; as Marx says, they are still attached to the navel string of the primitive community.'[31] Individualisation from the mass takes place through the emergence of the family from the gens.[32] Engels is able to mark out a distinction between the family and the gens, arguing for the primacy of the latter precisely because he sees the family as the procreative grouping, identified as a unit distinct from all other similar procreative units. In fact, neither gens nor totemic groupings would exclude the existence of quite distinctive households with rival interests. But, for Engels, this procreative grouping is in antagonism with the gens; it is the very structure of individual interests since it provides a rationale for the developing modes of accumulation.

The transformation of the gens originally unified by social and collective considerations rather than the individualism of the family, takes place partly as a result of the natural history

147

of the family, but also a result of distinctive economic conditions. Initially, hunting society, with sparse population, is divided only according to primitive social division, that is, the *natural division between the sexes*. This division, predictably, is the division around women's management of the home and men's involvement with hunting. Wealth, initially, is created by the men who 'discover' agriculture and the domestication of animals. In this way the high status which women had originally enjoyed is destroyed. The power supposedly invested in their control of lineage and their exclusive involvement with the household is wrenched away from them. Instead, power now accrues to property and property accrues to those who create it. This development transforms the relative statuses of the sexes. Another consequence in this gradual development of the means of production is that it inaugurates the first great social division, between those tribes where pastoral forms are quickly instituted and those which continue in their former ways. The production of milk, meat, skins and even surpluses of these lays the foundations for exchange to take place. The differentiation of pastoral tribes paves the way for exchange to become a regular institution.

The increase of production in all branches – cattle-raising, agriculture, domestic handicrafts - gave human labour the capacity to produce more than was necessary for its maintenance. At the same time, this required more intensive labour. Thus the social division of groups produced the 'first great cleavage of society' into groups of masters and slaves, exploiters and exploited. These factors coincided to install the father as absolute master and patriarch, ruling despotically over not only his slaves but also his family, enforcing monogamy, and all this in order to accumulate and transmit to his genetic offspring. The second great division of labour took place when, with increased production and the accumulation of wealth, there was increased specialisation, from which arises production directly for exchange, commodity production. The distinction between rich and poor appears beside that of slaves and masters. It results from inequalities of property arising from the dissolution of the collective families, and the appropriation of land, by individual heads of family –

land which was previously the collective possession of the gens.

Denser population necessitates closer consolidation of internal and external action. The confederacy of tribes everywhere becomes a necessity, involving the gradual fusion of tribal territories, thus constituting the basis of the nation. Greater military efficiency ensues, a development soon turned to plunder and pillage. In turn, this creates even greater sources of wealth and lays the foundation for the development of the hereditary monarchy on the basis of military prowess. Thus the free, self-ordering gens is gradually transformed into an organisation which plunders and oppresses its neighbours. Emergent divisions of labour are intensified and consolidated and the merchant class emerges. These conditions have now produced wealth in commodities and slaves, wealth in money and finally wealth in land with the *gradual establishment of hereditary property*. Land could become a commodity once the ties with the gentile constitution had been cut and money demonstrated this possibility. Thus citizens were increasingly divided into classes according to wealth. Confronted with these new forces, gentile constitution became an anacronism. The gentile constitution had grown out of a society which knew no internal contradictions, and possessed no means of coercion except public opinion.

It is in this context of disintegration that the state arises; 'the state arises on the ruins of the gentle constitution'.[33] It is clear that in many ways the theory of the dissolution of the gentile constitution gleaned from Morgan is added as substance to the philosophical ideas advanced by Marx in his very early writings. The state is still the abstraction by which the general interests of private property are expressed over and above those of individuals.

This new force, the political level, is qualitatively different from the forms of alliances which had characterised gentile society.[34] The state, for example, is based on territorial considerations; political society will be characterised by the implementation of public forces, such as the army. Finally, the state, in this outline, operates in the interests of the economically dominant class, which is therefore seen as the politically dominant class. It should be noted that these

149

interests are not the expression of individual interests; the activity of the political instance transforms these to an abstract representation of interests. It is at a definite stage of economic development that the cleavage of society into classes produces the necessity for the state; it is therefore formed in the process of class struggle.

The family as economic unit: monogamy and prostitution

The history of the family unit plays a crucial role in the emergence of a class-divided society and the emergence of the state. The decisive victory of monogamy is one of the signs that 'civilisation' is beginning: 'It is based on the supremacy of the man, the express purpose being to produce children of undisputed paternity; such paternity is demanded because these children are later to come into their father's property – his natural heirs.'[35]

The monogamous family in this account is first and foremost an economic unit, the unit by which property is both accumulated and transmitted in the interest of the private individual. A necessary concomitant of the monogamous family as economic unit is that the sexual relation involved in marriage always expresses its economic function. It is for this reason that prostitution in *The Origins* is simply the obverse of bourgeois marriage. Here the exchange of money expresses the true economic nature of the sexual relation in bourgeois society. Prostitution, in fact, acquires a privileged place in marxist writing on the family and the woman question. Prostitution expresses aloud the economic nature of the sexual relation in bourgeois society. The traffic in women (the title of Emma Goldmann's tract on prostitution) was a theme which ran through all the writing on women at this time. Lenin referred with disgust to the 'traffic in flesh', Bebel saw the rottenness of bourgeois society in the prevalence of prostitution. Kollontai and Eleanor Marx Aveling, both saw prostitution as expressing the 'commercialism' of contemporary marriage. Far from bearing witness to marxism's entrenchment in Victorian morality and sexual represssiveness, the centrality of prostitution was a facet of the mode of explanation of sexual relations and the family in marxist theory.

The economic function of the monogamous family is made quite explicit in *The Origins*. Monogamy,[36]

> was not in any way the fruit of individual sex love, with which it had nothing whatever to do; marriage remained as before marriages of convenience. It was the first form of the family to be based not on natural but on economic conditions – on the victory of private property over primitive natural communal property.

When monogamous marriage makes its first appearance in history, it is far from a delightful reconciliation between men and women. Instead, it announces a struggle between the sexes unknown throughout the prehistoric period. Where *The German Ideology* had suggested that the first division of labour is that between man and woman for the propagation of children, now these divisions can be elaborated as laying the foundation for the development of class society:[37]

> The first class opposition that appears in history coincides with the development of the antagonism between man and woman in monogamous marriage, and the first class oppression coincides with that of the female sex by the male. Monogamous marriage was a great historical step forward; nevertheless, together with slavery and private wealth, it opens the period that has lasted until today in which every step forward is also relatively a step backwards in which prosperity and development for some is won through the misery and frustration of others. It is the cellular form of civilised society in which the nature of the oppositions and contradictions fully active in society can be already studied.

Here, the function of the family in marxist theory is fully expressed. The possibility of the accumulation of wealth may have arisen through the technical development of society, in particular the development of agriculture and the domestication of animals. It is this development which generates a rationale for slavery. This in turn provides the conditions for subjection in the family. Yet it is the pairing family which provides private property with a calculating agency, the monogamous family, with its supposed exigency of natural, that is, genetic, inheritance. This alone provides

151

the motor for the emergence of structures of private property, hence the division of labour which will institute class divisions. Thus the relation of domination of women by men is a model for the oppression entailed in class relations without becoming class relations themselves. Engels's history is a new version of the theory of individual acquisitiveness as the natural basis of society. The emergence of the monogamous family constructed an economic unit of property which previously had not existed: 'The transition to private property is gradually accomplished parallel with the transition of the pairing marriage into monogamy. The single family is becoming the economic unit of society.'[38]

For Engels, *marriage* is an economic relation, and the pairing family will necessarily mean transmission in the male line. We have already raised fundamental problems with this; it assumes a universal history of the 'family', it assumes that marriage has the same function in all cultures; it neglects the fact the economic relations initiated by marriage may not be invested in the man and woman but in other kin; it suppresses the possibility of women as the locus of transmission of property; it neglects forms of holding property and structures of transmission which by-pass the procreative family. That Engels's theorisation should presuppose all these make his conclusions as to division of labour within the family and the relation of this to class division very suspect. Furthermore a natural level of division of labour between the sexes is presupposed, excluding consideration of this division itself as a construct.

Classes, interests and representations

This examination of Engels's *The Origins* shows how, in a certain tradition of marxism, the conceptualisation of the family was integrally related to the theorisation of classes, class interests, agency of possession and political representations. Formed in the convergence of early marxist political theory and later ethnological theories, the concept of the family fulfilled several functions for Engels. It was seen as an economic unit, with an economic rationality under a system of private property. It thus functioned as a structure which took the problem of the human agency of the bourgeoisie back one stage. But this supposed attempt to provide a non-human account of the possessive agency of the bourgeoisie was, in fact, built on presuppositions about the relations between the sexes which have made their theorisation difficult. These assumptions are: a natural division of labour between the sexes; a male psychologistic motivation to ensure trans-mission of property to genetic offspring; and finally, the capacity and desire of the male to submit the female to these exigencies. Thus the account which sets out to demonstrate the emergence of the power relations of the 'modern family' provides this account by assuming certain features of that contemporary family, such as marriage entailing the subordi-nation of women as chattel.

Several issues need to be sorted out before going on to examine the specific treatment of the woman question. These relate to exactly how sexual division is theorised in relation to other social divisions, such as class; how and why class relations are given analytic priority over other social divisions; and how the human agency of possession relates to class. All these are implicitly answered in *The Origins* and it is important to understand them since in the following chapter it will be argued that the failure to confront the specificities of sexual division was largely conditioned by the political and analytical priorities set by the proposed interrelation of concepts around the family. Three elements of the theory presented in *The Origins* will help clarify the way in which the concepts are interrelated: the treatment of social division in the notion of primitive communism; the question of why women do not constitute a class; and finally, the way in which familial relations are sometimes taken as a model for class relations.

Social divisions in primitive communism

In *The Origins*, the gentile constitution is taken as a form of social organisation where there is a distribution of social sur-plus in a communistic fashion. This form of distribution can be more or less complex, and the marxist tradition has some-times taken kinship relations to be the mechanism of redistri-bution of the surplus in more or less complex forms.[39] The distinctive hierarchies which might be entailed in kinship networks, such as hierarchies between juniors and elders, and between the sexes, are not theorised as antagonistic contradictions. The gentile organisation is still thought to be a communistic, essentially democratic form of social organisation. Class contradiction is theorised as arising from differential relations to the means of production in terms of ownership. Thus we have a very delimited notion of antagonistic classes and interests; these are defined primarily in terms of ownership of the social surplus.

'Communistic' is clearly an economic designation of a very particular kind limited to a description of the redistribution of the surplus to the collective. It excludes, or at least minimises, consideration of the forms of domination and subordination which accrue to other social divisions, for example sexual divisions. This designation has recently been submitted to the interrogation of marxist feminists considering work on so-called 'pre-capitalist' societies. Here it has been indicated how marxist writing on whether or not class relations exist within pre-capitalist societies has not taken account of the social division of the sexes.[40] Whether the consistent subordination of the female sex to the male sex should logically constitute women as a class is a complicated issue and must be treated with some caution.

Why are the sexes not classes?

In *The Origins,* the sexes are not theorised as economic interest groups, that is, classes, even though all the likely conditions seem to be present in the designation of pre-capitalist modes of production. There is the presumption of an essential antagonism whereby men seek to wrest control of women's reproductive capacity to ensure genetic self-perpetuation. Women are not thought to be subject to the same psychologistic motivations. These factors constitute women as a radically different group from men. Their effect is to place women in a different relation to the relations of production. First, women are excluded as normal loci for the transmission of lineage and wealth, if paternity is known. Second, 'the natural division of labour between the sexes' is theorised as a division whose effects mean that men not only produce wealth but also therefore control it. Yet, curiously, none of this is sufficient to constitute the sexes as interest groups. In classical marxist theory, interest groups are seen to arise through a structurally different relation to the means of production. In capitalism, for example, two groups are bound together through exchange – those able to initiate production of and to control surplus are differentially positioned from those who do not. Classes, then, are constructed as effects of relations of production, dependent on structurally different relations to the means of production.

Despite women's distinctive relation to the means of production, they do not appear as an interest group even though they are absolutely distinct in some pre-capitalist social formations in terms of wealth, labour, authority and control of lineage. Thus even though classes are defined in terms of differential relations within the means of production, women do not appear as a class with identifiable interests. There are two reasons for this: the treatment of family as economic unit and the contradictoriness of the theorisation of class agency.

The first is that the family is theorised as an economic structure which unites the sexes; thus women are seen as combined through marriage to the structural position of the husband or father. This combination of the sexes in an economic unit should alert us to other factors in the theorisation of classes and agency of possession. It is clear that it is the family which is seen as the economic subject of the bourgeoisie. The bourgeois class is not a group of individuals with identical relations to and interests in, the means of production – this much is clear from the idea of the state as abstract representation. Yet because classes are thought to arise out of economic interests, a form of agency is required. It is the family which, produced by marriage as an economic function (that is, providing the rational for accumulation and inheritance), provides this agency. The economic rationality of this agency is provided only, however, if the possibility of women as an interest group is suppressed. Thus a distinctive account emerges not only of economic, but also sexual, relations. Marriage is seen as an economic structure; it creates an economic unit and the structure of inheritance creates the possibility and motive for capital accumulation. The sexes, therefore, can no longer appear as sexes in terms of economic subjectivity. The sexual connection is thus theorised as a bond in which antagonistic contradiction is subsumed under the contradiction between economic classes.

Social divisions and classes

There seems to be a certain level of arbitrariness in the way in which classes are designated in pre-capitalist modes of production, if women cannot be theorised as a class despite a radically different relation to the means of production. That the sexes should be combined in an economic unit, the family, does not seem to be sufficient grounds to deny that sexual division may be a potentially antagonistic social relation. The industrial enterprise is an economic unit, in competition with others, yet it is theorised in marxism as a unit in which antagonistic agents are combined. That there seems a certain logic in applying the marxist concept of class to women has been demonstrated by the facility with which certain recent feminist theories could extend the marxist model of class to women.[41]

What is clear is that, in Engels's work, the sexual and familial bond is thought to override class distinctions; it constitutes men and women as an economic unit in spite of the fact that the imagery used to describe this unit is one of the slave master and his slaves. It is clear that certain elisions have been made to avoid knotty problems. The ideological bond which constitutes marriage relations and constitutes them in such a way that men have definite privileges is not seen as an antagonistic contradiction. This, it appears, can only arise from structural contradictions in the relations of production, positions which are only occupied *by workers and their families* or the bourgeois family, not by sexes. What begins to be apparent is that there is a hierarchy by which certain social divisions are designated antagonistic and others are not. Antagonistic divisions arise, it appears, exclusively from the production, distribution and control of surplus.

The reason why women are not theorised as a class in pre-capitalist society may, perhaps, be clarified by examining why they are not theorised as a class in capitalist society. Here it is explicit that the concept of class would not allow for sex differentiation. It is argued that the accumulation of wealth and the development of exchange relations in the form of exchange of commodities, result in the structure of capitalist appropriation of the surplus. It is argued that there is a necessity for 'free labourers', bound to the means of production through the wage form. Only by this process is the labourer bound to the means of production in the form of commodities that is, wages. It is the wage form which produces surplus value, and lays the foundation for extensive capital accumulation.

This position insists that surplus value is extracted from what Marx calls 'undifferentiated agents'; in other words, capital is indifferent to the sex or social status of the wage labourer.[42] Capital seeks only to maximise its surplus; differences in remuneration arise from the differences in the amount of labour required for production. Wages, therefore, are equal to the value of the necessities of the labour, or rather the necessities of the labourer and his family. Class division is constituted in relation to this process of extraction of surplus; either the control of surplus is given in the form of ownership or there is separation from the means of production.

Dating from the first appearance of *Das Kapital*, various writers have raised fundamental problems with this theorisation of the extraction of surplus and its relation to the theorisation of class.[43] The fundamental problem with a theory of value is that it does not take account of social and ideological divisions. First of all, labour is not the only thing that commodities have in common. Exchange is fixed by many categories; hence it is not necessarily the amount of labour time and the maximum surplus that will fix the exchange rate between commodities. What is more, as history has made abundantly clear, remuneration for labour is not decided by the cost of reproduction of the labourer's necessities; it can be fixed by the operations of monopolies; by trade union activity; by ideological divisions like the differences between the sexes. Thus even in the categories which are employed to designate the construction of two major classes, the questions of the effects of other social divisions appear as insufficiently theorised. It appears that these social divisions have been arbitrarily designated as subsidiary to economic class contradiction arising from the wage form and relations of production under capitalism.

It might perhaps be argued that the reason why social division other than economic class relations are assigned to a secondary place is because a marxist analysis specifies class as an abstract concept, given by the relations of production.[44]

In other words, under capitalism, class refers to the structural contradiction at the level of production between categories of separation from and possession of the means of production. Such, indeed, would be the Althusserian reading of marxist texts. However, this chapter has already outlined that in a certain tradition the family is brought in as a human agency of possession, being the embodiment of bourgeois economic rationality. This indicates how the status of agency of possession is rarely resolved as an abstraction. A final aspect of the treatment of the family demonstrates quite clearly that, as often as not, classes are theorised as relations between human subjects with certain capacities. This is the mobilisation of the metaphor of paternal power.

Patriarchal power and the relations between classes

Despite the fact that the relations between the sexes are not inscribed as class relations, they are nevertheless taken as the model of the form of domination between classes. We have seen how in order for the family to become an effective economic unit, women must be subjected and defeated. This form of subjection installs the economic rationality of capital accumulation, the monogamous family. This form of subjection, that is, domestic slavery, characterises all subsequent forms of subjection.

This indicates clearly the contradictory manner in which the subject of economic interests is thought of. At one level, as shown earlier, the operations of the state are presented as the abstract representations of the interests of private property. This functioning of the political level is the place where the interests of private property are expressed beyond the individual interests of the human agents which make up a society. It is also the level of class struggle in a society where the classes do not just line up and confront each other but are crucially interdependent in the production process. Yet in spite of this theorisation of the mode of operation at the political level as a specific representational level in which interests are not theorised as the capacities of human agents, this 'patriarchal' model indicates how the relation between the classes is sometimes thought of in terms of intersubjective dominance, along the lines of the patriarchal family drawn from comparative jurisprudence. Thus the relation between the classes is thought to be one where the outcome of the struggle between the classes is decided in advance by the capacities (power) of one human individual over another.

The theoretical limitations should be immediately apparent. The patriarchal family is simultaneously the cause and effect of class relations. It is the development of social forces, like the accumulation of wealth, which is said to give rise to the patriarchal family, yet patriarchal power (desire and capacity to overthrow women and their offspring) is the capacity by which one class gains control over the means of production. Thus ownership and control is given a human agency, and that agency is a capacity accruing to the patriarch of a patriarchal family.

The effect of this way of thinking has been especially difficult for marxism. It suggests that the relationship between classes is a relationship between human individuals, invested with certain capacities and attributes. Like the capacity to put others' labour to work and to control lineage, attributed to the patriarch in Engels's account, it is often suggested that the bourgeoisie have the capacity to determine the outcome of struggle by means of their control over the means of production. The mechanism by which this capacity is guaranteed is the state. Various criticisms have been made of this account of class relations.[45] Most obviously, the capacity of possession, that is, the ability to control and set the means of production in motion, need not necessarily be invested in a human subject. Marx himself realised this when he studied the joint stock company which had all the attributes of a capitalist agency. Yet significantly he could not decide that the joint stock company was capitalist precisely because it lacked an agency of possession, the bourgeois man and family.

In addition, this conceptualisation of classes has had a reductive effect on the assessment of class struggle in relation to the state, or political level. It becomes a struggle whose outcome is decided in advance, decided by the intersubjective capacity of the bourgeoisie. Where the position is accepted, it is usually moderated; the state reflects the interests of the ruling class since they have intersubjective capacities. However, the state will be overcome through the inevitability of the collapse of capitalist social relations.

This account contradicts other aspects of the theorisation of class and political representation, other aspects found even in Engels's text. The notion of a capacity (power) of a human agent which has the potentiality to decide in advance the outcome of a struggle rather obviates the theorisation of the political level as a distinct practice with its own specificity, that is, as an abstraction of the interests of a class against the interests of any one individual. It seems pointless to hold to the idea of the specificity of the political level and its representations yet simultaneously to insist that these representations express the interests of a group as some kind of capacity.

Conclusion

This chapter has shown how in a certain tradition within marxist thought the concept of the family was mobilised as an interlinking concept in the theory of the totality. In particular, it was used by Engels to account for economic subjectivity, and was used to explain the relation between classes and the state. The analytic priority of the family subsumed any separate consideration of the division between the sexes as an antagonistic division. Yet we have seen that logically the conditions were present by which the sexes could have been thought of as antagonistic groupings. It indicates the way in which marriage is assumed as an ideological bond by which the sexes are seen to be united and submitted *as families* to the primary social antagonism, that between the classes.

This treatment of the family and sexual division within the family points to broader questions within marxism. For even those accounts of the social structure which reject the necessity for a calculating economic agency such as the family, assume no less aspects of sexual division. The insistence on the extraction of surplus value from undifferentiated labourers is an account relying on the iron law of value. But even here there is ambiguity about the status of sexual division within the labour market. At some moments, value is extracted from undifferentiated agents. At other moments, the entrance of women into the labour market requires that the employer ceases to pay the 'family wage' and begins to 'exploit' a higher number of labourers. It is clear for a number of reasons that the abstract notion of value functions only if the ideological divisions structuring the labour market are ignored.

In addition, we have seen that although much of the marxist account is aimed at a conceptualisation of the state as the abstract regulation of class interests, the notion of class itself is often inflected by ideological notions of the relations between the sexes. A notion of patriarchy as inter-subjective domination is sometimes used as a metaphor for class relations. Thus we frequently encounter explanations of the family which in fact *presuppose* aspects of the patriarchal family. Not only is a natural division of labour between the sexes presupposed, but class society is interpreted according to a psychological investment of men in paternity. The net effect has been a systematic blocking of any revision of a marxist analysis which might include sexual division as constructed and antagonistic.

The problem of the arbitrary marginalisation of social divisions other than those given in strictly economic terms points to the organisation of theoretical work to predict political forces. Marxism has aimed at producing a theory of the social totality which would both designate and activate the industrial working class as the prime motor of historical change in the development of socialist social relations.

In this chapter I have concentrated on marxism as philosophy; within that philosophy a series of questions were subsumed to analytic priorities. In the following chapter I will be considering marxism as a political programme in its treatment of sexual divisions. It is here that the form of conceptualisation of the family just studied came into its own. This was the tradition which offered explanation of, and politics towards, the position of women. The following examination will show the extent to which the analysis of sexual divisions and the family have been tied to political objectives. It was the very centrality of the concept of the family and the way it meshed with other political objectives which rendered problematic the specific treatment of sexual division.

6 The woman question and the early marxist left

Introduction

It is clear from the previous chapter that the family, far from being an absent concept in marxism, was centrally related to other aspects of theorisation. Nor can marxism reasonably be accused of neglecting the specific question of women's position in society. However, that very integration of the family and, under the family, sexual relations, to the theories of class and political representation meant that paradoxically the issue of women's social subordination found a too easy place in marxist schemas. This theoretical presence has rarely been translated into political priorities and the evidence for this is twofold. On the one hand, there is the evidence of conservatism towards the family and sexual relations often encountered in socialist societies. On the other hand, there is the fact that attempts to change sexual relations have frequently been subordinated to other political priorities.

There appears to be a central paradox confronting any consideration of marxism's adequacy to deal with the position of women in society; why, given the theoretical importance of these concerns, were they rarely brought to the forefront in social and political programmes? Was 'the woman question' central only in so far as the history of the family and the theoretical consideration of the status of women were the bearers of all other considerations on social relations as outlined in the first three chapters? Or, was it the priority

163

given to the idea of the working-class party and economic class antagonisms which meant that 'the woman question' rarely became more than a theoretical debate? On the answers to these questions hangs the issue of whether marxism can ever be useful for understanding sexual division in society.

Some might say that marxism naturally neglects women's politics because marxists are mainly men and that men as an interest group would not seek to further women's interests. This is an argument which ignores the evidence. It would be difficult to ignore the commitment which socialism above any other political philosophy has shown to challenging the subordinate position of women in society. Rather than consider the family sacrosanct, marxism insisted on the variability of familial forms. And such has been marxism's concern with the position of women in society that those societies in whose development marxist theory has been crucial often afford women's *formal* equality a significant place in their constitutions.[1] Who can doubt that marxism, with such commitments, would in its history have been both a natural ally for feminism and, indeed, in some cases, the point of origin for some forms of feminism? Both in the centrality which it gave to the concept of the family and in its offer of understanding forms of subordination in society in a 'materialist' fashion, the question of the subordinate position of women in society has rarely been totally absent from marxism's concerns.

Marx, Engels, Lenin and Stalin all at some point considered the 'woman question'. Lafargue, the head of the French Communist party, wrote a book considering the history of women's position in society.[2] August Bebel, leader of the German Social Democratic Party, wrote *Woman under Socialism*, a book which was to have enormous influence in social democratic politics. All believed that equality between the sexes was integrally linked with a wholesale transformation of society into an egalitarian, that is, socialist, society. Nor did this mean that the specific struggle for equality between the sexes was neglected. Marx and Engels, for example, were responsible for such actions as an amendment to the minimum programme of the French Worker's Party of 1880 where a legal measure was added there to the economic and political demands for women's emancipation; 'The abolition of all paragraphs of law which . . . put women in a subordinate position to men.'[3]

Lenin initiated changes in marriage, divorce and abortion laws and frequently stressed the role of socialism in the 'emancipation' of women. In 1921, he celebrated International Women's Day with an article in *Pravda* insisting on the need for the struggle against women's oppression to be joined to the cause of socialist construction:[4]

> The main and fundamental thing in Bolshevism and in the Russian October Revolution is the drawing into politics of precisely those who were most oppressed under capitalism. . . . And it is impossible to draw the masses into politics without also drawing in the women; for under capitalism, the female half of the human race suffers under a double yoke. The working woman and the peasant woman are oppressed by capital but in addition to that, even in the most democratic of bourgeois republics, they are, firstly, in an inferior position because the law denies them equality with men, and secondly . . . they are 'in domestic slavery, they are 'domestic slaves' crushed by the most petty, most menial, most arduous, and most stultifying work of the kitchen and by isolated domestic, family economy in general.

A few years later, even Stalin is no less effusive in his insistence on the crucial role women have to play in advancing socialism.[5]

> The fate of the proletarian movement, the victory or defeat of proletarian power depends on whether or not the reserve of women will be for or against the working class. That is why the first task of the proletariat and its advance detachment, the Communist Party, is to engage in decisive struggle for the freeing of women workers and peasants from the influence of the bourgeoisie, for political education and organisation of women workers and peasants beneath the banner of the proletariat.

Why is it, then, with all this apparent concern for women's position in society, that the relationship between feminism

165

and socialism has been at best stormy, and the record of socialist countries in achieving equality between the sexes and the liberation of women ranges between somewhat limited to absolutely dire? In the following chapter it will be argued that socialist politics concerning the position of women were always limited by their political and theoretical priorities. Women were simultaneously viewed as a 'natural' group and at the same time submerged in the concept of the family and the political priorities dictated by the integration of this concept with those of the state and classes.[6]

The family, the labour market and 'true sex love'

The politics advanced towards the family in *The Origins* are characteristic of much subsequent marxist writing on the subject. The disintegration of the family is seen as a sign of the hypocrisy of the bourgeoisie, who champion the family but who use women as a source of cheap labour. Nevertheless, women's increased role in production is welcomed by marxists because it simultaneously offers women freedom from economic dependence (and therefore slavery) and consequently destroys the economic basis for marriage, hence undermining a cornerstone of bourgeois society. It is only through the destruction of the economic basis of marriage that free and equal sexual relations will be achieved. For although the proletariat have no economic motive for marriage, their marriages have nevertheless been influenced by the patriarchal ideology of bourgeois society, installing the father as absolute authority with the wife as little better than the chief servant. Once economic dependency has ceased to distort relations, all humans will be able to choose their mates in the same way as the proletariat, that is, uninfluenced by economic considerations and expressing 'true sex love' which, for Engels, is monogamous, heterosexual and permanent.

There are two elements in the political goals expressed here – two elements whose lack of necessary integration explain much of marxism's difficult relation with feminism. On the one hand, there is the concern with increasing women's involvement in production and the destruction of the *economic function* of marriage. On the other hand, there is a concern that the quality of the relations between the sexes should be transformed, in other words, a transformation of moral and sexual relations.

The insistence on the need for women to become involved in production is characteristic of much marxist writing on the family. This is because it is assumed that the family has an economic function which must be destroyed. Marx, for example, assumes a degree of inevitability for women's increased role in production. Women will necessarily be drawn into production, and therefore waged labour, in the logic of technical development. Although the capitalist ceases to have to pay a family wage, there are more workers available from whom surplus value can be extracted.

We saw earlier how Marx insisted that surplus-value is extracted from 'undifferentiated' agents and how the wage is supposed to represent only the value of labour power and the creation of surplus, being indifferent to social categories of value. At other times, however,[7] Marx starts out with an original 'family' wage, adequate not just for the reproduction of the labourer but for the reproduction of wife and children as well. Thus destruction of the family unit will be a source of increased levels of exploitation; the capitalist may initially have to pay more, but increased productivity will lead to higher profits. Increased exploitation will lead to increasing social contradictions and hence the eventual overthrow of capitalist social relations.

This position insists that marriage has an economic function belonging to a particular mode of production which must be overthrown. It led to the kind of politics advanced by Engels in the second half of his formulation, his moral politics. For Engels, as for many subsequent marxists, it is the economic element which is the source of oppression within marriage. Once this element has been removed, sexual morality will pursue its 'true' course, that of heterosexual, monogamous love.

Relations of production, sexual relations and feminism

The fact that marxists were prepared to consider sexual

relations as likely to change and to speculate on the possibilities under socialism, meant that marxism was open to the emergent discourses around sexual relations. These discourses were also profoundly structured by the debates about the family and sexuality which were traced earlier. Many socialists considered these questions to be central. There were also many sexologists who were socialists. Some socialist programmes even adopted quite radical perspectives on sexual relations.

But when this question was raised with any systematicity, as with Stella Browne in England, or Kollontai in Russia, marxism was distinctly unsympathetic to any specific intervention within sexuality. The explanation for this seems to be that the two aspects of marxist politics towards sexual relations – the destruction of the economic function of the family and the transformation of the relations between the sexes – were hegemonised by the first element. All aspects of the relations between men and women were deemed to be dependent on the economic function of marriage.

The reason for this hegemony was because marxism insisted at the level of theoretical and political necessity that the struggle for women's emancipation should be integrated to the struggle for socialism. In the previous chapter we saw how the marxist political priority was to transform economic antagonism and that the social division between the sexes was excluded from consideration. What is more, the insistence on the necessity for the transformation in the relations of production was translated into a political assessment of which forces will effect this transformation; that is, forces around the relations of production. In this assessment, the possibility of seeing a specific dynamic in the relations between the sexes disappears. The marxist conceptualisation of the family insists on a necessary relation between the relations of production and the oppressed condition of women, a relation mediated by the economic function of the family. In this tradition of marxism, there is an insistence that socialism must achieve the emancipation of women and that any true emancipation of women must entail socialism. The insistence on the theoretical integration of the two elements through the economic function of the family means that the differential effects of social relations on the sexes were suppressed.

This suppression of the possibility that the forms taken by sexual relations might entail different relations of power characterised much writing on the woman question by the early marxist left. There was an intense hostility to what was branded 'bourgeois' feminism, or to whatever attempted to examine sexual relations apart from the economic relations of production. The feminist movement, or, more correctly, movements, emerged in the second half of the nineteenth century. They aimed at transforming sexual relations regardless of economic relations. Some involved extremely radical criticisms of traditional morality and existing social relations. Others were confined to campaigns against legal and political discrimination. Feminism, then, as now, was by no means a homogeneous political movement with a clear set of aims and objectives. It encompassed a multitude of tendencies; movements for legal and political reform, gradually crystallising around the suffrage movement; agitation for sexual and moral reform; advocacy of and opposition to birth control; sometimes agitation for the elevation of motherhood. Quite often, feminism was no more than a relatively spontaneous organisation around disparate women's issues, for example the campaign which surrounded the Contagious Diseases Act.[8] The effects of such campaigns, however, was sometimes to produce far-ranging critiques of existing social relations.

A minimalist definition of the feminism encountered by the early marxist left was that it was concerned with the position of women in society. Elements within it were, however, completely beyond the theoretical scope of marxism. Questions of sexual behaviour, masculine behaviour, questions of control and expression of sexuality, questions of female autonomy were all in contradiction with marxism's hierarchy of analytic and political priorities given in the deterministic account of sexual and familial relations.

Marx's daughter, Eleanor Marx writing with E. Aveling[9] summed up the marxist response; the movements were 'bourgeois' since the solutions they offered were purely individualistic and would benefit only a small minority of middle-class women. None of these issues, except perhaps the agitation around the Contagious Diseases Act, had aimed at bettering the lot of all people and transforming social relations to the benefit of all people.

Yet for exactly the reasons for which they were attacked, these movements were problematic for marxist theory. What feminist movements attacked were forms of oppression and discrimination whose relation with the economic class relations was, at best, tenuous. These forms of discrimination affected women of all classes, that is, they affected woman as a sex. Changes in these relations could provisionally be secured without any changes in the relations of production. Collectivisation of the means of production, moreover, need not intervene at the level of sexual discrimination.

In the debate and activities which took place around the woman question in European social democracy we can clearly see the issues at play between the way in which marxist priorities sometimes get constructed and the woman question. In the ensuing sections an examination of feminist responses to August Bebel's *Woman under Socialism* will attempt to uncover what were the sticking points between this tradition of marxism and feminism.

Woman under Socialism

The period covered by this book, 1860–1930, was witness to the development of marxist political parties within Europe. Almost without exception, the 'woman question' was debated widely within these parties. The German Social Democratic Party (SPD), which came into existence in 1875, was at the time taken as the showcase of a marxist political party. It was a party which quickly gained immense working-class support and generated discussion of socialist strategy which was to be widely influential throughout Europe.

This is no less true of the consideration of the 'woman question'. Clara Zetkin, one of the leaders of the International Socialist Women's Movement was a leading member of the SPD. Her work was to be of importance for socialist women in their struggle for women's emancipation both during and after the Russian revolution. It was also to be influential on the policies pursued by the Austrian Social Democratic

Party which in 1926, even when the German party became increasingly indifferent to women's issues, produced an unusually radical party programme to deal with the position of women. It[10]

included a wide-ranging, integrated section on the position of women in society: in work, education, religion and family law. For the first time in any political party, a section on population policy advocated the legalisation and free availability of abortion as well as the free distribution of birth control information and contraceptive devices.

It was in the context of the SPD that Bebel wrote *Woman under Socialism*, which was to become the most influential marxist exposition of the position of women in society, being both an analysis of the sources of women's oppression and of strategies by which this could be changed. Kollontai referred to it as 'the woman's bible'. It would be difficult to overestimate the impact of Bebel's book; it was one of the principle factors which drew women in their thousands to the cause of social democratic politics, as Ottille Baader, a working-class activist in the SPD described:[11]

Life's bitter needs, overwork, and bourgeois family morality had destroyed all joy in me. I lived resigned and without hope. . . . News came of a wonderful book that . . . Bebel . . . had written. Although I was not a Social Democrat I had friends who belonged to the party. Through them I got the precious work. I read it nights through. It was my fate and that of thousands of my sisters. Neither in the family nor in private life had I ever heard of all the pain the women must endure. One ignored her life. Bebel's book courageously broke with the old secretiveness. . . . I read the book not once but ten times. Because everything was so new, it took considerable effort to come to grips with Bebel's views. I had to break with so many things I had previously regarded as correct.

This reaction was typical and accounted for the strength of a feminist presence in the early years of the SPD, a presence which recognised that the SPD was the only party to give any priority to the cause for women's emancipation: 'From bio-graphical material it is clear that an important motive in sustaining female membership was the perception of the SPD as the most consistent champion of women's equality in Imperial Germany.'[12]

Bebel's book first appears when the anti-socialist laws were in force in Germany,[13] yet it had reached fifty editions by the time of Bebel's death in 1913, and had been translated into innumerable foreign languages. Like Engels's *The Origins*, it is often referred to as one of the most formative texts of social democratic thought. Both owe their wide influence to the fact that they offer an outline of a general schema of marxist thought, dealing with the history of the family and the capitalist mode of production, suggesting the inevitability of its overthrow. But the texts were also influential not only because 'the family' and 'the position of women' occupied such crucial positions in the exposition of general accounts of social relations, but also because 'the woman question' was highly contentious in German politics. Issues of women's emancipation, the extension of franchise and women's posi-tion in the labour market were all issues which were debated regularly and fiercely at the German Workers' Congresses. Yet this period, where the 'woman question' was hotly debated, saw little real advance in making the issues raised about changing the position of women in society central to the socialist programme as a whole.

Traditionally, the question of women's emancipation had been treated sympathetically by socialists, the influence of Saint-Simonian thought being strong in Germany.[14] There was, however, an equally strong and growing current of thought which violently opposed women's role in production and argued for the separate spheres of influence of men and women. Both tendencies called themselves feminist, and in the early days of German social democracy, both these strands of thought, which later came to dominate the theorisation of the woman's question, were strongly represented. Such was the case, certainly, at the third conference of the German Worker's Association. On the one hand, arguments were made against women's waged labour both on the grounds that women's proper sphere of influence was in the home, and also on the grounds that women's competition lowered the average male wage. Yet in spite of the strength with which the position was held, motions were carried which supported women's emancipation and insisted on the need for women's increased role in production. Women should achieve independence and equal rights and statuses. These, it was argued, could only be achieved by women employed in serious work, equal with men at the work-place. These two dominant positions corresponded to the division among social democrats between the followers of Lassalle on the one hand, and the followers of Leibknecht and Bebel, who were both more directly influenced by Marx, on the other.

The Lassallean attitude was widespread among all the workers' movements at that time.[15] They argued that women should be excluded from industrial production as this would increase male employment, reduce unemployment and increase the average male wage. Women should be remunerated for their work outside production, that is, for their domestic labour. This attitude to female labour had been forcefully attacked by feminists. To make the improvement of women's position dependent on that of men's, 'flew in the face of all humanity and civilisation'.[16]

The emphasis which the Lassalleans put on the radical distinction between the sexes, by no means uncommon, corresponded closely with the emergent ideology of the constitutional difference between men and women where women are seen as bound by their reproductive capacity to domestic spheres of influence. This ideology, which became pronounced with the emergence of fascism in Germany,[17] was by no means confined to one political position. It ran from the radical Saint-Simonians who, like Bachofen, insisted on the female principle as the democratic and communistic principle across the political spectrum, to fascist writers like Klages and Baumler.[18]

Bebel and Leibknecht argued against this, directly influenced by Marx's arguments from *Das Kapital*; increased women's employment would be both the means to women's independence and an exacerbation of the contradictions between capital and labour since it would increase the level of exploitation. These two positions dominated the intellectual milieu in which the struggle over the women's question took place.

Although the conservative Lassallean position did not come to dominate, the positive attitude of the 1865 Conference was never again repeated. Indeed, in 1866, the German section of the International Worker's Association published a document with the approval of Marx and Engels insisting on women's place within the family:[19]

> The rightful work of women and mothers is in the home and family caring for, supervising, and providing the first education for the children, which it is true presupposes that the women and children themselves receive an adequate training. Alongside the solemn duties of the man and father in public life and the family the woman and mother should stand for the cosiness and poetry of domestic life, bring grace and beauty to social relations and be an enobling influence on the increase of humanity's enjoyment of life.

All future attempts to discuss the woman question vacillated between these two positions. 'Feminism' was claimed either to ensure women's increased role in production or to ensure women an honourable status in society through her position in the home.

As the social democratic party programme was drawn up, the struggle between these two positions intensified around the question of women's suffrage. For example, in Eisenach in 1869 the marxist amendment of 'all citizens' to the proposal of 'universal, equal and direct suffrage' for men from the age of twenty was rejected. However, the question of women's subordination did get on the agenda and many unions took up the issue later, with the emergence of a definite commitment to greater unionisation amongst women as one solution to the lack of political attention paid to women's specific problems. The Unification Programme of 1875, by which the German Social Democratic Party was founded, resulted in the compromise of 'all citizens over 20 years of age', and the prohibition of all female labour which was morally and physically detrimental.[20] This later position was elsewhere endorsed by Marx who advocated the exclusion of female labour from 'branches of industry that are especially unhealthy for the female body or objectionable morally for the female sex'.[21]

Thönnessen has noted that there was a significant gap between discussions and proposals within the party of equal suffrage and labour restrictions, and the translation of these into measures demanded by the SPD in the political forum. For example, protection for women was not demanded until 1877, nor female suffrage until 1895. There was an even greater period of time between when the SPD first presented the demands and when they were actually realised through legislation.

The basic position of the party remained unchanged until 1889. It was characterised by imprecise demands for equal voting rights for both sexes and, in the economic sphere, support for female labour with rational, that is moral, restrictions. Like many of the issues raised within the party, however, the women's question was overshadowed by the passing of the Exceptional Laws in 1878. These were in force for twelve years and were laws introduced by Bismarck, who, frightened by the advances which the SPD were making as an electoral party, banned the free assembly of socialists.

It was in this context that Bebel wrote his *Woman under Socialism* which appeared first in 1878 under the title *Women in the Past, Present and Future*.[22] It is a clear statement of the position which argued for the progressive function of women's increased role in production. Women's plight should be related to the general plight of the working class. Both have their source in economic oppression; both will be overcome when capitalist society is transformed into socialist society. Unlike Engels, however, Bebel partially raises the question of women's oppression *as a sex* and attempts to consider the social construction of sexual identity. This attempt was compromised, however, by a unifying notion of economic oppression which prevented any real formulation of the problems.

Bebel insisted that the source of all oppression was economic and like other socialists, he thought that marriage was an economic relation. Women are oppressed as a sex, but this oppression is because the 'natural relation' between the sexes has been distorted. Marriage, he wrote, should be a union that two persons enter into only out of mutual love, in order to accomplish their natural mission; in the modern world, however, this mission is distorted by the requirements of private property. Again, he sees prostitution as the obverse of marriage. Prostitution exemplifies the distorting effects of bourgeois marriage. It inverts the relations between the sexes, making women the seducers, a role which 'naturally' belongs to the men. Moreover, abstinence creates all sorts of 'perversions', such as homosexuality and pornography. Thus there is a situation where on the one side there is excess, resulting from unnatural abstinence, and on the other the horrors of the hard life of the proletariat whose family life is destroyed.

In the context of all these aspects of marriage, the increase of women's involvement in productive labour is to be welcomed. It is a social development which, in destroying the foundations of bourgeois marriage, points the way to the construction of newer and freer forms. Antagonisms are necessarily generated by the economic dependency of one group on another. Freer forms can only arise when private interests are overthrown, that is the overthrow of the bourgeoisie by the working class.

Socialist women and the woman question

Bebel's position was supported and developed by Clara Zetkin whose pamphlet, 'The Question of Women Workers and Women at the Present Time', in 1889, summarised the various writings on the women question from within socialism. Again, like Engels and Bebel, she was convinced that the only route to women's emancipation was women's involvement in production and the overthrow of the capitalist system. The question of women's emancipation was never, however, developed as a political priority within German social democracy. Frequently, demands for the improvement of women's position in society were limited to demands for protective legislation. Some feminists resisted this on the grounds that it deprived women of complete equality in productive relations, thus slowing down the inevitable collapse of capitalism. Despite the progressive programmes drawn up by the party after the repeal of the anti-socialist legislation,[23] in general the questions of women's social position received less attention in the years after the repeal of the anti-socialist law. Clara Zetkin sided with Rosa Luzemburg against what they saw to be the 'revisionist' direction gradually taken by the social democratic party. Their philosophy on the transformation of the position of women was closely bound up with a classical marxist theory of the total overthrow of capitalist social relations. Thus the defeat of that version of marxism was also a defeat of the woman question in social democratic politics.

While excuses could perhaps be made for the failure of the woman question to become anything other than marginal to SPD policy, *Woman under Socialism* had an enormous impact beyond Germany as well. The radical impact in the Austrian social democratic party has already been noted. In that country, the feminist platform had been strong enough to carry through radical measures designed to improve women's position. Alexandra Kollontai, active in the struggle for women's emancipation in Russia, described the book as 'the woman's bible' and freely admitted that this book had inspired her as to the importance of the woman question. Yet, ultimately the priority given to transformation of the position of women was no greater in a country which had achieved a form of socialism. Much of Kollontai's writing, as a socialist profoundly concerned with the subordinate position of women, is exemplary of the problems of attempting to formulate an analysis of women within marxism.

Kollontai was so violently antipathetic towards 'bourgeois' feminism and the suffrage movement, that she refused to call herself a feminist. Indeed, much of her early political activity involved speaking at meetings against what she called the pernicious and diversionary effects of bourgeois feminism. Kollontai had early decided, like Zetkin, in favour of the orthodox marxists against the 'revisionists'. This expressed a commitment to the notion of the increasing contradiction in the relations of production and the inevitability of the collapse of capitalism. Her work is interesting because it is an expression of the theoretical and ideological position of marxism in respect of the family which had been pushed to its extreme. It was pushed to an extreme because of political difficulties encountered in formulating the specificity of women's position within orthodox marxism.

Kollontai's early work, *The Social Basis of the Women's Question*, was written as an attempt to answer the feminist and suffragist movements from the perspective of marxism. It explored four themes, 'the fight for the economic independence of women, marriage and the family problem, the protection of pregnant women and women in childbirth, and the struggle of women for political rights'. Again, economic factors were taken to be the root cause of women's subordination. The property-orientated monogamous family expressed these economic factors. It is, therefore, 'the essential basis of the social stability of the bourgeoisie'.[24] Women's subordination cannot be resolved without a total transformation of the relations of production within capitalism:[25]

> There is no independent women's question, the women's question arose as an integral component of the social problem of our time. The thorough liberation of women as a member of society, a worker, an individual, a wife and mother is possible therefore only together with the fundamental transformation of the contemporary social order.

Kollontai's treatment of the question of sexual relations is often more subtle than the reductionism of this statement might suggest.[26] It is clear that Kollontai's political experience, both in exile in Europe in the years preceding the First World War, and in Russia during the Revolution and the ensuing civil war, raised a whole series of questions about strategy towards women and the family which went far beyond the analyses offered by either Bebel or Engels. Kollontai encountered the struggles of the SPD Women's Bureau, constantly fighting to keep women's issues on the agenda in Germany. She herself had to fight in Russia to establish the importance of work among women and for women. Finally, she experienced both male socialist's active resistance and the passive resistance of traditions and customs. All these contributed to the sense of the need to talk about the dynamic of sexual relations in their specificity. It was in this context that Kollontai, unlike many other marxists, was prepared to think about the work of the sexologists like Havelock Ellis, and psychoanalysts like Freud, which she had encountered in exile in Europe. It was in this context too that she argued the need for 'a psychology of love', a psychology which could explain the tenacity of old customary morality and sexual behaviour.

Kollontai's attempt to develop a specific account of sexual relations, yet remain faithful to what she saw as orthodox marxism, are revealing. They show the convolutions necessitated by dealing with sexual relations in their specificity and with women in their specificity while arguing still for their necessary relation to relations of production. Kollontai claimed that the family was undergoing changes in response to the social and economic environment. The effect of changes in productive relations had been to change ideas about the role of women in social life and to undermine sexual morality. Yet different class groupings respond differently to these changes and the different responses are exemplary of the roles which the bourgeoisie and working class will play in socialist revolution.

Faced with changes, the response of some groups is simply to defend the old forms of the family. For other members of the bourgeoisie, the middle-class intelligentsia, change is actively pursued. A more liberal sexual morality is sought and the traditional indissoluble marriages are replaced by the freer, more easily broken ties of civil marriage. Yet the ideology of these new forms of morality is extreme individualism and self-gratification. For the working class, it is a matter of passive adjustment to unfavourable circumstances – the old family forms destroyed by women's increased role in production, the proliferation of prostitution, extreme economic hardship, etc. But in keeping with their role as 'the progressive class', the response of the working class is also active and creative. For the destruction of the old family life and its replacement by forms of socialised labour has also the effect of setting collective or community values above family and therefore above individual values. A worker, she argued, never puts his family before his class; he will never break strikes for the sake of his individual family. The bourgeois man will, however, always put his family first. All acts of avarice and anti-social behaviour are justified in the name of protecting his family. Thus the working-class response to changes in sexual morality as a result of social changes again demonstrates their mission as the progressive class, the class in whose interests the socialist revolution is carried out.

Kollontai became increasingly interested in the problem of the subordination of *women as a sex*, a problem which she related to the sexual roles imposed by monogamous marriage. Increasingly, she looked to psychology for her critique of monogamy and attempted to develop questions of the dynamic of a monogamous relationship which went beyond the question of economic hardship. She argued for the need for psychic adjustment as well as social change to solve 'the sexual crisis'.

In this context she outlined three basic circumstances which distorted the modern psyche – 'extreme egotism, the idea that married partners possess each other, and the acceptance of the inequality of the sexes in terms of physical and emotional experience'.[27] In order to relate these circumstances to her economistic account of the family, she suggests an analysis of ideological forms as they themselves formed in the process of struggle.

The limitations on Kollontai's ideas are all too apparent. Although she attempts to invest ideological relations with a degree of autonomy, she nevertheless sees psychic forms – possessiveness, etc. – as an effect of a definite set of relations of production. Such an assumption ultimately rests on the idea that social structures generate certain definite ethical forms or forms of behaviour.

Kollontai's position is highly problematic even in the terms of her own argument. For she attributes to the classes different behavioural responses. How is it, then, that psychic responses may vary between classes when these responses are said to arise within the monogamous family, an ideological structure shared by bourgeoisie and working class alike? How can a model of the psychic structures of the monogamous family be drawn in ultimately the relations of production condition differential behaviour responses from the different social classes? Kollontai is contradictory. She insists on the tenacity of ideological forms, the monogamous family structuring emotions, needs and desires; at the same time she insists that the working class have a creatively different response because of their different relation to the means of production.

The contradictory nature of Kollontai's arguments do, indeed, point to what appears to be a consistent problem within marxist theory. In so far as marxism insists on the integral relation between relations of production and ideological forms like the family (where the relation is one of determination), an account of the latter can never properly be given. For if 'behaviour' or 'ideological' forms function for or reflect the requirements of the relations of production, however loosely their connection may be theorised, the structures which arise in those ideological practices are always reduced to reflections of the economic relations of production.

Nor was it simply a question of theoretical inconsistency. Kollontai saw her ideas at first resisted and gradually rejected in the tightening up of family law and morality during the late 1920s and 1930s. First, she was witness to the defeat of her general political sympathies, expressed in the Worker's Opposition, a group which opposed Lenin's economic and social policies. Under Stalin, however, even the possibility of such opposition disappeared and Kollontai in fact recanted on her earlier positions, being the only Bolshevik of the first Soviet who survived the purges. Far from having opened up the possibility of challenging women's subordination, increased conservatism towards both family and the position of women characterised the regime in the later years of Kollontai's life.

Women as sex

The grim instance of the failure of these issues to achieve any prominence in the building of socialism has given a certain historical justification to those feminists, branded by the socialist women as bourgeois, who criticised the attempt to develop a politics towards women based on marxist theoretical analysis. Alys Russell's[28] survey in 1896 of the treatment of the woman question within social democracy illustrates the terms of the hostility towards marxist feminism. The focus of her survey is the work of Bebel, in order to dispute his treatment of *women as a sex.* Russell argues that in so far as

Bebel takes sexual relations as procreative relations in order to derive women's evils from economic dependency, women as a sex disappear. The problems she raises are still pertinent for those arguments which seek to derive a politics of feminism from a marxist analysis of the position of women, even though the terms of her criticism derive from a very distinctive and limited theoretical and political milieu.

The first point of disputation is the doctrine that all political movements will derive from class interest groups, and that all politics are the effect of a struggle between the classes:[29]

> The attitude of SPD towards the women's movement is well illustrated by its criticism of the form which that movement has taken in England. It regrets that working women, owing to the activity of women in the upper classes, have failed to acquire any feeling of class consciouness, of solidarity, of confidence in their own powers. . . . Perhaps nowhere so much as in their attitude to this question are we made to realise the Social democratic doctrine of *Klassenkampf*; or class warfare, the doctrine according to which every political party is the party of a class, and every political movement, the exclusive movement of a class. What in England and America has been the movement of a whole sex, has in GSD been merged in the movement of the working class. Women are to have their rights not as a sex but as workers.

Alys Russell argues that in England, at least, the tradition of feminism has largely arisen from within an individualist bourgeois mode; it has been concerned with the rights of women, all women as a sex, typified by the work of J.S. Mill and William Thompson.

There is no necessity, she argues, for the struggle for women's rights to be bound to the struggle for socialism, insisting that the subordination of women can still be found in so-called primitive communistic modes of production. She attacks the marxist hypothesis of the matriarchate. Far from implying communism or the high status of women, evidence from matrilineal societies often reveal a system of male political dominance; 'these facts hardly coincide with Bebel's statement that mother-right meant communism, the equality of all.'[30] In addition, Alys Russell criticises the argument, so beloved of socialist feminists of this period, that the capitalist system must necessarily be superseded because of the impossibility of its contradictions and antagonisms yet that it is this system which provides the conditions for its own supersession:[31]

> The underlying idea of [Bebel's book], seems to be first that the recognition of women's equality with men is only a question of time, since women have already advanced so far and won so much for themselves; but secondly that they cannot attain this equality under existing social conditions. . . . It would seem that the first assertion rather destroys the second, and that Bebel in his desire to prove the capabilities of women, has stated that their success in attaining their ends so emphatically that the needs for a socialist society is but slightly felt. And certainly Bebel's main demands are capable of being satisfied under the present order of society. He really asks for no more than is demanded in countries by those advanced women who are not followers of Marx and whose suggestions are more practical than Bebel's.

Alys Russell points to examples of this contradiction which is a general contradiction of those theories which advance any inevitability to the logic of capitalism. For example, she suggests that women's economic independence could theoretically be secured by trade unions for the unmarried, and endowments of motherhood.[32] 'This latter though a socialist measure is, theoretically compatible with the private property. And the equal mental and physical training of the sexes, one of Bebel's chief demands is certainly possible in an individualist state of society.'[33] Her perspective is Fabian, and the Fabian idea of a socialist strategy towards the family was to reinforce women's position in the family by various state endowments. However, her criticisms undoubtedly isolated problems which have often worried feminists. As socialism is defined in terms of an upheaval of the relations of production between classes, there is no necessity that women's equality will be advanced by this route and none other. Indeed, feminism's discourse of 'equality' is one that starts from notions of citizenship and legality. It is, therefore, as she pointed out, profoundly individualistic.

In many ways, Russell's criticism does pinpoint central problems with marxist political analysis of that period. It pinpoints the difficulty of formulating strategy when analysis assumes that socialism will only be attained by a total transformation of capitalist relations of production. But since the conditions for this transformation are continuously produced by capitalism itself, it is not clear how best to formulate strategy to produce the conditions for transformation. Over this issue, German social democracy itself was completely split.[34] The aim of a socialist party was clearly to achieve a socialist economy, but how could this be achieved? By participation in existing capitalist political forms? Or only by revolutionary activity? The problems and divisions all sprang from an unresolved problem in the heart of marxism. What was the status of 'capitalist relations of production' and how did this general structural designation of a particular society affect the other social relations of that society? Could the interests of the 'progressive class' ever be advanced through the social forms which characterised capitalism? Where all were agreed, however, was that first and foremost socialism must be an expression of the interests of the working class, interests defined as collective possession of the means of production.

For Russell, the problems which this position created were political problems. Is it true that the interests of the working class, so defined, will advance women's interests? Surely the interests of women as a sex could also be advanced through alliance with more middle-class feminist groups? It was not at all apparent to her, for example, that the interest exhibited by some feminists in birth control and the radical implications this might have for women's sexuality are compatible with the socialist analysis advanced by Bebel. She formulated the problem in characteristically Fabian terms, pointing to a contradiction between individual and collective interests, which expressed itself in socialists' talk of the 'natural' sexual requirements, and simultaneous disinterest in birth control issues: 'even Bebel does not say how a communistic society

The woman question and the early marxist left

will reconcile the contradiction that must occasionally arise between natural instincts and duty as a citizen'. Unrestrained sexual satisfaction, she argued, could only be to the advantage of the male proletariat: 'Bebel's is the psychology of the proletariat, and when he insists on the necessity for the satisfaction of natural wants, he has in mind the man of few pleasures and little imagination.'[35]

For Alys Russell, deeply entrenched in eugenicist assumptions, Bebel's analysis presents a contradiction between individual/socialist state – the problem of the 'above averagely intelligent females' whose self-interest is not served by child-rearing. Yet, if scientific breeding of the race is to be cultivated by socialist (as she automatically assumes it should be), then surely these are the very individuals which socialism would most like to see as mothers:[36]

> Unless educated women are made to feel that child-bearing is a duty to the State, to which they must if necessary make some sacrifice of independence, and even happiness, it is difficult to conceive how even 'the perfect Socialist State' will be continued in the future without the deterioration of the race.

The argument is a curious one, crossed by so many strands of thought – the ideology of individual interests as the spontaneous product of a free-floating individual, the eugenicist belief in the necessity for the scientific planning of the race, the distrust of the language of class warfare and class interests and the belief that provisional alliances can be made, such as between middle- and working-class women to achieve provisional objectives. At the same time it touches on some critical area of the relation between feminism and marxist socialism. Feminism has often been steeped in bourgeois notions of equality, rights of citizenship, etc. Marxist socialism has just as often inscribed most traditional notions of the family and sexual relations into the heart of socialism. It is no more apparent now, than it was to Alys Russell, that the priorities developed by marxist political parties will do anything to challenge sexual hierarchies and the social forms of oppression related to those sexual hierarchies. Everywhere in

185

this exchange of positions, the need for a more radical conceptualization of sexual relations is apparent. The marxist tradition embodied by Bebel insists on the integration of feminist and working-class interests in the overall transformation of the economic structure of society. Thus more radical attempts to tackle sexual relations as specific and entailing distinct forms of subordination were either sacrificed by orthodox marxism to the politics expressed in *The Origins* or simply were unable to make themselves heard.

Conclusion

The integration of the family with theorisation of class and political representation, meant that the issue of women's subordination found an all too easy place in marxist schemes. We have seen in the previous chapter that the concept of 'family' in fact belonged to a tradition of speculation on general social relations. Through a certain sleight of hand, Engels made the position of women synonymous with the family. It was this which gave the woman question such a ready place within marxism but which blocked any real theorisation of women or any real acceptance of the centrality of transforming sexual relations. Because of the particular function which the family fulfilled in Engels's work – as the place of individual interest, the family also was easily submerged by socialism to some notion of individualism. It became the realm of freedom to which the state addressed its activities. (It is interesting to reflect that there is a high coincidence between statist notions of socialism and their adherence to traditional forms of the family – as if the family were sufficient expression of individual freedom.)

The bourgeois feminist approach of that period correctly specified on the one hand the non-reducibility of movements to transform the relations between the sexes to an economic (orthodox marxist) notion of socialism. On the other hand, elements of bourgeois feminism were able to stress the radical implications of birth control for women in a way that marxism was unable or unwilling to do, hamstrung by the lack of space possible for the theorisation of the relations between the sexes. In this way a more radical challenge was launched on the family from outside rather than inside marxism. At the same time, however, this feminism which, in the past, took a relatively technicist view of equality rather than striking at more fundamental inequalities, failed to see that the cause of all women cannot be bettered without a fundamental restructuring of social relations, including the ways in which the means of production are controlled.

We can conclude, then, that a certain tradition emerged within marxism, where the family was, paradoxically, both to the forefront of political and theoretical concerns, and, simultaneously, inadequately theorised. In so far as Engels's account of the family insisted on the analytic and political priority of the relations of production, the specific dynamic of relations between the sexes could not be adequately treated. For example, the insistence on the family as economic unit made it impossible to consider the differential effects of family relations on the sexes. Far from marriage binding the sexes together as an economic unit, marriage and the ideologies of sexual division have put the sexes in radically different positions. Men and women have different relations to the labour market, to child-bearing and child-care, and to the state. This tradition of marxism might argue that the state represents the interests of the bourgeoisie; it might equally well be argued that the state differently affects men and women, women constructed in a relationship of dependency on men.

This chapter has only briefly attempted to outline some of the arguments surrounding marxism and the woman question. Its aim has been both to demonstrate how analytic and political priorities have blocked the specific analysis of the sexual division as social division. Through this analysis it has been suggested that these priorities have constructed a hierarchy of social divisions, which if it remains in force will continue to block understanding of the specificities of sexual relations.

7 The patriarchal family in Freudian theory

Introduction

As with the history of early marxist thought, the development of psychoanalysis was profoundly influenced by the debates already traced in this book. Theories of the history of the family, and especially the patriarchal family, appeared in psychoanalysis integrated into an account of the construction of individual sexual identity. Unlike the other discourses examined, however, psychoanalysis did not assume 'sexuality' as an unproblematic category. Instead, sexuality is a central object of interrogation. It has been demonstrated that various accounts of the family or the history of the family rely on a notion of the sexual drive as a given, which has as its aim sexual reproduction. Concomitantly, men and women are theorised as having radically different aims and pleasures; sexual relations and sexuality are seen as the same thing, both deriving from absolute sexual difference in the service of reproduction.

In opposition to such theories, psychoanalysis proposed a radical re-examination of the concept of sexuality, questioning the centrality of sexual reproduction and the rigid distinction between men and women. Such is psychoanalysis' preoccupation with the study of sexual construction that it has often been accused of concentrating on sexual identity to the exclusion of the social context in which that identity might have been produced. The two following chapters attempt to explore what theory of the social determination of sexual identity is, in fact, proposed by psychoanalysis and why this theory is such a problem for other social sciences. Where psychoanalysis attempts to explain the determination of sexual identity by social relations, it turns to the debates already covered by this book. The following chapters will discuss whether it is the effects of this legacy which have compromised psychoanalysis's more radical claims.

This assessment would seem to be timely since recently it has been suggested that Freud's account of sexual construction is not, in fact, an account of a universal and timeless process which unfolds itself regardless of the culture or historical moment into which an individual is born. Instead, it is seen as a theory of sexual construction within a historically finite period – a cultural period, loosely designated 'patriarchal'.[1] As such, it can be taken as an illuminating account of sexual construction within a delimited period. Grounds clearly exist in Freud's own writing to justify this interpretation since he goes to considerable lengths to place the taboo on incest and the castration complex – so important in his account of sexual construction – within the context of an actual history of the human family. Yet it is precisely this element of Freud's work which is steeped in presuppositions of earlier debates and we need to ask whether a return to these elements is making most use of the radical aspects of Freudian theory.

In various interpretations Freud's own claim for the universality of his argument is either dismissed or reinterpreted. Where dismissed, it is claimed that Freud was mistaken in projecting a useful and accurate, but strictly delimited, account on to all societies.[2] Where reinterpreted, universality is modified on the grounds that, *as yet*, there have only been patriarchal societies in which women have been dominated as a result of their reproductive capacities.[3] As a result, so the argument runs, although Freud's claim for universality is incorrect, it is understandable since it reflects reality. A final element has been introduced in reinterpretations of Freud's hypothesis of the evolution of the human family. Structuralist re-readings[4] of Freud stress that the myth of the evolution of the human family from primal horde to patriarchal family is strictly metaphorical; Freud, simply lacked the concepts necessary to dispense with an evolutionist schema.

Several questions need to be asked of these contemporary

usages of Freudian theory. What, for example, was the precise relation between the concept of patriarchy and other aspects of Freudian theory? It is this study which will be able to tell us the extent to which the concept in psychoanalysis is usefully assimilated to a positivist notion or a historical or cultural phase, 'patriarchy'. It will be able to explore whether this interpretation of Freud's actual history of the human family in fact compromises the deconstruction of sexuality which is evident elsewhere in Freud's work. The subsequent chapter explores the effect of a theory of the actual history of the human family on psychoanalysis' relation with other social sciences. It also discusses the problems entailed in attempts to reduce the significance of Freud's account of the human family. These problems are acute for structuralist reinterpretations which, in suggesting that this element of Freud's work should be treated as metaphorical, have neglected the effects of this account on psychoanalysis' dealings with the social sciences. Neglecting this effect does not deal fully with the ambivalences in psychoanalysis, but perhaps more seriously, it fails to challenge the terms in which the social sciences have formulated their opposition to psychoanalysis.

Phylogenesis: Freud's history of the human family

In 1920, the first edition of the *International Yearbook of Psychoanalysis* was published in England under the editorship of Ernest Jones. The impact of psychoanalysis was already widespread; in England and America it had been championed for treatment of war trauma. With the defeat of Germany in the First World War, the editorial explained the inappropriateness of continuing publication using German as the international language. Until the war, the main organs of psychoanalysis had been *Das Jahrbuch der Psychoanalyse* and *Imago*.[5] Under the careful editorship of Ernest Jones, the new international journal pursued a rigorous policy by which all books dealing with the interpretation of mental phenomena were automatically reviewed. Into this category came all books published in the area of psychology *and* anthropology, which was clearly seen at this time as an area of the human sciences from which psychoanalysis had much to gain. During this period, the journal is characterised by an impressive orthodoxy: every relevant text is reviewed either collectively or by individuals in order to establish its actual or potential relationship to psychoanalysis. The systematic treatment of sociological and anthropological material reveals psychoanalysis' claim to be a science capable of explaining all cultural and social phenomena. *Imago*, still published in Germany, advanced this; the journal concentrated on the application of psychoanalysis to the mental sciences.

From a very early stage, psychoanalytic thought had established an interest in many of the same objects as those studied by the anthropological literature of the time (myths, sexual practices, rituals). But psychoanalysis entered forcibly on the picture of anthropological debates when, in 1913, Freud published *Totem and Taboo*. Here he added his account of the history of the human family to the multitude of versions already in existence. The pressing question which confronts us here is why Freud felt the need to relate his discoveries of various psychic (sexual) complexes in the individual to a hypothesised account of the history of the human race.

During the years prior to the publication of *Totem and Taboo*, psychoanalysis had constituted itself as a radical intervention in medical discourses. Through its assessment and treatment of neuroses, a conception of sexuality and sexual behaviour had been advanced which cut across existing medical definitions. Treatment of nervous diseases had previously insisted on constitutional derangements,[6] such as the designation of hysteria as a disorder of the womb, or sexual problems as the effect of constitutional disorders, like 'constitutional homosexuality'. Psychoanalysis, in opposition, refused the divisions between 'neurotic' and 'normal' people. It was the theory of sexuality which constituted such a radical departure for psychoanalysis from other medical discourses. Freud insisted that most 'neurotic' disturbances could be traced to the early sexual experiences of childhood, and that neurotic structures were only a variation of those structures by which all humans acquired their sexual identity. From his clinical studies, he concluded 'that a disposition to perversions is an original and universal disposition of the human sexual instinct and that normal sexual behaviour is developed out of it as a result of organic changes and psychical inhibition occurring in the course of maturation'.[7]

In the course of elaborating this account of neuroses, psychoanalysis developed a theory of the construction of sexual identity which radically challenged virtually all other contemporary accounts. Instead of masculinity and femininity assumed as irradicably different somatic and psychic states, Freud advanced a non-essentialist theory of sexuality. He insisted that the sexual behaviour of children of both sexes was indistinguishable. The infant is initially bisexual; there is no given object of the sexual drive. The child is, in fact, 'polymorphously perverse', seeking all forms of sensual gratification. Both girl and boy child initially pass through the same dominant phases of erotic stimulation. Sexuality exclusively in the service of reproduction, that is, heterosexual genital sexuality which is so much taken for granted in other discourses, is problematised by psychoanalysis. Psychoanalysis insisted that reproductive sexuality is an outcome which had to be explained rather than the yardstick by which all other 'perversions' were to be measured: 'Thus from the point of view of psychoanalysis the exclusive interest felt by men for women is also a problem that needs elucidating and is not a self-evident fact based on an attraction that is ultimately of a chemical nature.'[8] The prehistory of infantile sexuality uncovered by Freud was that of infantile incestuous wishes directed to the parent of the opposite sex and polymorphous perversity. Both of these had to be repressed in the construction of genital heterosexual attractions. It was the process of this construction which formed the conscious and unconscious mental activities of any individual. In this account, two complexes were specified as formative in infantile sexuality: the Oedipus complex and the castration complex.

In *Totem and Taboo*, Freud related his discoveries of the Oedipus complex and castration complex in the individual unconscious to a hypothesised account of the history of the human race. Here, he turned to the two obsessive themes of contemporary anthropology; the study of totemism and the prohibition on incest. He argued that the boy's fear of the father, which put an end to the boy's incestuous wishes on his mother, and his consequently ambivalent relation to the father, were emotional structures which could be found at a more general cultural level – in the totemic structure of religion and the prohibition of sexual relations between members of the same totem clan. Freud argued that the individual instance was precisely an effect of a racial pre-history.

The myth which Freud hypothesised was as follows. Siding with Darwin's followers, he suggested that pre-cultural man lived in and roamed around with a horde under the dominance of one strong male. This strong male, or primal father, copulated at will, regardless of biological ties, punishing any of the other males who tried to usurp his privilege. In their common dissatisfaction, the sons united and finally murdered the father. They they ate him. After their action, the sons realised that their deed was awesome. The other side of their ambivalent relationship towards their father gained the upper hand: their feelings of affection and admiration, and because of this, an intense guilt. Such guilt led to the restoration of the father's original prohibition against the sons enjoying their mothers and sisters. What had been previously prevented by the actual existence of the father was now prohibited by the sons themselves. Accordingly, the sons became guilty of the two crimes which, Freud claims, are the only two which 'primitive society' takes seriously – incest and murder. The repression of the wish for the father's death and for sexual relations with the mother correspond to the repressed wishes of the Oedipus complex.

Freud suggests that a long period of time elapsed between the murder of the primal father and the restoration of his laws. During this period, as a result of the initial horror at the deed, the women of the tribe became dominant. Not only was descent organised through the mother, disavowing the role of the father, but this period was also characterised by the worship of mother-goddesses. The restoration of reverence for the father was accompanied by the recognition of paternity. The admittance of paternity to consciousness is described by Freud as the advance to culture, *the* advance which constitutes human civilisation.

Freud's hypothesis draws in several levels of concern. On

the one hand, it attempts to 'solve' anthropological problems with psychological data. On the other, it mobilises anthropological data as a solution to problems interior to psychoanalysis. Totemism is seen as a facet of the emotional relationship with the father – the product of the desire to restore to the father his former revered position after the murder. The taboo on incest has strongly practical motives. Once the father had been removed and the sons were in a position to enjoy what had previously been the exclusive possession of the father, they immediately became competitors with each other. Each wanted to take the position of the father. Their only option was to renounce the women they desired.

Freud's account joined the multitude of contesting definitions about the 'meaning' of mother-right societies and the practices of exogamy and incest-taboo. Matrilineal societies are described as regressive stages following the trauma of the primal murder. The incest-taboo and the concomitant practice of exogamy are the reinstatement of the father's law, without, according to Freud, the father's tyranny. But Freud's hypothesis is also more than another version on the universal history of the family. The terms in which he couches his hypothesis are strikingly similar to the terms in which he accounts for the 'prehistory' of the infant which, before repression, requires the forgetting of infantile active sexuality. There is a stage of primitive promiscuity and incestuous activity before the intervention of civilisation. 'Advance' is won at the cost of sexual renunciation and patriarchy is recognised.

Innumerable objections, both theoretical and empirical, can be, and were, raised to the Freudian hypothesis. It was subject to the same objections to all unilinear evolutionary histories. It commits the additional crime of ethnocentrism, attributing to different family organisations degrees of primitiveness. Finally, there is very little evidence to suggest that totemism and the sacrificial meal occur together. However, it is not the disproving of proving of Freud's hypothesis which interests me here, but rather the need to understand its function in and effect on psychoanalytic theory. All of the obvious criticisms of Freud's tinkerings with anthropology were raised at the time of the publication of *Totem and*

Taboo.[9] Some anthropologists disputed the factual evidence, some challenged the crude evolutionism, others questioned the validity of using individual 'psychical' complexes as a base for making deductions about 'primitive' social organisations. Yet in spite of all these criticisms, Freud not only adhered to his theory of the 'real event' at the origin of social life but also returned with a vengeance to the theme in the last book he ever wrote, *Moses and Monotheism.*

Moses and Monotheism resumes the concluding theme of *Totem and Taboo* where Freud explains his compulsion to provide a phylogenetic account of the structures of the individual unconscious, that is, an account based on a history of the human race:[10]

> It is not accurate to say that obsessional neurotics,
> weighed down under the burden of excessive morality, are
> defending themselves only against psychical reality and are
> punishing themselves for impulses that were merely *felt*.
> Historical reality has a share in the matter as well.

Here Freud summarises the psychoanalytic compulsion to elaborate a history of the human race. It is in order to solve the problematic issue of whether or not unconscious structures are acquired through each individual's identical experience or whether psychic structures can be acquired without individual experience.

This problem remained crucial and Freud attempted to solve it in various ways. At some moments, he insisted on a real history of the family – the phylogenetic account – as a solution to the status of the real event. At other moments, however, he developed a notion of primal fantasy. Suggestions, however, that Freud simply abandoned the real event are contradicted by his last book, *Moses and Monotheism*, where he returns to the theme of an actual history underlying individual and social psychic complexes.

Real event to primal fantasy

His early work with Breuer on hysteria[11] had led to Freud's positing the importance of early sexual experience in the determining of neuroses. At that time (1893–5), however,

Freud was maintaining that what his studies had shown was the frequency of a 'traumatic' event in childhood. It seemed from his researches that countless so-called neurotics had been seduced in early childhood by parents and that neurotic and obsessional behaviour in adulthood could often be ascribed to such a traumatic event. Later Freud abandoned this idea, declaring that either all fathers had to be deemed potential rapists, or the foundations of female hysteria and neurosis had to be looked for elsewhere. The real problem with the theory of infantile trauma was not so much the unlikelihood of the frequency of such occurrences and the concomitant difficulty of establishing whether or not the events actually took place. It was also the theoretical problem that a trauma, a disturbance of sexual development, suggests a maturational account of sexuality in which too much sexuality too soon will have disastrous consequences.

In response to these problems, Freud reinterpreted the data of primal trauma as the effect on primal fantasy: instead of the commonness of parental seduction, it was necessary to posit the frequency of the fantasy of seduction. In 1914 Freud gave the following account of the transformation of his theories:[12]

> If hysterical subjects trace back their symptoms to traumas that are fictitious, then the new fact which emerges is precisely that this psychical reality requires to be taken into account alongside practical reality. This reflection was soon followed by the discovery that these fantasies were intended to cover up the autoerotic activity of the first years of childhood, to embellish it, and raise it to a higher plane. And now, from behind the fantasies, the whole range of the child's sexual life came to light.

In the movement from traumatic event to fantasy of seduction, Freud reinforced a notion of *psychical reality*, the effects of which could be just as violent as those resulting from an actual traumatic event. There were two assumptions inextricably linked with the idea of psychical reality. First is the relationship posited between the child's own sexual activity and sexual inquiry, and the production of fantasy. Second is the implication of the absolute status of psychical reality: 'We shall have to conclude no doubt that psychical reality is a particular form of existence which is not to be confused with material reality.'[13] The notion of psychic reality posed a critical problem for psychoanalysis. How could the psychic life and the unconscious be seen as the result of the individual's history if fantasies are not seen as rigidly dependent on actual events. The typicality of fantasy had to be accounted for without assuming that all individuals spontaneously produced the same fantasy.

Such problems underlay the fact that Freud's theoretical shift from real event to primal fantasy was by no means as smooth as he seems to suggest in *History of the Psychoanalytic Movement*, where he represents the discovery of the Oedipus complex and the castration complex as the natural and easy successor to the preliminary idea of the parental seduction. Instead of a real trauma, the Oedipus and castration complex could be seen as structures governing infantile fantasies. In fact, for some considerable time Freud worked with two parallel ideas. The first was the idea of a childhood sexuality which was ultimately rooted in biologism, an idea present in *Three Essays on Sexuality*. The second was a more subtle account of the Oedipus complex and castration. Freud reached this through self-analysis, and wrote about it systematically in *The Interpretation of Dreams*. It was only gradually that the notion of psychic reality was established as something other than the reflection of the biological drives of infancy. Even the early accounts of the Oedipus complex can not be freed from the accusation of biologism. They posited that the Oedipus complex – the attraction to the parent of the opposite sex and the jealous hatred for the parent of the same sex – resulted from an essential attraction by one sex for the other, and a 'givenness' of sexual rivalry between members of the same sex. Much of Freud's writing must be seen as concerned with resolving the problem of the relationship between the actual experience of the child and the production of fantasy.

'The Wolf Man' and *Totem and Taboo*

Freud's case-study published under the title *From the History of an Infantile Neurosis* (1918) sheds interesting light on the tension between the actual event and the role of fantasy in the individual history. Much of the first half of this lengthy and detailed case study is taken up with 'a detour through the prehistoric period of childhood',[14] using the symptoms of neurotic behaviour and the material of an early dream. The dream analysis of the little boy is highly elaborate, tracing associations which establish a precise date for the dream, the eve of his fourth birthday.

From the wealth of material produced by the associations of this dream Freud constructs both the wishes underlying the dream – the wish for sexual satisfaction from his father – and the terror that the satisfaction of this wish would entail castration like his mother.[15]

> Of the wishes concerned in the formation of the dream the most powerful must have been the wish for the sexual satisfaction which he was at that time longing to obtain from his father. The strength of this wish made it possible to revive a long-forgotten trace in his memory of a scene which was able to show him what sexual satisfaction from his father was like; and the result was terror.

What the analysis entails at this point is that the child recalls an earlier experience where, at (according to Freud's calculation) one and a half years old, the child had witnessed his parents making love, with the father behind the mother. The child makes sense of this observation when he is four, not when he is one and a half: 'His understanding of them was deferred but became possible at the time of the dream owing to his development, his sexual excitations and his sexual researches.'[16] Freud is well aware of the possible criticisms, centring on what possible sense a tiny baby could make of such a scene. He argues first on logical grounds that it must have been a reconstruction: a tiny child does not form such an understanding of events around it. Second, never in analysis is this 'event' produced as a memory but is always reconstructed. Despite this doubt cast on the nature of the recollection, Freud insists that 'It did take place as I suggest.'

Yet, at the very moment of insistence on the actual occurrence of these events, Freud suggests an alternative: 'There remains the possibility of taking yet another view of the primal scene underlying the dream – a view, moreover, which obviates to a large extent the conclusion that has been arrived at above and relieves us of many of our difficulties.'[17] The child may not have actually witnessed the act of intercourse between mother and father, as Freud suggested. He must have witnessed an act of intercourse, but not necessarily between his parents but perhaps between animals. Then the anxiety about castration emerges not from the actual sight of the mother during intercourse but as a result of other elements, for example, the sight of his sister, and a threat of castration by one of the servants in response to the boy's sexual activity.[18]

> we cannot dispense with the assumption that the child observed a copulation, the sight of which gave him a conviction that castration might be more than an empty threat. Moreover the significance which he subsequently came to attach to the postures of men and women in connection with the development of anxiety, on the one hand, and as a condition upon which his falling in love depended on the other hand, leaves us no choice but to conclude that it must have been a *'coitus a tergo, more ferrarum'*. But there is another factor which is not so irreplaceable and which may be dropped. Perhaps what the child observed was not copulation between his parents but copulation between animals, which he then displaced on to his parents, as though he had inferred that his parents did the same thing in the same way.

Thus at the crucial moment of claiming the 'reality' of the child's observation of parental intercourse, Freud turns away, offers an alternative solution in which the child combines various observations to produce a fantasy of the act of parental copulation. Here, because of the particularity of the child's experience, the fantasy is sufficient to generate intense anxiety – an anxiety which arises not from any *observation*, but from a form of understanding which is provoked in the fantasy.

The question of the real event is central to the Wolf-Man; the text hesitates between the deduction of an actual event and its dismissal on the grounds that the violence of the effect can be produced by fantasy. Significantly, Freud dismisses the distinction between fantasy and real event by appealing to his phylogenetic schema:[19]

> I should myself be glad to know whether the primal scene in my present patient's case was a fantasy or a real experience; but, taking all other similar cases into account, I must admit that the answer to the question is not in fact a matter of very great importance. These scenes of observing parental intercourse, of being seduced in childhood, and of being threatened with castration *are unquestionably an inherited endowment, a phylogenetic heritage*, but they may just as easily be acquired by personal experience.

Experience, then, is not a vital element of the development of the individual, either of the 'neurotic' or of the 'normal' individual. Where experience fails, the gaps are supplied by phylogenetic data. Freud is evidently working with a notion of 'reality' as that which is represented as having existed, this can be supplied equally well by phylogenetic data as by actual experience. Thus, at a crucial moment, Freud appeals to the schema laid out in *Totem and Taboo*, which text corresponds to precisely the same concerns – how is it that the individual's psychic life is structured despite his/her individual experience.

The same problem already exists in the 'Wolf-Man' which will reappear in *Moses and Monotheism*. Freud's phylogenetic schema leaves him still puzzling how to account for the transmission of memory of the real event – and indeed over the problem that the real event is simply pushed further back into prehistory. His discomfort with this solution is clearly demonstrated in the concluding passage of *From the History of an Infantile Neurosis:*[20]

> I am aware that expression has been given in many quarters to thoughts like these, which emphasise the hereditary, phylogenetically-acquired factor in mental life. In fact, I am of the opinion that people have been far too ready to find room for them and ascribe importance to them in psychoanalysis. I consider that they are only admissible when psychoanalysis strictly observes the correct order of precedence, and after forcing its way through the

strata of what has been acquired by the individual, it comes at last upon the traces of what has been inherited.

He is certainly not happy with the solution of instinctual or archaic traces which remain in his schema being the only way of providing for the transmission of common structures of experience. Yet he can neither attribute the transmission to spontaneous production of identical fantasy, nor accept that each individual is radically different according to that individual's experience.

Castration and representation

The function which phylogenesis fulfilled was to account for general cultural structures. It is clear, however, that Freud was grappling with the idea of the real event as real in so far as it is represented as having existed. This is confirmed by the way in which the status of recollection is rejected in analysis and replaced by the idea of the reconstruction of the event or fantasy in language.

Two factors in Freud's work, emphasised in much of his later writing, displace the notions of the real event and phylogenesis. These reveal Freud's attempt to account for the general structures of the unconscious without resorting to a phylogenetic account. Freud insists on the unconscious in analytic practice as a structural field which can be reconstructed since it handles, decomposes and recomposes its elements according to certain laws. Increasingly, he attempts to elaborate the status of these laws around two factors; infantile sexual theories and the castration complex.

Infantile sexual theories

As told by Sophocles, the original Oedipus myth provided indications of what became a central feature of Freud's account of infantile sexuality. Oedipus is asked to solve a riddle: 'What travels on four legs at dawn, two legs at midday, and three legs at dusk?' Oedipus was the first to provide the correct answer: 'Mankind'. His answer was fatal for that half-human, half-animal form, the Sphinx, which had posed the question. Already in the strange centrality attributed to this question in the Oedipus myth is an indication of what is tragic in Oedipus. It is his 'knowledge'. Oedipus goes on to '*know*' his mother in the carnal sense and therefore to know what, including the pleasure of his mother, is involved in the act of intercourse and his own conception.

The theme of sensual knowledge is confirmed by the presence of Tiresias, the blind prophet. In Greek mythology Tiresias had become a woman as a result of his having seen two snakes in the act of copulation. Seven years later – only after having seen the snakes again – he had been restored to manhood. The Gods, Jove and Hera, in an argument about the relative pleasure obtained by men and women while love-making, agreed to consult Tiresias; he, alone, was in a position to know the answer. Tiresias's reply was that, if love had ten parts, then men had one part while women had nine. Hera was so incensed about the betrayal of the 'secrets' of womanhood that she caused Tiresias to become blind. Jove, in pity for the predicament of Tiresias, compensated him with the gift of prophecy.

What is symptomatically present in the Oedipus myth is not just an example of how a man may unconsciously desire his mother and 'hate' his father. There are also the questions of female sexuality and pleasure and of the 'knowledge' of social categories of sexuality. The *tragedy* of Oedipus is that he goes on to find what man literally is; he literally knows the pleasure of his own conception, and the punishment is the symbolic castration of blindness. The 'tragedy' is not just the punishment for incestuous desires, and hatred of the parent of the opposite sex if it should be carried through. Rather, it is the tragedy of the non-intervention of sociality, in the form of the recognition of parental categories. In the normal course of events, the knowledge of paternity would put an end to the male's incestuous desire by the threat of castration. Oedipus' desire cannot be structured. Oedipus' 'knowledge' of and his subsequent inquiry into his origins Freud finds paralleled in all children. With the normal child, acceptance of the social institution of paternity puts an end to the child's involvement with the mother and structures desire according to social exigencies.

In Freud's work it is possible to see a modification of the trauma theory as the cause of neurotic behaviour in favour of an interest in the relationship between the child's sexual and aggressive behaviour and the production of sexual theories. I have suggested that this was so in the 'Wolf Man', but it is equally obvious in Freud's essays from 1908. In the essays, *On the Sexual Theories of Children* (1908), *Family Romances* (1909), *Some Psychical Consequences of the Anatomic Distinction between the Sexes* (1925), *Fetishism* (1927), *Female Sexuality* (1931) and *Femininity* (1933) the emphasis is increasingly laid on the sexual *theories* of children. What becomes important is how a mythical history is constructed by which the individual advenes to desire. Increasingly, the concern is with the theories about the importance of having or not having a penis. Castration and its implications in relation to feminine sexuality became central to this interest in sexual theories.

In positing the importance of inquiry, and of theory, Freud was far from replacing an essentialist notion of biology with an essentialist notion of a thirst for understanding: 'A child's knowledge on this point does not awaken spontaneously, prompted perhaps by some inborn need for established causes; it is aroused under the goad of self-seeking instincts that dominate him.'[21] In *The Sexual Theories of Children* Freud described these self-seeking instincts as aroused by fear and anxiety, for example, the birth of another child or, damage caused to narcissistic self-identification by anatomical distinction. Freud describes these provocations in identical terms to those used to describe his notion of primal trauma or fantasy. Sexual theories are provoked by early injuries to the ego (narcissistic mortifications) and relate to the sexual and aggressive nature of the child.

The provocation to thought itself by infantile sexual theories is intimately linked with Freud's idea in the phylogenetic texts of the provocation which the social category of paternity provides for intellectual advance. In the texts on infantile sexuality Freud makes it clear that the faculty of thought which takes its initial form as fantasy is never the result of any natural maturational process but is constructed *by the fantasies themselves* as a result of narcissistic injury.

In 'normal' development the anxiety produced by the fact of anatomical difference would coincide with the threat of castration brought by the father, or, for the girl, with disappointments in the mother. With 'neuroses', anxiety would set in process fantasies on sexual difference, remaining always in opposition to the predominating forms of sexuality. Thus Freud's analysis of male homosexuality revolves around the male child's initial and unshakeable fantasy that his mother has a penis, and, equally for fetishism, the structure of the latter is provided by the disavowal that the mother lacks a penis.

Freud does not separate fantasies from the text presented to the analyst, neither the text of neurotic symptoms, nor the text of dreams. He was increasingly interested in the structuring function which castration plays; it is seen as the nodal point around which the text is arranged. It becomes possible to describe certain definite forms the analysis will take, since the account of the individual's history has to be presented in and across language; it has therefore been submitted to the structuring effect of castration. Freud hovers over equating representation itself with the emergence of sexual theories provoked by narcissistic injuries, relating to the problem of sexual differences as embodied in the castration complex.

The castration complex

Freud's work shows a progressive displacement of concern with the Oedipus complex by a concern with the castration complex as structuring of primal fantasy and, therefore, as provocation for thought in general. This suggests that we should see castration as providing the condition for thought/ representation and as structuring individual and group experience.

In 1923 Freud's *Infantile Genital Organisation* added the importance of castration and of the phallic phase to his discovery of infantile sexuality. In that paper he acknowledges the shortcomings of the *Three Essays on Sexuality*. This is not merely because of the lack of discussion of the phallic or genital phase. It is primarily a criticism for having failed to take into account the implication of his theory of bisexuality and of the identity of the sexual activities of boy and girl. This is the *difference* of infantile sexuality from its adult outcome: both boy and girl undergo the same processes, are subject to the same drives, aims and activities. Both have active sexuality which is auto-erotic, or bound up with the mother, and which seeks sexual satisfaction. The identity of development is not confined to oral and anal phases of interest, but extends to active genital interest, for boys in the phallus, for girls in the clitoris.

It is not simply Freud's general theory of sexuality which has undergone revision; the specific problem of *female sexuality* has emerged and has implications for a general theory of sexuality. It is not coincidence that in his later writings on sexuality Freud concentrates on the question of female sexuality.

Two very dramatic factors now emerge from following through the implications of bisexuality. First, the girl-child must undergo a very radical change in the *form* of her sexuality – from active to passive, from clitoral to vaginal. Second, if the girl-child experiences the same desire as the boy-child for the mother, she must therefore undergo a very radical change in the *object* of her desire – from mother or woman to man. This is, then, the point of no return for biologism. No longer can the theory retain any notion of the essential attraction of each sex for the other, or of the essential antagonism for the same sex.

One element clearly demonstrates the displacement of the Oedipus complex by the structuring function of castration on the final forms of sexuality in Freud's theory. This element consists of the failure of Freud ever to solve the problem of non-symmetry between the Oedipus complexes of the boy and girl. The Oedipus complex for the boy is a growing but constant factor. As is the girl-child, the boy is bound up sensually with the mother, and, because active sexuality coincides with phallic activity, there emerge fantasies of sexual involvement with, or 'marriage' to, the mother. Only the threat of castration brought in rivalry by the father against the child's sensual involvement, coincident with the child' realisation of anatomical differences, forces the child to renounce the mother. For the girl-child, however, the process is reversed. For her, the castration complex has to be placed *before* the Oedipus complex since she too is linked sensually with the mother and undergoes an active development of phallic sensuality. Only with her discovery of anatomical distinction, threatening the girl's narcissistic image, does the girl-child renounce the mother and turn to the father. Increasingly, it is castration which in Freud's theory of sexuality structures desire, producing the 'final outcome' of reproductive sexuality. Castration can be seen as the point of organisation (or of disturbance) of the text by which the child represents its access to desire. Consequently, the moment of castration (the discovery of anatomical distinction) is synonymous with the possibility of representation. With the discovery of anatomical distinction and the elaboration of sexual theories, the child takes up a social distinction.

This rather cursory examination of aspects of Freudian theory has revealed two different but co-existent interpretations of the structural status of the unconscious. One insists that structures in the individual unconscious can be accounted for by a real event, and general structures can be accounted for by a 'real event' in human prehistory. The other suggested that the real event becomes real in so far as it is represented as being real. It appears that Freud increasingly thought the possibility of representation was synonymous with the discovery of castration; it is this which structures conscious and unconscious identity.

The structuralist re-reading of Freud has insisted that the notion of the real event should be interpreted in the light of the second series of preoccupations, castration and representation. Writers like Lévi-Strauss and Lacan insist that the phylogenetic hypothesis was elaborated because Freud did not have the concepts needed to formulate a theory of culture as signification. According to Lacan, such a theory would account for the structural nature of the unconscious without resorting to either of two impossible alternatives. On the one hand, there was idealism, with the idea that all individuals somehow spontaneously produce the same fantasy; on the other was the option Freud was forced to take – the phylogenetic hypothesis.

Lacan suggests that what Freud's account is concerned with is, in fact, the problem of anatomical difference and its relationship to the horizon of culture and signification. Because such concepts were not available to Freud, he was forced to fall back on a mythical history of the race, unconsciously remembered by all human beings. Both Lacan and Lévi-Strauss suggest that Freud, unlike many of his contemporaries, had realised that the prohibition of incest and the requirement of exogamy were inseparable movements, in some way *fundamental*, and the very structures which determine the construction of sexual identity and the unconscious. Unhappily, Freud's own writings do not always sit easily as potential structuralist texts. For not only does Freud hold to the phylogenetic account, but at the end of his life he wrote *Moses and Monotheism*, taking the phylogenetic account further by attempting to relate this pre-history to the actual history of the Jewish race.

Freud had always argued that religion and forms of religious behaviour – whether 'primitive' religion in the form of totemism or the religion of advanced 'cultures' such as Jewish or Christian monotheisms – exhibited structures which directly parallel the structures of behaviour revealed by individual neurotics. In *The Future of an 'Illusion'* (1927) and *Civilisation and its Discontents* (1930) Freud continued with this emphasis, describing religious ideas as patently infantile and at odds with reality, and attacking the social institutions of religion as 'the forcible imposition of mental infantilism', inducing mass-delusion and preventing the structures from appearing as individual neuroses. Religious doctrines carried with them the stamp of the time in which they originated; that is, in the ignorant childhood days of the race.

This theory of religion clearly included an account of the 'real event' as mythical horizon. Its emphasis was, however, on religion as collective neurosis, the projection of infantile preoccupations. In *Moses and Monotheism*, however, Freud adds a further element. He attempts to add the former concerns to an *actual history* of the events which determined the *particular* form of Jewish monotheism. It is this which suggests that there was never any easy solution for Freud as to the relative determination of particular histories and general cultural structures.

Moses and Monotheism shows the complexity of elements in psychoanalysis; there is the problem of the apparent universal structure of the unconscious; the problem of the real event; the status of history. The text shows that psychoanalysis cannot simply be claimed either as a positivist historical account of patriarchy or as an account of the universality of psychic structures.

History in *Moses and Monotheism*

In 1934 the first draft of this book was published under the title *The Man Moses, a Historical Novel*. The title served as a warning as to the status of the reference to history in *Moses and Monotheism*. Ernest Jones reports how dissatisfied Freud felt with his account of the life and social origins of Moses and of the origin of the Jewish 'tribes': [22]

> Experts would find it easy to discredit me as an outsider. . . . It won't stand up to my own criticism. I need more certainty and I should not like to endanger the final formula of the whole book which I regard as valuable, by appearing to found the motivation on a basis of clay.

At this point Freud decided temporarily to abandon the project, making the significant comment that 'I am no good at historical romances.' It should be noted that the final formula of the book reiterated *Totem and Taboo*'s argument on the coincidence of individual neuroses, religious practices and the hypothesised 'origin' of society. Here Freud also argued that the violence of the effect of Jewish religion can only be understood in terms of the particular history of the Jews. This specific history, he claims, produced the conditions for simultaneous 'advance' to monotheism and patriarchy. The history of the Jewish religion is argued in terms of 'over-determination'; the point of its emergence being a structure of coincidences, repetition of the act at the origin of culture, and definite material circumstances.

Freud's hypothesis of 'the actual history' of the Jewish race and religion can be summarised as follows. Freud starts with the 'outrageous' claim that Moses was an Egyptian and not, in fact, a Jew as the biblical tradition would have it. The religion which Moses brought with him was external to the Jewish people. It was the religion of worship of the Egyptian sun-god, Aten, which had become a monotheistic religion for a very brief period under the Egyptian pharaoh, Akhnaten. Moses perhaps had been a noble or priest from the exiled Akhnaten regime who formed an alliance with the oppressed Semites. He became the leader of the Semites but in the course of political rivalries was murdered by them. The Semites formed an alliance with other nomadic or dispossessed tribes. The religion of Aten was at first subsumed in the religion of the worhip of Yahwe, a fierce Volcano god. After a period of latency, the original forms of the Egyptian religion were restored. These forms were monotheism, rejection of the after-life, and the taboo on any representation of the god. All these forms, Freud claims, bear startling resemblances to the short-lived appearance of monotheism in Egypt. The precondition by which these forms re-emerged was provided by a historical coincidence. Another leader, son-in-law to the Midianite Jethro, emerged: he happened to be called Moses as well.

Freud argues that there are a series of historical accidents by which the history of the Jewish peoples replay the events at the origin of human culture – the murder of the primal father. Such a repetition provided the means of working through, and thereby resolving, the guilt at the original murder. An 'advance' in what he calls Geistigkeit (spirituality or intellectuality) is then secured.[23] This advance is both the recognition of the social category of paternity and permanent establishment of a single father-deity. Patriarchal monotheistic cultures are thus brought closer to the truth of the original traumatic deed, and therefore to a greater degree of neurotic resolution. Freud has substituted, or so it appears, a hierarchy of degrees of neurotic resolution for a hierarchy of degrees of primitiveness.

What is the status of this *specific* history of the Jewish people which Freud is so at pains to establish? Can his account of the development of the rigidly patriarchal and monotheistic culture on which our own is based be taken as occupying the same status of a positivist history of the development of patriarchal cultural forms? Positivist history interprets the representations found in texts by means of rules and procedures intended to determine the veracity of the record. It aims to eliminate distortion and to read back through the record to the real conditions of which it is the representation. In this case, it would seek to find a historical social formation characterised by paternal rule and dominance. Freud's methods are indeed a very long way away from such a positivist method of historical investigation. Several elements in the text of *Moses and Monotheism* demonstrate how Freud proceeds to his historical account. They reinforce the conclusions which I have begun to draw as to the status of the real event in Freudian theory.

Textual distortion

In its implications the distortion of a text resembles a murder: the difficulty is not in perpetrating the deed, but in getting rid of its trace.[24]

Unlike positivist history, which sets out to eliminate distortion by some appeal to a higher truth – oral accounts, statistics, economic conditions etc., – Freud treats the text as the analyst treats the speech of the patient. He expects to find the meaning of the text, *within* the text, not outside the text, as positivist history would expect. This is not, however, to expect transparency as if 'the text represents what really happened'. Instead, it seeks to reconstruct the meaning through processes of association, through displacements, through contradictions and repetitions. Analytic procedure accepts the patient's text always as already *re-presentation* going on to investigate the structures determining the re-presentations through displacements and distortions occurring in the text. It seeks neither to eliminate the distortion, nor correlatively to read back to the original event, but to construct the fantasy/event in the discourse addressed to the analyst. What is displaced at one point will appear in another place in the text.

Freud accordingly takes the biblical narrative neither as

historical truth nor as the total fiction of mythology. Distorting purposes can be deduced largely from the texts themselves, since quite often what has been suppressed or disavowed will appear elsewhere in the text. An example of textual distortion is given in the very notion of the 'chosen people'. This differs from any other religious mythology because the god chooses a people after a long period of absence from them. Freud here deduces another distortion resulting from the strange formation of Judaism by an Egyptian. It is an intelligible distortion if it is presupposed that Moses the Egyptian *chose* the Semites when he set out to escape Egyptian persecution.

Freud will not leave the notion of distortion at the level of the intrusion of political motives in historical representation. He supposes further both that the scriptures are a combination of historical and political evidence with mythological structures, and that, as myths, they may be assumed to possess elements of the typical myth.

The distortion of the typical text

The initial historical postulate that Moses was an aristocratic Egyptian derives from the deviation of the hero-myth of Moses from other myths of heroes. It is, in other words, a deviation from the average legend, the outline of which Freud derived from Rank's *Myth of the Birth of the Hero*, (1909).[25] This is thought to have profound links with the psychic life of the child: it has obvious parallels with the 'family romance' by which, through fantasy, the child embellishes its origins.

Freud accepts Rank's account of the typical legend, claiming that it is related to the problem of paternity. The hero is born against his father's will, is often cast out and returns to overcome the father. A classic version of the legend involves the exposure of the hero, often in a casket, from which he is rescued to be brought up by humble parents in place of his natural ones. Freud does not omit to emphasise the recurrent symbolism of birth which adheres to stories about casting out on to the water. In *Family Romances* (1909) he argues that the typical myth or legend has direct parallels in the psychic life of the child. Here, in fantasy the child often assumes that his/her real parents are only adoptive, he/she being descended from royal or noble blood. In fact, when the child realises the irrefutability of maternity, there is attributed to the mother a rich sexual life in order to replace the real father. Freud suggests that these infantile explanations or theories are the embodiment of, and to some extent, the resolution of contradictory impulses towards its parents. A typical example of such contradiction is the early over-estimation of the father which gives place to disappointment and, quite often, fear or rivalry. The child's 'fabrication' of royal descent by which the natural father becomes a foster-parent, corresponds according to Freud with the complex of over-estimation/disappointment and rivalry.

In contrast to this typical structure, the legend of Moses reveals striking dissimilarities and reversals. Moses is born of humble parents and rescued from the water by the aristocracy. Freud attributes to these dissimilarities the status of distortions of a typical text. Such distortions can be accounted for as being the eruption of certain features of a historical nature which, for political reasons, have undergone transformation. What is here being suppressed is the Egyptian origin of Moses. Under the pressures of nationalism the 'false' parents are made out to be Egyptian: hence the distortions to the usual form of the story.

Already we are confronted by a somewhat unusual assumption about the historical event. Family romances were thought by Freud to be located predominantly in the relations of desire within the family. Yet he uses the distortions operated on the typical romance as the evidence of historical events. The historical narrative has to be seen, in this case, as a reconstruction – a combination of typical structures, political forces and material circumstances.

The analogy between the individual and the group

As he does with much of the so-called historical evidence in *Moses and Monotheism*, Freud justifies his appear to 'typical legends' on the ground that religious observances, myths, etc. all have their bases in the same structures which underlie individual neuroses. Religious forms correspond with the complexes accruing to parent/child relations, castration anxiety, and events of a sexual nature.

It has already been argued that Freud takes religion to be a collective neurosis. This parallelism between individual and group neurosis in fact provides the whole 'flesh' of *Moses and Monotheism*, and is even mobilised to explain historical facts. Freud has the puzzle of accounting for the long period between Moses' exile from Egypt and the eventual acceptance of monotheism. This suggests a period of latency from which Freud deduces the need to forget a traumatic event. He deduces the murder of Moses, 'confirmed' by numerous references to disobedience amongst the Semites. Because of the murder of Moses, the father-figure, the Jews accidentally repeated the primal murder. Repetition of that deed, together with other repetitions, allowed a partial return of the repressed in which the working through allows reverence for the father to be reinstated. Hence the Jews 'advanced' towards patriarchal monotheism.

Again Freud is worried about simplistic claims for the universality and identity of human experience: 'We find ourselves in the realm of group psychology where we do not feel at home.'[26] However, he insists on an original event, and much of the latter part of the book is taken up with puzzling how knowledge of this event can be passed from one generation to another. Freud talks loosely of 'tradition', which he sometimes equated with oral records which preserve the memory of an event when written records disavow it. This is not adequate to explain the colossal lapse of time between the murder and the establishment of monotheism, nor can it account for the far-distant memory of the primal murder. Freud is found trying to establish a notion of tradition understood as unconscious memory traces, just as the individual preserves memory traces of an event which he/she could never recall. This notion of tradition as 'archaic traces' hovers on a biologistic account of the transmission of human culture.

The reason for Freud's persistence with the notion of archaic heritage related to his refusal of two opposed theories. One is 'culturalism', the other is that of universalism, supposing that an individual spontaneously fantasises complexes and mythical formations, because human experience is timeless and universal. Freud wanted to avoid taking up either of these positions: the first, because it could not account for the tenacity of an individual's complexes or, indeed, for their waywardness in relation to material circumstances; the second because it would contradict precisely the great discoveries of the unconscious, the effect of the 'pre-history of the individual' on the psychic life of the adult.

It was always the phylogenetic account which saved Freud from the awesome problems of empirical refutation of his thesis – from the empiricism which questions whether each individual has 'to see the other sex's genitals', or whether each has 'to hate and fear his father'. The reactions to early traumas are often not individual, but 'fit in better with a model of a phylogenetic event': 'The behaviour of neurotic children towards their parents in the Oedipus complex and in the castration complex abound in such reactions – which are intelligible only phylogenetically.'[27] Whatever the motive for Freud's adherence to the theoretically dubious notion of phylogenesis, the use of parallelism between individual and group psychology is hardly a basis for the deduction of 'real historical events' according to the positivist historical schema. Freud's use of the notion of tradition in the analogy between the group and the individual is, even at an explicit level, contradictory. It even opens on to an idea that the structures of the Jewish religion which are analogous to individual structures and complexes are simultaneous with the moment of a group's writing its history.

The position of the father and the advance in intellectuality: the Freudian notion of patriarchy

Perhaps more obviously than most one contradiction stands out in a generally confused text. It is that if monotheism emerged as a political factor, the condition for unity in a disparate empire, in Egypt under the pharaoh Akhnaten, why should the emergence of Jewish monotheism necessarily be tied up with the repetition of events of a pre-history; that is, the murder of Moses, the father-figure? The answer relates to Freud's conception of an 'advance in intellectuality/spirituality' and to the institution of patriarchy. While Egyptian monotheism was a temporary phenomenon, arising perhaps from political expediency, Freud attributed to Jewish monotheism the status of a permanent 'advance', established as the result of the overdetermination of circumstances by a series of repetitions, of which the principal repetitions were the repetition of the murder of the father and of the name of Moses.

According to Freud, these repetitions permitted a part return of the repressed – of those events which had existed only in 'tradition', in archaic memory-traces:[28]

> Fate brought the great deed and misdeed of primeval days, the killing of the father, closer to the Jewish people by causing them to repeat it on the person of Moses, an outstanding father-figure. It was a case of 'acting out', instead of 'remembering', as so often happens with neurotics during the work of analysis.

Freud argues not only the origin of monotheism in patriarchy through the institution of a monotheism entailing a lasting 'advance' paralleled, if not produced, by paternity as a social institution. Moses does not simply re-awaken the childish image of the father, but his murder and gradual reinstatement make possible the other side of that ambivalent love/hatred relationship of which the 'hate' side led to the original murder of the primal father.

Freud's conception is, however, invariably more complicated and interesting than this banal account of religion as the projection of infantile desires and anxieties. Interest attaches to the conception of patriarchy which is employed. where Freud relates his notion of advance, to the recognition of paternity as a social institution; the recognition of the father's role in procreation, and therefore of the father-place, marks society's advance from pre-history. In Freud's evolutionary scheme this advance is equated with the reinstatement of the original father's desires and prohibitions. Reverence for the father's desires is gradually recognised in the form of totemism. The point at which patriarchy is reinstated, nevertheless under the exigency of the exogamic exchange of women, is what constitutes the advance to sociality itself.

Reference is made here to the advance from pre-history to

history, just as Freud could write of the child's pre-history before s/he acquired consciousness. In *Moses and Monotheism* the analogy is explicit where Freud speaks of the identity of the words for conscious/conscience in both French and German. He claims that such identity bears witness to the identity between the acquisition of consciousness and the development of conscience or guilt at the moment of the original act of parricide. The identical recognition of paternity which provoked the category of thought was, in other words, inextricably bound up with guilt and 'religious feelings' ascribed by Freud to the complexes related to the primal father and his murder.

The conception of 'advance' is linked not so much with any notion of progress, or of higher forms of society, but more with the process of how the child acquires a place in society through a capacity for thought provoked by the father's position and, therefore, by the categories of marriage relations. The evolutionary schema of *Moses and Monotheism* generalises this constantly repeated process to an original event – phylogenetic account – so that it will not appear as a spontaneous and given product of the human child. What is significant is the symbol of fatherhood and its relation to abstract thought, rather than the literal father.

One aspect, in particular, of *Moses and Monotheism* does indeed belie the aim of a phylogenetic account. This is the argument's circularity. Freud asserts that intellectual/spiritual advance is achieved in the establishment of a patriarchal culture. Now it becomes possible in part to remember and reverence the original father. Logically, however, no such decisive emergence of patriarchy can occur, since the dominance of the father's control of marriage relations was 'originally' always present: it had simply been in abeyance following the act of parricide. The origin of patriarchy is presumably explained by presupposing the existence of patriarchy originally! In a significant moment in *Moses and Monotheism*, Freud himself comes to recognise the problem:[29]

> In the case of some advances in intellectuality, for example in the case of the victory of patriarchy, we cannot point

to the authority which lays down the standard which is to be regarded as higher. It cannot in this case be the father since he is only elevated into being the authority by the advance itself.

This brief comment fundamentally undermines the whole evolutionary schema outlined at such pains in the rest of Freud's text. This contradition does certainly indicate that the category of paternity is being invoked in a more complex relationship with kinship, castration and the sexual theories of children than would be apparent from the phylogenetic account. What is important about this fundamental contradiction in the account of the emergence of patriarchy is the light it throws on the category of paternity. First, it reveals that, at the basis of the advance to human culture, it is not the dominance of the fathers as a political group that signifies. What is significant is a prohibition on incest and an exhortation to exogamy. In other words, Freud's evolutionary account, unlike those of some of his contemporaries, was to show neither the inevitability of patriarchy nor the 'primitiveness' of matrilineal society. It was to demonstrate the fundamental importance of incest-prohibition and of exogamy.

The structural status of kinship

Lévi-Strauss has laid claim to this account in Freud as in fact describing the structural nature of human culture. The status of these structures was first elaborated by him in his *Elementary Structures of Kinship* (1949). In this book, Lévi-Strauss takes issue with the so-called functionalists, who refused to examine kinship as a system. Functionalists, as we have seen, concentrated on only the functions of particular institutions and on beliefs in particular societies. Lévi-Strauss, opposing them, argues that kinship does possess a systematicity. It consists of the apparent universality of prohibitions and of prescriptions for categories of marriageability. Nor is is just that all societies observe rules of some kind. Rules always involve some prohibitions against marriage within the clan or group and a prescription for marriage outside that group. Thus in all societies – matrilineal or patrilineal – it is possible to distinguish certain regularities. Women are exchanged according to a certain order, marriages being permitted with certain kin or with certain members of the same tribe or neighbouring tribes, being forbidden with other kin or other members of the same or neighbouring tribes. Faced with this apparent systematicity, Lévi-Strauss suggests the analogy between kinship relations and linguistic relations, as described by structural linguistics. They are made up of the same elements: systems of difference, signs, relations of exchange. In other words, Lévi-Strauss conceives of kinship as a system of communication guaranteeing the possibility of reciprocity and, therefore, of integration between self and others. In such a system, women are exchanged as signs.

Lévi-Strauss correctly suggests that Freud's phylogenetic account is so contradictory precisely because it cannot produce these terms. Paternity is not about forms of subordination on the basis of sex – legal, political or intersubjective. It features so irreducibly because, for Freud, kinship relations (incest-prohibition and exogamy) were the forms of fundamental classification. They were synonymous with thought itself. Thus the conceptualisation is premised on a primary conceptualisation – that of the social rules of marriage – which is premised on the recognition of the father's role. Thus I have indicated several areas which in *Moses and Monotheism* warns us not only against equating Freud's account with a positivist notion of history, but also against interpreting Freud's account as describing patriarchy as it is usually defined – that is, as the political, legal and intersubjective dominance of men as a sex.

Conclusion

The aim of this chapter has been to understand how Freud's history of the family relates to his theories of sexuality and the unconscious. It has been argued that Freud resorted to a phylogenetic explanation of the 'generality' of unconscious structures. This was in order to solve the question of the status of the 'real event' in the determination of the individual psyche. It was in elaborating this phylogenetic account that he turned to his contemporary debates about patriarchy and the origin and development of familial forms.

An examination of Freud's last work, *Moses and Monotheism* has, however, indicated that extreme caution must be employed in translating Freud's account into a description of a real historical phase, patriarchy. For even *Moses and Monotheism*, where Freud himself turns to the problem of 'real history', is an immensely contradictory text. And even this text ultimately seems to be preoccupied by what Lévi-Strauss has correctly formulated as the structural status of kinship. Freud's own insistence on the 'real event', both the phylogenetic account and the attempted outline of history, however, warns us equally against any simplistic neglect of this feature of his work. It was far from being a minor element in his work, and was, in fact, his theoretical solution to the apparent universality of the complex. I have attempted to indicate that two explanations of this ran parallel through Freud's work: that which favoured the structural status of castration and representation, and that which sought real historical explanations for the determination of the human psyche.

It is important to guard against any simplistic rejection of Freud's concern with the real event. This is not because it seems to me to be a particularly useful or indeed plausible account of human development. On the contrary, I am interested in Freud's concern with this level for two other reasons. One is that orthodox Freudian adherence to this scheme has determined the form of psychoanalysis' engagement with the social sciences, and it is around this question that the debate has occurred over the universal applicability of psychoanalysis' findings. It is here that psychoanalysis has been extremely limited by its use of evolutionary accounts of the patriarchal family. Second, Freud's own ambivalence on the question of the determination of the psychic complex seems to me to bear witness to a series of still unresolved questions about psychoanalytic theory.

In the following chapter, the engagement which psychoanalysis had with other human sciences will be considered. In particular, it will consider the way in which the dogmatic adherence to the account of literal history of the family compromised the more radical investigation of sexuality and the social structure which is evident in other aspects of psychoanalytic theory.

8 Psychoanalysis and anthropology: the interpretation of social practices

Introduction

Freud, as we have seen, refused to abandon his phylogenetic theory of the general structures of the unconscious. Although some elements in his argument justify reading it as a metaphor for the structural status of the incest-taboo and castration, Freud adhered to 'the time-honoured heirlooms of evolutionary anthropology'. He equated patriarchy with civilisation. He postulated a stage of maternal dominance, corresponding to the dominance of the sensual before the triumph of intellectuality. He insisted, too, on a unilinear history of the family. What is more, he persisted in these assumptions despite early chastisement from anthropologists for neglecting the criticisms to which evolutionary theory had been submitted; 'there really is a great deal of ethnology not at all represented by the authors whom Freud discussed'.[1]

In spite of the all-too-obvious limitations of Freud's theory, it was to be psychoanalysis above all other psychological theories which had an impact on some developments of anthropological studies of the family. Writing on the impact of psychiatry on American Anthropology, in 1944, one commentator insisted that psychoanalysis alone had made any systematic impression: 'certainly from the study of anthropological literature one gets an overwhelming impression that it is only psychoanalytic writers who are extensively read by anthropologists in this country. One would be hard pressed to discover five citations to nonanalytic psychiatrists.'[2] The psychoanalytic impact was not, however, a radical challenge to assumptions about the nature of sexual relations. Its influence was especially great in the development of studies of behaviour and personality within American anthropology, seen clearly in the writings of the 'culture and personality' school.

For many, particularly for marxists, this influence has been seen as deeply regressive. It emphasises a universal psychology and studies of behaviour as opposed to the social and economic structures of any given society. Psychoanalysis is seen by its opponents as applying a universalising account of the family and sexuality crudely to any cultural form. Especially as it has appeared within anthropology, psychoanalysis has reinforced the significance of the biological family as repository of individual emotions, instincts and psychology. From the point of any interrogation of the social construction of sexuality, psychoanalysis can hardly be seen to offer a radical perspective. Rather than generating a radical interrogation of sexuality, the legacy of psychoanalysis has been a long and sterile debate over the universal applicability of its findings about the human family. Positions have polarised around whether 'typical' emotional complexes like the Oedipus complex are universal, or whether emotional structures and obligations vary within different cultures.

The history of the early relation between psychoanalysis and anthropology is extremely revealing. It is clear that at first both disciplines envisaged a profitable exchange. Throughout the exchange, psychoanalysis vacillated between two forms of analysis, often in tension with one another. On the one hand was the attention to symbolism, insisting on the importance of sexuality and refusing to accept sexual positions as 'givens' or as simply culturally determined. On the other hand, there was the deep commitment to a universal history of the family. It was ultimately this commitment which won. Psychoanalysis emerged with an apparently entirely reactionary commitment to the universality of the nuclear family. This chapter sets out to investigate how it happened that psychoanalysis adopted such a sterile position when at a certain level it appears to have had enormous potential for investigating sexuality in sexual relations.

The Significance of Psychoanalysis for the Mental Sciences

The Significance of Psychoanalysis for the Mental Sciences was a highly influential monograph by Rank and Sachs, published in 1913.[3] It bears witness to the claim made by psychoanalysis itself for its applicability to objects tradition-ally studied by the social sciences. The claim was made not only by psychoanalysts, but also by some social scientists. From the publication of *Totem and Taboo* until the Second World War, there was a long period of exchange between psychoanalysis and the social sciences. Psychoanalysis was frequently cited as the discipline which, developed in con-junction with the traditional social sciences, could constitute a genuine 'human science'. The position was found surprisingly often among marxist writers of the period.[4] Given the impact of psychoanalysis in the social sciences, this aspiration now seems startling.

The claim made in *Totem and Taboo* that the 'beginnings of religion, ethics, society and art meet in the Oedipus complex'[5] stood in the background of psychoanalytic interpretations of social practices; it ultimately was the claim on which a psychoanalytic orthodoxy was founded. Freud himself had already established an interest in analysis of myth and cultural form, primarily through his work on religion, but, apart from the phylogenetic texts, he did not deal directly with anthropological data. It was left to his followers who were quick to extend his discoveries to a whole range of issues within the social sciences. Yet, these applications did not occur in a haphazard fashion. They occurred in the same period in which the orthodoxy of the psychoanalytic institutes was formed; it was the orthodoxy characterised by the early years of the *International Journal of Psychoanalysis.* Freud's rivalries and allegiances were formative in the development of an orthodoxy and, contrary to the structuralist re-reading, Freud clearly gave his support to some of the more literal interpretations of the phylogenetic account.

It was for this reason that, rather than move out of the debates around the emergence of the biological family, psychoanalysis remained with them and indeed emerged with a more systematic commitment to the significance of the biological family. Interestingly, the major dispute within the orthodox interpretation of sexual relations was around the question of female sexuality[6] and not around the significance of the biological family in the interpretation of cultural phenomena.

Dreams and myths

In its interpretation of mythical representations, it is possible to see quite clearly the two contradictory aspects of the psychoanalytic project. On the one hand, the approach undermines many of the assumptions of previous interpretations of symbolism. On the other hand, there is a crude interpretation of symbolism in terms of universal schemas of human sexual development.

The fundamental interlinked discoveries of psychoanalysis – infantile sexuality and the unconscious – had been made through a notion of indirect representation which underlay the interpretation of symbols. It was through the analysis of symbolic processes like dreams, that regular confirmation of the unconscious had been provided. Dreams were the 'royal road to the unconscious'. Like neurotic symptoms, jokes, puns and dreams regularly demonstrate another modality of signification, that of the unconscious thoughts. Their existence cuts through any differentiation between normal and abnormal mental processes.

In *The Interpretation of Dreams*, Freud had challenged previous interpretations of dream symbolism. He argued that those phenomena like dreams, jokes, and neurotic symptoms, previously consigned to the unknown and therefore unknowable, are, in fact, meaningful phenomena. They are in a direct relation to waking thought. The difference lies primarily in a modality of signification; the unconscious processes exploit the plurality of language, making connections which evade conscious thought, in order to avoid censorship. Dreams have both manifest and latent content. The manifest content of the dream are the images, words, sounds which can be fairly instantly recalled on waking, often having their origin in the dreamer's experience of the previous day. These are a series of seemingly arbitrary signs, sounds and images whose totality has the character of a rebus. Yet beyond the apparent arbitrariness and strangeness, analysis is able to induce the associations which will lead to the latent concerns of the dream.

From this process it was possible for Freud to deduce certain characteristics of dreaming and therefore of the relation between conscious and unconscious thought. The unconscious is a modality of signification which is characterised by distortion. The manifest content is seen as the product of the dream work, distorting the complex of the dream's concerns into something acceptable to the conscious self. There are two means by which this distortion is effected; the activities of condensation and displacement. Both these activities are available because of the structure of representation itself. Because representation is itself only a process of differentiation, new relations can constantly be constructed. The activities of the dream work are seen to be the effect of two fundamental features of dreaming: the imaginary satisfaction of desires which would be unacceptable to the conscious mind, and the process of censorship which prohibits that desire from conscious expression.

Previously unintelligible forms of behaviour like obsessional or neurotic behaviour become explicable as systems of displaced signs by which the individual produces a compromise formation between desire and its prohibition. Freud himself set the scene for suggesting an identity between these individual forms and general social forms, particularly in his analysis of religion as neurosis. In asserting that sociality was achieved only through the painful process of renunciation and repression, Freud's discoveries were extended to general social forms.

Rank and Sachs in *The Significance of Psychoanalysis for the Mental Sciences*, insisted that psychoanalysis' special claim in the interpretation of cultural forms is this treatment of the symbol. The symbol, they argue, can be seen as a social expression of repressed material. It is a 'special kind of indirect representation', especially suitable for disguising unconscious material. 'Its essence consists in the possession of two or more meanings, as it has itself also arisen by a kind of condensation, an amalgamation of individual characteristic elements.'[7] The symbol for this argument is essentially unconscious but is a compromise formation with the requirements of culture, therefore it 'lacks in no way the conscious determinants which condition in various degrees symbol formation and symbol interpretation'.[8] Discussing this article, Ernest Jones[9] adds that 'true symbolism', being a compromise formation between unconscious desires and social determinants, would always entail shock in its decipherment. From this perspective, myths, legends, religion, art, philosophy, ethics, law, all become forms of expression of the unconscious. These processes of representation are united by their common structure of fantasy, determined by sexual preoccupations:[10]

> Freud came to consider these apparently heterogeneous products of man's psyche from a common viewpoint. They all have in common the relation to the unconscious, to the psychic life of childhood, and to sexuality; they have in common the tendency to represent a wish of the individual as fulfilled: in common are the means of representation, which serve this end.

The impact of such claims was instantaneous, not just within psychoanalysis, where Freud's ideas were readily applied to ethnographic data, but also within anthropology. W.H.R. Rivers, initially a psychologist, who came to specialise in ethnology, wrote on *Dreams and Primitive Culture* in 1918.[11] Here he sought to extend further the comparisons which had already been made between dreams and myths. All the processes, he claimed, which Freud lays out as the processes of dream work correspond closely to the representational processes found in myths of 'primitive' societies. They share the same processes: dramatisation, the condensation of ideas in symbols, rituals as displaced expression. They share the same functions of disguise and censorship compromised with wish-fulfilment. Finally, they share the same content, an expression of sexual concerns. Rivers, though highly critical of evolutionary assumptions about primitive social organisations, is still happy to base his analysis on 'mental infantilism' of some groups. Their cultures more readily express themselves in this 'concrete' form due to their primitive mentality.

The possibility of viewing 'these apparently heterogeneous products of man's psyche from a common viewpoint'[12] threw open a while field for psychoanalytic interpretation. Freud's pleasure in welcoming Otto Rank, into the early psychoanalytic circle is revealing. Rank lacked a medical background but was welcomed as bringing a broad cultural knowledge. The followers were not slow to carry out the intentions of the master.

The symbolism of myths

As soon as psychoanalysis began to attract a following, publications appeared applying Freudian theory to the material of myth and ritual. Rank wrote the *Myth of the Birth of the Hero*: Abraham tackled the Prometheus myth in *Dreams and Myths*; Jones wrote several articles on symbolism in myths; Silberer's *Problems of Mysticism and its Symbolism* appeared in 1917[13]; books by Reik, Money-Kyrle, and Roheim appeared not long after.[14]

All these books and articles turned around a similar problem: what was the relation between individual and collective unconscious representations? Abraham suggested that myth is the dream of the people and a dream is the myth of an individual. 'The dream is a piece of superseded infantile mental life' and 'the myth is a piece of superseded infantile mental life of a people'.[15] Rank saw myths as images intermediate between collective dreams and collective poems: 'in mythical or religious phantasies a whole people liberates itself for the maintenance of its psychic soundness from those primal impulses that are refractory to culture . . . while at the same time it creates . . . a collective symptom for taking up all repressed emotion'.[16] In the previous chapter, we saw how, in the *Myth of the Birth of the Hero*, Rank turned his attention to the hero legends in a number of different cultures. The typical legend, he claims, is a structure of symbols by which various repressed primal impulses are expressed. Hero legends are the symbolic expression of a series of preoccupations which have a direct correspondence with the fantasies of small children and neurotics. The determinants are: early overestimation of the parents, followed by rapid disillusionment; sexual rivalry in which hostility felt towards the parents is represented as aggression by them through a process of projection; fantasies about the birth-process; and finally wish-fulfilment whereby the father, as sexual rival, can be killed. These determinants often condense in one symbol. Thus the recurrent theme of exposure on the water is an overdetermined symbol, condensing infantile speculation on the process of birth with fears of the parents' hostile intentions. The symbol of exposure embodies the fear of a hostility so powerful that the hero's birth itself will be fraught with danger.

Artistic representation could also be understood as symbols produced by indirect representation. The symbols used in art also arise in the structure of fantasy. Ernest Jones analysed symbolism in Christian art, turning his attention to the recurrent symbolism of the Madonna's conception through the ear.[17] This is the representation of the immaculate conception as the breath of the Holy Ghost entering the Virgin Mary's ear and causing her to become pregnant. For Jones, the symbol requires interrogation: why is breath endowed with this strange significance?

Several elements recur in the variations on this symbol. To the forefront are the representations of the message of conception as a dove, the offer of a lily, or a stream of air to the Madonna's ear. Jones sees these as the displaced or inverted representations of certain obsessions, primarily infantile anal obsessions. The displacement has taken place through connotations; the elements are privileged in their suggestion of excretory preoccupations. Warmth, sound, odour are constantly connoted through notions of breath, air, mouth. These connotations can also be produced as the inversion of what is represented: the pure lily, the odourless flower suggests the inversion of strong smells. The preoccupations with breath suggest the mouth and processes of introjection like eating. They also reveal their inversion – evacuation. These chains of association suggest an over-determined symbol in which are condensed various infantile scatological preoccupations producing a fantasy of birth as shitting. The mother eats food, her stomach swells, something is passed from her body through her anus.

Such fantasies are repressed by the adult consciousness but remain as sources of excitement and stimulation to the unconscious. Symbols formed as a compromise allow the fantasy to be represented but in a form acceptable to the conscious mind. Thus the satisfaction obtained from religious and artistic forms is a sublimated satisfaction. Jones points to the final process of evasion by which these preoccupations are transformed into acceptable material. Both religion and art are conceived of as the highest expression of human mind. Again, this can be seen as an inversion: what they deal with are preoccupations which the socialised mind regards as the 'lowest' and most disgusting:[18]

> If we regard the theme as a whole, we cannot but be impressed by the ingenuity and fine feeling with which an idea so repellent to the adult mind has been transformed into a conception not merely tolerable but lofty in its grandeur. In the endeavour to represent the purest and least sensual form of procreation that can be imagined, the one most benefitting to the Creator himself, the mind worked surely on the soundest lines by reaching for its basis to the crudest and grossest idea obtainable.

Jones's treatment of symbolism is at its most subtle here. In many places he falls back into a notion of symbolism as mimetic substitution, such as evident in his analysis of the meaning of salt, as representing semen.[19] Here, however, he treats symbols as indirect representation, complexly over-determined, employing all means to evade censorship.

Applied to the social practices of so-called primitive peoples, the psychoanalytic interpretation is no less ingenious, though equally problematic. Instantly, the psychoanalytic approach to the hoary old 'problems' of evolutionary anthropology overturns the assumptions that rites and symbolic practices can be explained by a unilinear history or as a direct expression of a social function. Evolutionary anthropology had insisted on treating the *couvade* as a rite masking the transition from mother-right to father-right whereby the father claimed rights to the child. Reik, in *Ritual*, examines the variety of practices which have come under the title, the *couvade*. These include not only the simulation of labour pains, but also elaborate rituals carried out by men supposedly to protect women in child-birth. The latter include precise food taboos as to what the father may or may not eat during the pregnancy. Reik ignored anti-evolutionary attention to the diversity of these practices, and insisted that all the rituals were connected; they were expressions of unconscious processes, compromises by which men can express fears and antagonism awakened by child-birth in a socially acceptable fashion.

Reik uses what psychoanalysis has been able to uncover about demonic representations in religious thought. Here psychoanalysis has been able to demonstrate the process of projection at work. While 'God the Father' is clearly a projection of infantile overestimation of the father, that overestimation is never the only aspect of a child's feelings. The male child is also profoundly antagonistic towards the father who is sexual rival and potential threat. Clinical psychoanalysis had shown how 'neurotics' frequently attributed to other people antagonistic impulses which they themselves feel. This is often at the basis of persecution complexes and paranoia, where the individual, unable to admit aggressive feelings in the conscious mind, projects them outwards as hostility directed against her/himself. Neurotics frequently feel intense bodily pain which is neither simulated nor false. It is real in the sense that it is imagined as real. Again these pains can often be traced to compromise formation between severe hostility felt towards another and intense guilt at these fantasies of violence. The imagined pain is turned against the subject her– or himself. The contradictory impulses are thus deprived of their gravity and tension if the unconscious part of the impulses (usually the hostile tendencies) can be projected outwards from inner perception to the external world.

In the case of religious representations, it is not the individual but the demons who are thought to have wicked intentions towards the father. The individual's intentions are left as 'pure'; protecting the father from external threat. The common coincidence of *couvade* practices with ideas about protection from demons led Reik to speculate on a similar origin:[20]

If therefore we look upon demons as the projection of a person's latent hostility, we must conclude that in this heightened fear of demons among many people, lie reactive feelings of punishment and remorse which conceal and over-compensate wicked wishes directed against the lying-in woman.

This process of projection becomes critical in some customs, like a Turkish practice where the man spreads a ring of fire around the hut to ward off evil spirits, an act where 'the confined women become seriously alarmed'.[21] The almost open hostility which accompanies these acts can readily be found in many other *couvade* rituals. Swords and other weapons are placed under the beds of the labouring women; arrows are shot over their huts. The introjection of the intention to harm the women produces customs where men dress in the women's clothing and writhe around simulating the pains of child-birth. The man internalises the pain wished on the woman, and experiences it pleasurably.

Finally, the dietetic *couvade* can also be understood in just this way. Again, this can be illuminated by the study of neurotics. Here elaborate rituals and taboos on certain foods or eating habits, are often justified on the grounds that if they are not observed a certain person will come to harm. They bear witness to repressed aggressive impulses towards that person. The suppression of these impulses increases the intensity of the masochistic instinctual component. The *couvade* practices ultimately, however, bear witness to the triumph of tender feelings towards the woman and child.

Underlying the aggression felt towards the child and towards the mother for bringing the child into the world is fear of retaliation. For the birth of the child, particularly the first child, reawakens the father's feelings of hostility to his own father, feelings of sexual jealousy, rivalry and hatred so great that it included a desire for the father's death. It is fear that these feelings will in turn be directed against himself that causes the father's hostility towards his offspring. At this point, Reik turns again to the phylogenetic account, offering an amplification of the primal horde hypothesis:[22]

> After the murder of the father, which was the most important event of primitive development, perhaps of human development the brother clan was formed. After successful detachment from incestuous objects . . . each of the brothers took one or more wives. The child who resulted from this new union awakened its father's memory of that outrage, since the child was a result of a breach in the paternal prohibition and made the son himself the father. His guilty conscience was changed into the fear of retaliation. The memory of the father found its primitive expression in the belief that the newly arrived child was the father himself, who had come to take revenge on his murderer.

But for these reasons the hostility is always more than fear of retaliation. It is also fear of the small child's incestuous feelings towards his mother, incestuous feelings which the father had to abandon. Thus the rites of pregnancy and pain performed by the father are overdetermined by also being a denial of the mother's role in childbirth, a very different notion of displacement of birth-rights from mother to father. The 'real meaning' has nothing to do with a transition in political rights. It corresponds to the father's fantasy of having given birth to the child and is a nullification of the mother's role in the child's birth. Thus social rituals are understood as symptoms which are 'complexly overdetermined'. A series of events like the birth of a child or its reaching puberty may provoke a 'return of the repressed'. Thus return is accomplished in a distorted form as 'structures in the nature of a *compromise* between the repressed ideas and the repressing ones'.[23] Crucial in this production of social rituals is sexuality – incestuous desires, sexual rivalry and anxiety.

This outline of three psychoanalytic interpretations of myths, artistic representations and social rituals has attempted to isolate what is distinctive about the psychoanalytic interpretation of social practices. This distinctiveness reveals both strengths and weaknesses. On the one hand, it reveals a radical approach to the notions of representation and sexuality. Symbols are indirect representations, complexly overdetermined by a series of sexual preoccupations which seek compromise formations with social forces. For this reason the idea of representation challenges that on which so many of the other theories examined in this book are based. It posits a notion of representation where the activity of the means of representation is not *reduced* to the service of other social functions. It is rigorously anti-functionalist, resisting the idea that symbolic practices simply reflect other social practices. Furthermore, these psychoanalytic interpretations insist on the importance of sexual anxieties and relations underlying some social practices, privileged as bearers of these concerns. Unlike other theories examined, the psychoanalytic interpretation does not present an 'unproblematic' theory of sexuality. The acquisition of sexual identity is a problem. Fantasies of pre-genital sexuality and desire are ever-present forces on which society is precariously perched.

However, these interpretations also reveal the elements which have led to the distrust of psychoanalysis. Here is a commitment to the worst kind of evolutionism translated into a comparison between adult and infantile mode of thought; 'primitives' represent infantile thought and Western capitalism represents adult thought. Of course, given the psychoanalytic logic of the ever-presence of repressed infantile wishes, then these divisions are sometimes dissolved: 'there are enormous differences, but these are not so much between child and adult as between modes of thinking which are present in both'.[24] In general however a hierarchy is implied; some cultures have 'resolved' sexual anxiety and rivalry to a more successful degree than others. The theory pulls towards a correspondence with theories of the 'mental infantilism of savages'.

Finally, these psychoanalytic interpretations rest on an adherence to a universalistic account of sexual preoccupations. They neglect the specificity of cultures. Even though there is a place in the theories for a notion of the particularity of each culture – after all, compromise formation takes place as a result of social exigencies – this perspective tends to give precedence to universalising theory of sexual constructions. Specific social forms may be the forces by which certain

233

wishes are repressed, yet social forms themselves are frequently posited as the result of compromise formations. It is both sociality which entails certain wishes to repressed, while at the same time social symptoms are themselves the product of compromises with these wishes. There is, in other words, a necessity posited to the outcome of development. This tension between the necessity of sexual development and the specificity of cultures came to the surface in the tension between phylogenetic and ontogenetic interpretations of culture which will be dealt with later in the chapter.

A number of writers quickly recognised that psychoanalysis was advancing a rigorously deterministic account of social forms. W.H.R. Rivers, for example, noted that psychoanalysis' theory of individual development exactly paralleled the rigorously historical approach to social forms of modern anthropology:[25]

> Both agree in basing their studies on a thorough-going determinism according to which it is held that every detail of the phenomena they study, whether it is to be the apparently fantastic or absurd incident of a dream or to our eyes the equally fantastic and ridiculous rite or custom of the savage, has its definite historical antecedents and is only the final and highly condensed product of a long and complex chain of events.

That psychoanalysis insisted on this rigorous determination of all social forms by the sexual history, either of the race or of the individual, was simultaneously psychoanalysis' distinctive 'discovery' and the reason for major splits within the movement. The splits with both Adler and Jung had their origins in Freud's insistence that accounts of individual conscious and unconscious could only be explained by a rigorously deterministic account of sexual history.

It is this rigorous account of sexual determination which interests me here. For it seems that the *form* which this account took was determined by the orthodoxy formed in the discussion of the history of the family. In the writings on symbolism there is a tension which is general in psychoanalytic writing. At one moment, it insists on the complex overdetermination of symbols and the importance of sexuality whose outcome is not decided in advance. At the next, it insists on a real universal history of sexual organisation determining all social practices. In what followed, it becomes clear that sexuality was conflated theoretically with the history of the family.

The conflation of sexuality and the history of the family

It will already be apparent that in some interpretations, psychoanalysis turned 'naturally' to the phylogenetic hypothesis. In some cases, the commitment was literal; for others, it was more ambivalent. The ambiguity in these interpretations reflects the unresolved status of the complex. It has been argued that Freud's retention of the hypothesis reflects a commitment to the history of the family as objectification of *complexes* and not *instincts*; it represents a commitment to the priority of culture over instincts or nature. Yet as we will see, the orthodoxy which emerged stressed precisely the opposite – the priority of a necessary history of the instincts in a given familial form over the cultural complex. The orthodoxy arose partly as a result of the particular form in which Freud resolved the cultural referent of complexes, that is, the phylogenetic account. This solution engendered an interpretation of the complex as emotions connected with a real history of the family – that is, transitions in the procreative unit. It is for this reason that psychoanalysis has such a hopeless reputation for universalising generalisations as to the human family and its complexes. Partly, however, the emergence of a crude orthodoxy was in response to the crudeness of the critics of psychoanalysis, a point which will be dealt with more thoroughly later.

Flügel's *The Psychoanalytic Study of the Family* demonstrates quite clearly how easily the psychoanalytic notion of complexes could be interpreted as describing complexes of typical emotions arising from a real nuclear family. His book argues that emotional conflicts generated by actual conflicts and rivalries within the procreative family determine the human psyche. These emotional complexes can be reduced to two fundamental impulses and their conflicts; 'the two principal poles of emotions, love and hate which coalesce in the

Oedipus complex'.[26] These typical emotions of the human family, and the various ways in which they are resolved, are thought by Flügel to structure all social institutions, beliefs and activities: the puberty rites, men's clubs and secret societies of 'savage' societies can also be interpreted as social reconciliations of desire and prohibition, a 'reconciliation based on the renunciation of incestuous desire and on the establishment of common love and interest between those of the same sex'.[27] Lack of resolution of conflicting impulses results in various forms of 'anti-social' behaviour. This interpretation gave rise to the mobilisation of psychoanalysis as an explanation for 'anarchy', 'communism', trade union activities etc.: 'the influence of displaced father-hatred is probably in large measure responsible for the fact that strikes and other crude forms of rebellion against authority in industry occur principally among the working class where the tyranny of the father is often of a primitive and repressive type'.[28] It does not require a close analysis to reveal a theoretical slide has occurred: it is no longer the effect of sexuality on representation, but a question of the typical emotions generated by the procreative nuclear family. These emotions and practices are pushed back beyond social institutions and practices as the very explanation of those practices.

Although Flügel was something of a populariser, his conclusions were by no means atypical. Indeed his book was one whose success gave stimulus to the publication of psychoanalytic material by the Hogarth Press in England. Similar interpretations could be proliferated. Moreover, this approach was not lamented within the Institute. Freud himself not only refrained from criticism of such interpretations but elsewhere endorsed those who worked from the position that the family, the nuclear procreative family, is the referent underlying all social forms.

Of especial significance here is the fact that it was this aspect of psychoanalysis' trajectory which attracted attention from the social sciences. Chapter 4 has already shown the interest which Malinowski and Seligmann began to take in the dynamic of the 'basic family'. Where anthropologists took an interest in psychoanalysis, it was for an account of the way in which emotional complexes arise in different cultural forms, and the way in which wider cultural values are transmitted through the basic family. In other words, it was on a terrain similar to that which prioritised the complex as the product of a real nuclear family.

Malinowski's attempt to apply psychoanalytic concepts to anthropological investigation attracted particular attention. The debate which took place as a result of Malinowski's work was extremely important for the history of the relationship between psychoanalysis and anthropology. To each side, it was a debate which revealed the weakness of the other's position. For many, especially from the side of anthropology, it marked the point of no return for an integration between the two. For all, it marked a polarisation between so-called universalising and so-called culturalist explanation which has haunted the social sciences since.

The universality of the Oedipus complex: the Jones/Malinowski debate

In the early 1920s, Malinowski published a series of articles about the Trobriand Island, where he had made a study of matrilineal social organisations. In these articles he attempted to modify psychoanalysis as a means of discussing the collective sentiments at the basis of Trobriand society. In 1925, Ernest Jones replied to this modification in the article 'Mother-right and the Sexual Ignorance of Savages'.[29] Malinowski answered Jones, together with a reprint of the original articles, in *Sex and Repression in Savage Society* (1926). After the exchange with Jones, Malinowski's attitude to psychoanalysis hardened irretrievably. He declared himself to 'be no longer impressed with the claims of psychoanalysis'. Jones's reply had convinced Malinowski that psychoanalysis was, in fact, incompatible with anthropological investigation. The debate drove a wedge between psychoanalysis and speculative/anti-evolutionary theories which proves almost impossible to dislodge. Taking as its central object the complex of typical emotions and the possibility of their variation in non-European cultures, the positions polarised between cultural relativism and the universality of emotional forms.

In the original essays, Malinowski's sympathy for psychoanalysis can probably be traced to his interest in the collective sentiments of social groups.[30] He had already outlined a decisive rejection of some of the themes and ideas of nine-teenth-century ethnology. He is no longer concerned with 'the primitive' versus 'civilisation'; nor is he preoccupied with 'transitions' from mother-right to father-right societies as explaining certain features of human evolution; in short, he is no longer concerned with the exposition of 'origins' of an institution as an exhaustive explanation of that institution. It is 'sociology' which can demonstrate the material nature and function of culture, a sociology which pays proper attention to the differences between cultures.

Malinowski argues that the heterogeneous elements of material culture are to be understood as institutions and systems with definite functions. He nevertheless suggests that it is not sufficient to analyse culture and the transmission of culture purely by reference to its institutions. Institutions produce certain sentiments which are transmitted through culture and form an integral part of that culture. It is from this perspective that Malinowski seeks to appropriate psycho-analysis.

Initially he praises the potential of psychoanalysis for providing the link between psychological and biological sciences and sociology. Though the most developed part of psychoanalysis may as yet be the science of the individual mind, this should by no means preclude a reconciliation with sociology. According to Malinowski, 'Psychoanalytic doctrine is essentially a theory of the influence of family life on the human mind' where we are shown 'how the passions, stresses and conflicts of the child in relation to its father, mother, brother or sister result in the formation of certain permanent mental attitudes or sentiments towards them'.[31] From this it should be possible to elaborate on the sociological nature of family influence and to understand the consequences of the complexes, inaugurated in the family, for society as a whole.

For Malinowski, the issues are simple. He is indebted to psychoanalysis 'for the discovery that there exists a typical configuration of sentiments in our society and for a partial explanation, mainly concerned with sex, as to why such a complex should exist'.[32] However, the family is not the same in every society; its 'constitution varies greatly with the level of development and with the character of the civilisation of the people, and it is not the same in the different strata of the same society'.[33] In fact, the organisation of reproduction, the relations of descent and power invested in these relations differs so fundamentally in both form and function that we can only ever talk of families:[34]

> There are differences depending on the distribution of *power* which, vested in varying degrees in the father, give the several forms of patriarchy, or vested in the mother, the various sub-divisions of mother-right. There are considerable divergences in the methods of counting and regarding *descent* – matriliny based on ignorance of fatherhood and patriliny in spite of this ignorance, patriliny due to power, patriliny due to economic reasons. Moreover, differences in settlement, housing, sources of food supply, division of labour and so on, greatly alter the constitution of the human family among the various races and peoples of mankind.

Such diversity can only mean one thing: the sentiments produced by family life must also vary. Freud's account of the complexes produced by the human family must only apply to a society organised along patriarchal lines, where fear of the father would produce forms of anxiety. The *emotions* described by Freud surely cannot apply to a society like the Trobrianders, where 'we have the independent mother, and her husband, who has nothing to do with the procreation of children, and is not the bread-winner and who cannot leave his possession to the children, and has no established authority over them'.[35]

Malinowski proceeds to a detailed description of Trobriand society, looking for the differences in the emotional development of children resulting from the different social structures. The society is matrilineal. Paternity is either not recognised or of no great social significance in terms of entitling the subject to power, authority or social standing. Descent is reckoned through the mother's kin. When the father dies, his property passes not to his biological children but to his sister's offspring. In accordance with this form of descent, the greatest social authority for the children is not their father but their maternal uncle. Finally the taboo on incest is not a bilineal taboo, entailing prohibitions on any biological relative, but a unilineal taboo. In this context, the greatest object of prohibition is between those in the same descent group, not between parents and children. Accordingly, Malinowski argues that the typical complexes which are found in Trobriand children and adolescents is fear of the maternal uncle, who is, after all, the source of authority, and a prohibition on incest which is strongest between brother and sister. He claims to have established 'a deep correlation between the type of society and the nuclear complex found there'.[36] Such a conclusion points to the mutual assistance which anthropology and psychoanalysis should be able to give each other. Psychoanalysis is to be modified. The aim is not to seek for 'the universal existence of the Oedipus complex but in studying every type of civilisation . . . [to] establish the special complex which pertains to it'.[37]

Ernest Jones replied promptly, disputing Malinowski's 'findings' as a distortion of psychoanalysis. He argues that it is not possible to limit Freud's discoveries to one culture only – Western culture. Jones bases his defence of the universality of the Oedipus complex on the issue of knowledge of paternity in Trobriand society. Jones accepts a more cautious approach to questions of authority, power and descent, than assuming that matrilinearity resulted only from ignorance of procreation. At the same time, he shares earlier evolutionary anthropologists' concern to understand the implications of indifference to paternity, which is regarded as so strange that it must offer some explanation of that society as a whole.

Jones agrees on the need to break up any easy conflation between authority, inheritance, succession and residence. Moreover, it is easy to acknowledge that there is no correspondence between mother-right societies and ignorance of paternity. But Jones uses the available material to demonstrate that there is plenty of evidence of a *form* of knowledge of procreation – hints, statements, forms of symbolism which all betray an awareness of the act of procreation and its biological significance. The knowledge is similar to that of a child. Jones takes theories of spirit conception to displace knowledge of the father's role in procreation for a specific purpose. It is suggested that mother-right societies and their belief systems function to repress knowledge of fatherhood. The function of this repression is to displace the conflict – the Oedipal conflict – felt between the boy and his father. Aggression actually directed at the father is displaced on to the maternal uncle who is invested with power. By this displacement the biological father can become a '"beloved", benevolent friend'.[38]

This process is seen as a form of 'decomposition', similar to that found in psychoneuroses where various attributes can become detached from the original figure and incorporated into another one which then personifies those attributes; 'the process serves the function of unloading affect in a relationship where it might have unpleasant consequences and depositing it at a safer distance'.[39] Thus in the case of mother-right societies, there is a decomposition of 'primal father into a kind and lenient father on one hand, and a stern moral uncle on the other'.[40] Nor is it chance that it is the maternal uncle who is set up as father substitute. He, after all, was the object of the mother's early incestuous desires and is already therefore a sexual rival of the son. Jones directly contests that the incest taboo exists between different subjects because of differential relations of power, that is, the incest taboo does not serve as a function of descent groups and their hierarchies of authority. According to Jones, this is a travesty of the Freudian position which he claims places familial emotions at the basis of all social institutions:[41]

> [Freud] regards the relationship between father, mother and son as the prototype from which other more complicated relationships are derived. Malinowski on the contrary puts forward the idea that the nuclear family complex varies according to the particular family structure existing in any community. According to him a matrilineal family system arises for unknown social and economic reasons, and then the repressed nuclear complex consists of brother and sister attraction, wtih nephew and uncle hatred; when this system is replaced by a patrilineal one, the nuclear complex becomes the familiar Oedipus one.

The problem with Malinowski's sociologism, according to

Jones, is its inability to explain the origins of social forms; the emergence of matrilineality is apparently an arbitrary matter which equally arbitrarily produces a series of emotional complexes bound up with power and authority rather than sexuality:[42]

> in my opinion . . . the matrilineal system with its avunculate complex arose . . . as a mode of defence against the primordial Oedipus tendencies (rather than) for unknown sociological reasons with the avunculate complex as a necessary consequence and the Oedipus complex appearing only when the patrilineal system was subsequently introduced. The forbidden and unconsciously loved sister is only a substitute for the mother, as the uncle is for the father. On Malinowski's hypothesis the Oedipus complex would be a late product; for the psychoanalyst it was the *fons et origo*.

This position was to become inextricably tied up with psychoanalysis: it stresses the genetic aspects of the family against the social issues. It insists that all societies will share some version of the same complexes. It argues that the mode of resolution of these complexes will determine the forms of social organisation. This was a totally literal interpretation of *Totem and Taboo.* All societies are seen to bear the mark of the original murder, the guilt and the structuring function of the father's desire. That is why Jones can see the establishment of patriarchy as a 'real advance' bearing witness to a partial remembering and reconciliation of guilt. It is this which underlies his extraordinary and offensive conclusion:[43]

> The patriarchal system as we know it, betokens acknowledging the supremacy of the father and yet the ability to accept this even with affection, without having to have recourse to a system either of mother-right or of complicated taboos. It means the taming of man, the gradual assimilation of the Oedipus complex. At last man could face his real father and live with him. Well might Freud say that the recognition of the father's place in the family signified the most important progress in cultural development.

The obvious criticisms of Jones have all been made already – the assumption of the eternal nuclear family, the determination of social institutions by family structures, the 'geneticism' which assumes that the biological is more important than the social, and finally an evolutionism which assumes that Western patriarchal forms are the highest form of society. Such have been the justified responses within anthropology.

But beneath the limitations of Jones's position and his adherence to the nuclear family as the referent behind all psychic structures, there are more interesting issues at stake. First is Jones's adherence to the idea that certain social relations entail sexual anxieties and their resolutions; sexual relations are not seen as always the effect of some other real 'material' relations, which is the essence of culturalist arguments. Moreover, in keeping with the psychoanalytic attention to symbolic forms, it is not the case in Jones's argument that symbolic practices mirror the 'real' social relations, nor that they are some obscuring mythification. Instead, symbols are 'overdetermined'; they are the effect of condensations or displacements of other concerns, embodied in such a way as to escape censorship.

Second, Jones's arguments unlike so many other examined in this book evades crass 'rationalist' explanations. Even the more radical writers like Engels and Havelock Ellis had used notions of sex-antagonism exacerbated by economic requirements to account for mother-right forms. Jones, though steeped in evolutionary prejudice, insists that sexual relations are neither 'givens' nor reducible to being effects of other social relations. Sexual identity is a problem; its resolution is a work basic to any given culture.

These, however, are no more than charitable implications for Jones's work. He remained committed to a crude evolutionary account of the procreative family as the referent underlying all cultural forms. And what is interesting about this fact is its inevitability, given Freud's adherence to a phylogenetic account. Freud insisted on this history precisely in order to maintain that the complex was the point of sociality itself. But the terms in which it was elaborated committed psychoanalysis to a thoughtless theoretical position with regard to the family. Malinowski's culturalism is

243

clearly problematic for an account which lays claim to discovering the mechanisms by which human sociality is achieved. Psychoanalysis cannot just abandon this claim, confronted with the functionalism and cultural relativism which annihilates any systematicity to structural complexes.

Yet the extraordinary literalness and ethnocentrism of Jones makes him an easy target for Malinowski who, in his reply, gives the psychoanalytic theory of culture more systematic attention. There are several aspects of the thesis advanced in *Totem and Taboo* which Malinowski challenges as incompatible with any progressive anthropology. It is only ignorance which leads analysts to prioritise the biological relations over the social relations. He also challenges the fundamental assumption of the primal horde, arguing against Darwin that humans and apes cannot be conflated. More seriously, he disputes the idea of a collective mind or race memory and finally, he points out the impossible circularity of Freud's arguments.

Anthropology, as Malinowski understood it, opposed these reactionary notions and argued for the detailed examination of different cultures and the functions of institutions and beliefs within those cultures. In spite of the problems with functionalism outlined earlier, Malinowski's point is valid in this instance. Freud himself wavered and hesitated between tradition on the one hand, and race memory on the other, not fully prepared to accept the implications of either. As Jones takes it up, there is no room for equivocation. He commits himself firmly to a reading of *Totem and Taboo* where racial memory of the original deed forms an integral part of the interpretation of social institutions.

But even if we abandon the theoretical premise of racial memory, the myth of the primal horde itself is of very little use. Apart from its breaking with certain evolutionary hypotheses, the transition from primitive promiscuity to mother-right to father-right (a hypothesis which Malinowski also finds unacceptable), it offers only impossible contradictions: 'But it is obvious that if the complex has preceded all cultural phenomena, then a fortiori the totemic crime, which is the cause of the complex, must be placed still further back.'[44] Malinowski picks up on the problem of the logical impossibility of the 'primal' father which Freud himself questioned in *Moses and Monotheism; Sex and Repression* thus represents an effective and systematic dismissal of the literal level of *Totem and Taboo.*

It is interesting that Malinowski concludes his engagement with psychoanalysis with a reappraisal of the debate on matrilineality versus patrilineality, dissociating himself finally from the evolutionist concerns of how and why patrilineality emerged out of matrilineality. Malinowski instead asserts that both are equally valid modes of reckoning descent with certain advantages accruing to them; in fact, contrary to popular belief, Malinowski asserts that, on balance, the matrilineal system has certain advantages.

The debate between Malinowski and Jones, then, had a significance beyond that of a minor exchange of articles. Both had a grasp of the issues involved in the question of matrilineal society, which went beyond that of many of their contemporaries. Both, in different ways, broke with dominant evolutionist theories of society, both cut across the notions of sex antagonism and the 'interests' of sexed groups. And because both were intelligent exponents of their particular ideas, they were to exercise an influence on the future development of their disciplines. The position taken by each exposed the limitations of the other in the debate. After it, Malinowski rejected his initial sympathy with psychoanalysis and apologised for his misguided enthusiasm. Indeed, *Sex and Repression in Savage Society* marks a definitive turning-away from all the grandiose claims of evolutionary anthropology towards the demand for detailed empirical study of different societies and the functions performed by institutions within those cultures. Psychoanalysis, unimpressed by the attempt to reduce the unconscious as a structural field to an effect of culture, rejected Malinowski's position and held out for the irreducibility of the typical complex.

Phylogenesis to ontogenesis

Jones and Malinowski held antagonistic and mutually exclusive positions but they were opposite poles of a similar concern. Because for both, it is a question of what is the external social referent for the production of individual emotional complexes. Jones properly defends psychoanalysis' claim to have discovered the structural field of the unconscious and in order to make this claim, he must adhere to the general necessity for repression. Yet he attributes this necessity to the universality of the nuclear family, in which conflicts between the biological father, mother and child generate the structural complexes of the unconscious. No wonder Malinowski and functionalist anthropology should chide psychoanalysis for its ignorance of the variety of form and function of the family. No wonder a wedge should have been driven between psychoanalysis and those branches of anthropology seeking to provide an account of human relations which did not assume those human relations a priori, but looked at them in the context of the other social relations in which they occurred. These culturalists versus universalist arguments have been replayed with equal lack of resolution, on countless occasions, within and outside psychoanalysis.

The divisions they produced were such as to engender some of the most violent splits and allegiances within psychoanalysis. Reich and Fromm both insisted that the Freudian account was strictly delimited. What it in fact described was the structure of emotions within a patriarchal culture. Reich, in pursuit of his themes of 'happiness', insisted that repression and neuroses were only present in patriarchal societies. Patriarchy was seen as vital to upholding an authoritarian class structure and it was in the service of this structure that sexual repression was effected. It was a point on which Fromm agreed.[45] Reich used Malinowski in *The Invasion of Compulsory Sex Morality*[46] to argue that the natural state is one of libidinal satisfaction; only patriarchy induces repression and this is an effect of social and economic forces. He sides with Malinowski to insist that sexual conditions flow from the social and economic organisation of a given society.

Both Reich and Fromm suggest that the economic motive for patriarchy is the existence of class-relations; these are exacerbated in capitalism but present since the origins of private property. In capitalism, the state plays the role of the authoritative father, and has dealings with authoritative fathers at the heads of patriarchal nuclear families. The ideology of capitalism is that of repression of the libidinal economy. Both Reich and Fromm insist on the image of the matriachate, benevolent and democratic – an altruistic love

246

based on a community of interest rather than individual appropriation. These ideas were to form a powerful current in German marxism before and during the war. Under the impulsion to interrogate fascism, German marxism was shot through with themes of maternal democracy upheld against the repressive authoritarianism of patriarchy. Until Reich's expulsion from the KPD in 1932, even the more orthodox end of Communism had time for such theories. They were to have a lasting effect on the history of marxism through their impact on the Frankfurt school, whose quest for a marxist psychology is deeply embedded in the themes from these debates. Much remains of importance in these debates, in which theories of patriarchy are brought forward as an integral part of analysing contemporary capitalism.[47]

However, there is also an uncritical slide in these arguments between repression and oppression; it allows the hypothesis that sexual repression is the product of a particular epoch. This is radically incompatible with the psychoanalytic interpretation of the structural status of the unconscious. Moreover, these positions replay the problems of culturalism; the commitment to cultural relativism minimalises the points of conflict and lack of resolution in any individual. From a culturalist perspective, individual complexes are always the end product of the overall intention of a social structure which seeks to reproduce itself. Moreover, by these means, a division between individual and society is reinforced.

While Freud's own writings were often more ambiguous than some of the exponents of the universality of the patriarchal family, it must be admitted that orthodox Freudianism partly defined itself in a response to these criticisms. Freud gave his full endorsement and financial assistance to Geza Röheim, the Hungarian analyst who did anthropological fieldwork. Röheim's writings serve as a monument to the reductionism implicit in the psychoanalytic interpretation of social practices, what Reich called 'a catastrophic use' of psychoanalytic data in ethnology. Röheim's work is of importance for several reasons; one was his position as the ethnologist of Freudian orthodoxy; another is his 'solution' to the status of phylogenesis; finally there is his impact on American anthropology.

Röheim was heralded by psychoanalysts as the practical

Psychoanalysis and anthropology

anthropologist and analyst who would remedy psychoanalysis' embarrassing lack of empirical data. He produced several enormous tomes on Australian society and his field trips were financed by Freud in collaboration with Marie Bonaparte who also wrote psychoanalytic interpretations of ethnological data.[48] A special edition of the *International Journal of Psychoanalysis* was given over to his 'findings' in 1932.

Australian Totemism 1924 is a quite extraordinary and unreadable book, revealing an uncompromising and literal adherence to the Freudian hypothesis. All symbolic practices of the Australian natives are to be interpreted as expressions of sexual concerns; they are 'a result of a compromise between the libido and repression'.[49] Different social groups could be classified according to the degree of successful resolution of sexual complexes. Thus Röheim concluded that Australia was peopled by two waves of immigration. The first was characterised by a successful resolution of the Oedipus complex, the second by the return of repressed elements and therefore an unsuccessful resolution. Röheim asserts the existence of the primal horde and primal murder with extraordinary literalness; 'there is no doubt as to it having happened'.[50] So literal, in fact, is his interpretation that in *Australian Totemism* he can add to Freud's account the fact that the primal father must have been killed with stones since most primitive people use stones as their principal tools.

His discussion of the primal event also sets the scene for its removal. Answering Malinowski's derision, Röheim suggests that:'the Freudian picture is intended to be compressed and dramatic representation of the facts, The "father" stands for generations of fathers and "the brothers" for generations of brothers'.[51] What Röheim argues is that the murder of the father was a frequently repeated event; further, that its traumatic effects were felt not by the brothers but by their children who witnessed the murder:[52]

Thus the primal battle becomes a very comprehensible trauma; for, among higher apes, the child clings to the mother in terror and is often squashed in the fight. According to Zuckerman, the primal fight and the primal scene immediately succeed each other. The young in the ape horde are treated as sexual objects from the beginning.

248

> There is no shortage of traumatic experiences, both real
> and libidinal. We have assumed that damages had occurred
> in the observers by the repression of infantile experiences.

As far as Röheim is concerned, the phylogenetic account is
virtually interchangeable with an ontogenetic one; the
repeated primal scene whose successful repression constitutes
the dawn of sociality is also the history of the individual.
Here the protracted infancy and dependency sets the scene
for premature sexual trauma such as witnessed in "the primal
scene'. Thus the phylogenetic account is only a generalised
representation of the ontogenetic account. In fact by 1943 in
The Origin and Function of Culture Röheim has entirely
abandoned phylogeny for ontogeny.

Röheim's argument reinforces an idea of a universal constitution of the human being. The difference between social
structures can be explained as the product of a frequently
repeated infantile trauma. In the case of some Australians,
the practice of the mother of sleeping across her child would
produce a particular complex of sexual feelings and conflicts.
However, these cultural differences could be premised on a
basic unity to human psyche life; 'It would seem . . . that the
psychic unity of mankind is more than a working hypothesis,
it is so obvious that it hardly needs proof.'[53] It is a small step
from this to discarding any reference to actual events at
the origins of human culture: recurrent complexes can be
explained by assuming common responses to different
cultural conditions. What has moved to the centre of the
stage is an account of the different 'personalities' resulting
from the differential structuring of the complex, premised on
a basic unity to human responses.

The responses within anthropology to psychoanalysis were
varied. In England, the interest taken by Malinowski, W.H.R.
Rivers and the Seligmanns did much to establish an early
exchange between the two emergent disciplines. As a result,
however, of the sort of exchange embodied by the Jones/
Malinowski debate and the hegemony of structural functionalist approaches, psychoanalysis ceased to have any real
credibility within English anthropology. In America, however, it was a different story. The interest in psychoanalysis
came later, with cautious endorsements from Kroeber and

Boas who asserted that 'some of the ideas underlying Freud's psychoanalytic studies may be fruitfully applied to ethnological problems'.[54] It was, however, with Röheim's 'solution' to the phylogenetic account that psychoanalysis began to appear with some systemacity, being a formative influence in the Culture and Personality theories within anthropology.

Writers like Ruth Benedict, Margaret Mead and Edward Sapir were at the forefront of developing these interests. An interest in biographical accounts had already emerged as a valid methodology within American anthropology, and under the influence of writers like Röheim this was transformed into an interest in recording personality types produced within different cultures. The approach was and is in many ways an unhappy combination of what is worse in all approaches. On the one hand, there is an emphasis on extreme cultural relativism – in which at best anthropology can only be descriptive of psychological forms. On the other hand, it relies on a notion of a universal human psychology: psychoanalysis is employed as a universalising account of the emotions generated by the basic human family. Cora Du Bois, commenting on the relations between anthropology and psychoanalysis, isolated this problem of explanation imposed by ontogenetic accounts of human culture:[55]

> Are we to assume that the psychological change preceded the cultural change? Or is it necessary to assume the priority of one or the other. If we assume the priority of cultural change, then psychological interpretations of culture are purely descriptive and not explanatory. If we assume the priority of psychological changes, we are faced with the problem of accounting for their origin.

This quotation neatly summarises the problems which cannot be resolved within an approach which simultaneously stresses cultural relativism and the universality of psycho-sexual complexes. In general, anthropologists opt for the theory as the basis of 'descriptive' accounts in which speculation as to the origin of psychological forces was suspended. And in this guise the work gained strength within anthropology. Despite the contribution which writings like Margaret Mead's have made to stressing cultural relativism, particularly within the question of sex roles, in general the work cannot be seen as providing a particularly radical contribution to the theorisation of social relations. What has been accomplished in this theoretical perspective is a stress on psychological factors at the cost of understanding the social and economic dynamic of a given culture. More particularly, however, it has reinforced a theoretical split between individual and society, in which the individual is synonymous with the family and the organisation of the sexual instinct.

Conclusion

These last two chapters have dealt with the place which theories of the family had in psychoanalysis. The last chapter dealt with the way in which a history of the family was mobilised to account for the generality of the psychic complex. It was, however, demonstrated that it was possible to read Freud's ideas in a different, perhaps less reductionist way, that which was indicated by Lévi-Strauss, who saw Freud as having stumbled on the relations between kinship classification, representation and the regulation of sexuality.

In this chapter, however, I have argued that it is not really possible to argue, as the structuralist tradition has done, that we can simply ignore Freud's ambivalence about the 'real family' and the real history of that family. In the history of the debate between psychoanalysis and anthropology, it is easy to see that the commitment to a real history of the family was far from a minor or insignificant element in psychoanalytic interpretations of cultural forms. Some aspects of the approach to cultural forms treat sexuality as a distinct irreducible element in cultural forms. Other, perhaps more typical, approaches stress that cultural forms and corresponding sets of behaviour have been determined by a real history of the family. The terms in which the cultural theory of psychoanalysis was formulated – terms culled from debates on the family outlined earlier – compromised radical notions of sexuality and the unconscious with Freudian theory. In so far as the social sciences have found a place for psychoanalysis, it has been in seeking a universal account of individual behavioural development, in which sexuality is seen as having a universal form determined by a real history of the family. The opposition to this account has been formulated largely by a crude culturalism. The criticisms of psychoanalysis launched from this position are not only often not much better but use exactly the same problematic. This problematic is that there is a real history of the family – which in this case is variable. Sexual structures are to be understood by reference to that empirically observable unit. Both these positions have reinforced a division between individual and society. There is a real empirically observable unit which is the outcome of, or the determinant on, the behavioural forms characteristic of sexuality.

In the previous chapter, it was argued that Freud elaborated his phylogenetic account precisely in order to stress that the psychological complex must be understood at the level of culture. The complex would be the instinct duplicated at the level of culture whereby it would be impossible and unnecessary to speculate on the original form of the instinct. The fact of the complex would annihilate the distinction between individual/instinctual behaviour and cultural forms. However, the radical implication of this approach, particularly for an analysis of the problem of sexual division, has never been developed. This is partly an effect of the history of psychoanalysis' relation with the social sciences, partly as an effect of the form in which the structuralist re-reading of Freud has been advanced. The problems with the structuralist theory will be discussed in the following discussion of the theorisation of sexuality.

Conclusion:
sex and social relations

This book has been motivated by several questions. Why, it has been asked, do contemporary discussions of sexual relations constantly run aground over a polarisation between 'universalist' and 'culturalist' explanations? What caused this sterile polarisation? Finally, are these the only two explanations of sexual relations? If not, on what terms could a study of sexual relations proceed? Before these last questions can be answered, which is the purpose of this final chapter, it will be useful to summarise the main findings of this book.

The traditional views of sexual relations

Contemporary discussions within feminism suggest that a new theory of patriarchy is needed to explain the dynamic of power in sexual relations. Yet it has become clear that this would not be a new approach to sexual relations at all. In fact, the history of how conceptualisation of sexual relations developed was virtually synonymous with the history of the study of patriarchal relations. The intensification of the discussion of the family and kinship in the second half of the nineteenth century created the terms — and the limitations — for how sexual relations are now theorised.

Our contemporary understanding of sexual relations was formed when dominant explanations of society in terms of the patriarchal family dissolved. A debate ensued, which had definite political and social conditions of existence. It was obsessed with a study of the historical relations between the sexes. At times, the debate became political. This was because the real object of these debates was the question of how alliances are formed between individuals, or between individuals and groups. In the nineteenth century a new space was formed where these questions were pursued; this was the space of the 'natural'. Sexual relations, theorised as on the border between nature and culture, became the privileged site for this speculation on how human society arose.

These discussions of sexual relations held absolutely fixed ideas about sex and sexual identity. Sex was heterosexual, reproductive activity and even those theories which argued for primitive promiscuity at the beginnings of human society, never questioned the different sexual entities of men and women. Men and women were seen as radically distinct groups with different sexual identities and interests. These sexual interests were combined — either amicably or antagonistically — into the practice of marriage and reproduction, the practice on which all civilisation was seen to rest.

Transformations in relations between the sexes, embodied in the family, were taken to be the clue to all human history. The objects which these theorists pretended to study, that is, non-Western societies, had in fact disappeared under the weight of speculation on the whole history of humanity as embodied in relations between the sexes. There were compelling reasons why, within anthropology, violent criticisms were made of these general histories. Anthropologists had to counter some of the extraordinary claims which had been made during the course of these debates.

Criticisms were made against the wild speculations of the 'armchair anthropologists'. And these criticisms remain pertinent today. For anthropology at the turn of the century reacted correctly against the 'illegitimate' separation of one social practice from the culture in which it arose in order to produce a universal history or sexual relations. Anthropologists began to object to the way in which a practice like bride capture was taken out of its context to furnish a hypothesis about relations between sexes over the history of humanity. Such was the tangle of assumptions surrounding the study of these practices that, in general, anthropologists began to express reservations about the validity of any speculation on a common origin and development of the human family and therefore human society. Anthropologists began to study different societies as complexes of elements interacting in a functioning totality. A segment cut through any society would reveal the interaction of elements within that society. It would no longer be legitimate to perform spectacular mental acrobatics to separate one practice from its culture and use this as the basis for a universal account of human history.

The criticisms are still valid; a universal history of humanity usually has to privilege one element – such as sexual relations – by which a diversity of cultures can be united. This means that before the study can be started, an assumption has already been made, that is, that sexual relations are the significant element in the development of all social phenomena. But cultures may attribute vastly different values to different practices, despite their superficial similarity. The criticisms made by anthropologists at the turn of the century made it clear that it would be necessary to understand what meanings any given culture gave to their practices, without imposing meanings on these practices.

However, some aspects of these criticisms were also inhibiting for any development of an understanding of sexual relations. For many general questions were put aside as well in the rejection of grandiose claims. On the one hand, the emergence of modern anthropology correctly insisted on the numerous different types of family organisation. Kinship relations are not just variations on one basic form, but are different relations, entailing different obligations, meaning different things, and distributing power and property differently in different cultures. On the other hand, although these claims were important, they engendered a form of argument which is somewhat sterile from the perspective of contemporary feminism. The refusal of any explicit account of determination in favour of a detailed account of the necessary interrelation of all elements of a culture, retarded the interrogation of how power and domination arise. A series of issues were not raised – issues about the unequal power between the sexes; how kinship might reproduce or construct sexual inequalities; and the role which kinship might play in organising reproduction. As we saw, one of the factors contributing to the absence of such questions was, ironically, the consolidation of a distinctive notion of the procreative family.

While opposing theories of an original family and challenging universal histories, a space was left open for theorising the individual as separate from society. Thus, even those positions which rigorously opposed psychologism and concentrated on social relations, laid themselves open to ideas of the individual as a pool, or reservoir of behaviours, needs and instincts. Not surprisingly, sexuality was consigned to the realm of the individual, a fact which has facilitated explanations of sexual relations in terms of instincts and essential sexual constitutions. The criticisms made of wild theories of the family were dominated by two theoretical assumptions. One was this conceptual split between the individual and society. The other was the refusal of explicit accounts of how society was determined, while it was simultaneously suggested that there was, in fact, a diffuse causality. Some practices like religion, marriage, and family forms were thought to be determined by more material practices such as the holding of property, and economic relations of production.

Accounts of sexual relations were, however, no more adequate from those disciplines which superficially appeared to avoid the problems of the position outlined above. On the one hand, marxism offered a rigorous account of the way in which relations of domination and subordination were determined; they were to be explained as effects of the economic relations of production. Psychoanalysis, on the other hand, offered a non-essentialist theory of sexuality. Both these theories, however, have been shown to be extremely limited in their explanations of the relationship between sexual arrangement and social formation. Marxism's insistence on the analytical and political priority of economic social divisions rendered its theory of sexual relations open to essentialising accounts. Psychoanalysis concentrated on a detailed account of the construction of sexual identity in sexual regulation but adhered to a universalising account of the familial determination of sexual forms.

Both marxism and psychoanalysis claimed totalising explanations for the form taken by sexual regulations. Neither paid attention to the emergent criticism of unilinear theories of the family. This blindness reveals the place occupied by a universal history of the family in both theories. The universal history of the family was made necessary by other aspects in the theories; they were mobilised as specific theoretical solutions, to provide totalising accounts of elements within the social formation.

Within marxism it was, paradoxically, the centrality of the conception of the family which in fact blocked any systematic understanding of the family from the perspective of sexual division. In the study of marxism's treatment of the woman question, it became apparent that there was a requirement for the conception of the family to fit in with an overall conception of the interrelation between elements within the social formation. This conception of the totality of social arrangements was seen to emerge from a series of political priorities specified by the theory, political priorities which appeared in their full inadequacy when confronted with the woman question.

For psychoanalysis, the family was conceptualised in a particular way in order to theorise the relationship between the instinct, the complex and society. There emerged an account of the history of the family and the universality of the emotions within the procreative family. The account compromised other more radical conceptualisations of sexuality within the theory. In so far as orthodox psychoanalysis offered an account of social relations, it was taken to describe a complex of emotions resulting from a real nuclear family. This position was at the basis of some of the formative divergencies within psychoanalysis, divergencies which simultaneously reveal the proximity of the discourses under scrutiny and their divergence through different forms of attention.

Within orthodox psychoanalysis, the result was that the radical non-essentialist notion of sexuality gained only a very limited place in accounts of the relationship between sexuality

and social forms. Initial bisexuality was posited as the pre-
cursor of the final reproductive outcome of sexual construction, and a source of subversion of that reproductive
outcome. Far from embracing the precariousness of sexual
identity as a constant element within social relations, orthodox psychoanalysis returned to the idea of universal history
of the family which had determined the reproductive outcome of sexual identity.

The critics of this orthodox psychoanalytic history of
the family also failed to develop the implication of initial
bisexuality. The critics of the orthodox position on the
family compromised the idea of the structural status of the
unconscious through their espousal of 'culturalist' arguments.
These arguments were subject to the same problem as those
found within marxism. In other words, they fell prey to
implicit forms of essentialism, either by presupposing that
anatomical difference was a sufficient basis for a coherent
adoption of social roles or by failing to take account of the
tenacity of sexual construction with the social formation.

In the exchanges which took place between the discourses
traced here, several elements are striking. One is the extent to
which all these discourses were limited by the terms set by
the earlier discussions of the family. Anthropology alone
attempted to deconstruct the general theories of these earlier
debates but left untouched any critique of the conceptualisation of sexuality. Cause or effect of social relations,
heterosexual reproductive sexual identity tended to be presupposed at the heart of its studies.

What is also striking in the history of these discourses is
the way in which the division of attentions affected in the
emergence of different discourses meant that some investigations disappeared altogether. Psychoanalysis tried to
investigate the construction of sexuality as process and contradiction. This, however, has no place in the social sciences.
Sociology rarely explores sexual relations at all. The typical
object of study is the household – an institution assumed to
function unproblematically on reproductive sexual relations.
An amorphous commitment to the idea of determination of
sexual relations by other social forms tended to be offered
as sufficient explanation. Anthropology has paid endless

attention to the variety of sexual organisations but has rarely addressed the radical implications of psychoanalytic theories of sexuality. Where psychoanalytic theories appeared, they appeared either under the regime of culturalism or under the regime of a universalising psychology. Marxism has an attention to the construction of social identity and to detailing historical circumstances, but it has constructed a theory where under the importance of the family, the social contradiction between men and women is only thought of in essentialising terms.

Divergencies and divisions: the determination of social life

The division of attentions has made remote any chance of explanations of certain phenomena. It becomes difficult to explain hierarchies between the sexes, the cause of different statuses, the determination of different familial forms and their effect on sexual behaviour while delivering a historically specific account. Some discourses have concentrated on sexuality in isolation from society; some have simply taken sexuality for granted as the reproductive instinct. Various discourses have offered various proofs and forms of explanation as to what is specific about women as a sex; how a society constructs sexual division; and what are the determinants on the forms taken by sexual division. Yet all these various proofs are compromised; they do not deliver a historically specific account of these processes. The reason underlying this compromise is that all these discourses, apart from psychoanalysis, rely on a notion of sexual identity (and therefore sexual regulation) as pre-given.

Wherever a theory functions with a given notion of sexual organisation, it necessarily implies something eternal about the differences between men and women. This implication makes it virtually impossible to provide an account of how sexual status and division is produced within a given historical moment. Even with a rigorous culturalism, which insists on the variability of sexual identity and relations, there is a problem of presupposing sexual characteristics. For even where the individual is taken to be a *tabula rasa* on to which sexual identity is written, there is a problem where men and women are assumed to take up coherent roles. For here, too, it is suggested that anatomical difference guarantees the roles required by different arrangements of the social. Despite this apparently common limitation, there have been violent divisions between modes of explanation. Within the social sciences, for example, there is division as to how social forms, like marriage, the family, beliefs, and so on, are determined. It is a debate as to whether social phenomena are adequately accounted for by reference to the interdependence of social institutions or whether those social institutions can themselves be explained by the characteristics of individuals, that is by the needs, instincts and forms of behaviour of individuals.[1] The theorisation of social phenomena involving sexual behaviour has been plagued by this division and there is good reason for this.

The book has shown how, in the development of studies of the family, sexual regulations were taken as regulations on the borderline between nature and culture. It has been argued that the resolution of the place of sexuality in the social sciences was achieved through the agreement that sexual regulations were on the borderline between nature and culture. As such, they came under two major arguments between modes of explanation within the social sciences. On the one hand is the division between explanations which take their starting point either as the individual or society. On the other hand, there is the concomitant discussion as to how social phenomena are determined, that is, either by the characteristics of an individual or by reference to the inter-relation of social institutions.

These dominant discussions under which sexual regulations have been treated in the social sciences frequently polarise around a series of sterile divisions, divisions exemplified by the Jones/Malinowski debate. The problem is presented in terms of whether patterns of sexual behaviour are derived from a universal human imperative or whether they are conditioned by the interaction of elements within a particular culture. Posed in another way, it is the question as to whether sexual behaviour is natural (instinctual) or socially conditioned.

It is to be hoped that this book has shown that these

options were structured by dominant ideological principles. Under the theoretical division between individual and society, sexual behaviour has been consigned to the realm of the individual. Sex has been taken as belonging to the realm of the behavioural, the emotions, biology. This consigning has taken place primarily because the heterosexual reproductive instinct has rarely been questioned. Sexuality and the heterosexual act are often taken to be synonymous. It would not be an exaggeration to say that virtually all social phenomena entailing sexuality — marriage, the family, the household — have been assumed to operate on the basis of this so-called fundamental instinct. A conceptual separation then becomes possible on the grounds of a division consolidated in the social sciences between the so-called social and the so-called individual realms.

This conceptual division has structured the debates within the social sciences. In general it would be correct to say that there has been a division between discourses which start from those areas deemed 'the individual' and those which start from the social. Such a division itself points to the assumptions as to what is usually taken to be a social science. It is a discourse whose primary object of attention is the interaction of social elements. However, it is apparent from the argument made here that while this might be the primary object of interrogation, there is an unresolved space whereby explanations from the so-called individual sciences can and do creep in. This is precisely the division between individual and society, and between two dominant modes of explanation. Thus even within discourses like sociology or anthropology there is still division as to whether the individual should be explained as a substantive to be accounted for by the sciences treating emotions, instincts and behaviours, or whether these phenomena should be explained by the particularities of a given culture.

Whichever side of the division is espoused marks a failure. Amorphous or rigorous determination leaves a space which can be filled by one of two options. Either nothing is said about sexuality except society determines the social manifestations of sexual relations, in which case the objects to be studied are the so-called determinant forms. Or, ironically, biological and psychological capacities are presupposed but not discussed explicity. Those theories which start from the realm designated 'the individual', and refuse the assumptions of determination (like psychoanalysis) appear to be falling into universalising and naturalising claims.

These divisions around the question of sex have a dull note of familiarity. They are none other than the divisions between nature and culture, the individual and society. It is the old 'nature versus nurture' debate and it encompasses our understanding of sex because sexual behaviour has been consigned to the realm of the individual, while sexual relations are taken to be a crucial part of culture. Thus the two modes of integration of sexual behaviour in some discourses of the social sciences are in fact witness to the non-theorisation of sex. The lack of any substantial theorisation of the construction of sexual categories, sexual relations and sexual hierarchies is the result of this classification and of the conceptual division between individual and society.

Two points should be made if there is to be any advance in our understanding of sexual relations within society. The first is that sex cannot be consigned to the realm of the individual; the second, that the division between individual and society is purely conceptual. It is a conceptual division which must be displaced if we are to develop an understanding of how sexual division can be the basis for oppressive relations.

Sex: individual or social?

The division between the individual and society is a theoretical division, based on the way in which areas of investigation have been carved up between different discourses. On the one side, there are a number of phenomena which are deemed to be individual — instincts, behaviour, needs, emotions, desires, fantasies. These phenomena are usually thought to be found in the so-called primary situation or procreative group. On the other side are the phenomena deemed to be social — the economy, ideological (collective) beliefs, institutions and customary social forms. Sexuality has, in general, been consigned to the side of the individual, whether it is taken as cause or effect of social practices. However, even if one accepts this conceptual division, it would be difficult to confine sexuality to this area.

Sexuality does not only concern forms of behaviour and personal desires. Everywhere sexuality is defined publicly. Most obviously, sexuality appears in public customs, like marriage. It also appears in a number of discourses and practices in a less obvious way. Governmental policies on housing, population, and education all in a variety of ways, concern the definition and regulation of aspects of sexual behaviour. One has only to mention the kinds of houses made and provisions for families within housing policy, or the sex segregation within education to realise that public policies are constantly engaged in the task of defining and redefining sexual behaviour.

Even the areas such as the economy, carefully detailed as the social, crucially involve sexual definitions. Within contemporary Western society, the wage paid for male labour is a family wage[2] regardless of the marital status of the recipient. This has important correspondences with other aspects of the economy; it constitutes women as a low-paid group; it marks out sexually ghettoised areas of employment; and it constructs relations of economic dependence of women and children on men. There is no way in which any study of the economic relations of contemporary society could afford to neglect the sexual division and sexual organisation which provides its logic.

How sexuality is talked about, displayed and organised is a central feature of social existence. Moreover, there are many forms of behaviour and desire which cannot be attributed to an 'individual' conceptually separated from society. While pornography, for example, may address a hypothesised individual, it is an aspect of public arousal of desire.[3] It participates in a very definite ideology of male sexual needs which re-inforces the form taken by sexual division in our society.

Psychoanalysis has even undermined the idea that what we think of as the most personal and intimate aspects of behaviour can be attributed to the spontaneous production of individual. Even that most individual form of behaviour, fantasy, is taken by psychoanalysis to be a form of hallucinated sexual satisfaction which cannot evade reference to the complexes by which sexuality enters social existence.

The function of these brief points is to indicate that sex cannot be confined to the realm of the individual behaviour. Sexual division and definition is a crucial element in our contemporary social organisation. Hierarchies and forms of social life are arranged around these divisions. Moreover, even those elements of the 'individual' are seen by psychoanalysis to be pre-structured by the social complex. The instinctual, in other words, cannot be abstracted from the complex.

Yet more extensive criticism could, however, be made of the conceptual division between individual and society, and these criticisms are important for clearing away major obstacles to developing non-essentialising notions of sexual relations.

Why the division between the individual and society is a problem

One immediate problem which strikes us confronted with the division between the individual and society is that a theoretical space has been constructed in which elements like behaviour, desire, fantasy can be thought as somehow separate from society. It becomes possible to think of the individual as somehow outside society.

It is clear that to think about it in this way constructs a false problem. In so far as we talk about the human we refer to a living creature, existing in society. Even the unborn child has a place decreed to it. For example, in our society, the practice of patrilinearity means that the child will be given the father's surname. There is nothing in the child's first engagement with the world that is somehow outside society, everything that occurs is part of a social structure: the practices of child care; the ways in which affection is displayed; who cares for the child; and in what way care is given. The statement seems like a truism and would certainly be received as such by the majority of social sciences, yet a separation is still affected. Certain elements of human and social behaviour are thought to be subject to forms of explanation, which start from this hypothesised individual. For as long as this separation is maintained the endless tedium about the relative determination of nature and nurture will roll on.

Recent attempts to explain all of culture by reference to biological explanations (socio-biology) have been rather successful. This indicates the extent to which the social sciences, despite their commitment to social determination, have left open a space into which snugly fit psychological and biological explanations, with their universalising and reductionist views.

Both the claims and the counter-claims share one assumption on which the conceptual division is operative. Both the idea of the individual as *tabula rasa*, whose behaviour, emotions, desires are conditioned by social forces; and the idea of individual instincts, drives and needs which are expressed in social forms, are operative on one condition. The condition is that a homogeneous individual is supposed to exist; in other words, that there is such a thing as a coherent individual which can be accounted for either in terms of an identity, a social role, a sum total of behaviour, or an instinctual disposition. Agent of social roles or perpetrator of the selfish gene, it assumes a coherent subject as outcome or origin.

But if psychoanalytic theory has taught us anything, it is that such a proposition cannot bear scrutiny. It has shown how the idea of a coherent subject is a fantasy. For in bringing to light unconscious processes, it has demonstrated that conscious or public identity is only a tip of an iceberg. Symptoms, dreams, modes of expression like jokes, all bear witness to other modalities of desire, repressed perhaps but in a continuous relationship with conscious representation, disrupting, displacing, seeking satisfaction or expression. There are several points of importance in this account. One is that not only is identity a construct, but it is also continuously and precariously reconstructed. Any aspect of behaviour or desire will only ever be a moment in a process; the exact opposite can frequently be revealed co-existing in the unconscious. In addition, as has been demonstrated earlier, psychoanalysis has undermined essentialist notions of the instincts. In stressing that the complex must take precedence over the instinct, Freud has demonstrated that 'instinctual' behaviour never has pure expression. The variability of the object through which instinctual satisfaction is sought clearly demonstrates the inseparability of instinct from the object by which it finds satisfaction. Such a distinction clearly places the instinct under the primacy of sociality. There is never any activity which 'expresses' instinctual behaviour. Sociality and its renunciations confront us only with the instinct displaced and fluid, defined in the object through which it seeks satisfaction.

The conceptual division between individual and society assumes that, on the one hand, the elements under the term individual are somehow pre-social, and, on the other, that the individual is a coherent and homogeneous entity. This is presupposed by biological explanations, by psychological explanations and even by explanations which assert that the individual is culturally conditioned (for this too assumes a presocial empty space filled up with coherent social roles). Attention to the discourse of the unconscious, however, reveals contradiction and conflict. This is an important discovery from the point of view of conceptualisation of sexual relations, for it undermines the possibility that any sexual practice could be the expression of any one pre-given instinctual drive, for example, the expression of reproductive interests. Freud has shown much too clearly that the acquisition of reproductive, heterosexual positions is a painful process whose outcome is extremely precarious. Psychoanalysis has demonstrated that there is nothing essential about the sexual drive of male and female.

The Freudian account shows that the very process by which the sense of individual identity is acquired is the process by which social position is achieved. Lacan has further elaborated this, indicating that a sense of individual identity is only acquired through the acquisition of social position. Crucial in this is the acquisition of position of sexed subjectivity, not given by an intrinsic sexual disposition, but constructed through our entry into a culture polarised around anatomical difference. The psychoanalytic account does not deny the sense of individual identity. However, it recognises this as a construction, precisely an element in taking up a social position. Male and female positions are constructed through the acquisition of social identity. Thus psychoanalysis simultaneously shows how the sense of individuality is only acquired by becoming a fully social subject. Yet at the same time, it shows how individuality is precarious, contradictory, only maintaining coherence by holding fiercely to a socially defined and fixed role.

The reason why it is important to challenge the notion of the centred subject produced in the individual/society division is because it is one of the ways in which essentialist notions of sex operate. The fantasy of a coherent individual — behaviour, instinctual disposition, social role or whatever — allows for an idea of sex as a consistent, coherent feature which unilaterally affects men in one way, women in another. This is self-evident in biological and psychological explanations. But even the idea of cultural conditioning productive of roles presupposes something essential; it suggests that men and women are constructed differentially by a given society. Superficially, this argument would not appear to support essentialist notions of men and women, but in fact it does. For how is it that a society unilaterally affects anatomical women in one way, and anatomical men in another way? And what is it about that anatomical state which guarantees that anatomical men and women will consistently take up these roles, as social men and women?

Against this, the psychoanalytic hypothesis has very radical implications. It would seem to suggest that any analysis which implied a homogenous subject, however theorised, will ultimately lead to a reductionist notion of sexuality. This suggestion presents a serious problem for some of the recent attempts to advance the understanding of sexual relations in society. Aware of the inadequacies of previous approaches, recent writings on the construction of sexual identities and hierarchies have suggested the need to 'integrate' various aspects from various disciplines in order to produce an adequate understanding. When examined closely, however, these theoretical mergers, like the one offered between Marx and Freud, do not seem adequately to avoid the pitfalls of dominant and traditional approaches to sexual relations. They often neglect the consequence of making grandiose claims about patriarchy or the relations between the sexes. Frequently they fail to challenge elements like the division between individual and society, or the diffuse notion of determination. Most accept the idea of the homogeneous individual as source or support for social structures. The legacy of these assumptions constantly threatens to compromise the search for new ways of examining sexual relations.

Patriarchy or the relations of human reproduction[4]

The concepts of relations of human reproduction and patriarchy are once more beginning to dominate attempts to theorise sexual relations in society. These concepts are crucial to those explanations of the subordinate position of women in terms of essential characteristics of men and women. These suggestions return to identical terrains, and identical problems, to those traced already in the nineteenth century. The concepts have also been advanced as solutions to problems within marxist theory. Here they offered as possible explanations or descriptions of the 'relative autonomy' of human sexual relations from the economic mode of production. Concentration on the relations of reproduction appears as a response to two things. One is quite simply the inescapable evidence of a very definite relation between women's subordinate position and the role of child-bearer and child-carer. Assumptions about women's child-bearing and child-rearing capacity seem to underlie practices like the family wage; hence they underpin women's economic dependency and oppression as well as the ghettoisation of women in low-paid work.

Confronted with the seemingly unavoidable relation between many social practices and women's role as reproducer, it has seemed logical that reproduction should be a primary site of investigation. But there is another reason which should be apparent from the rest of this book; the emphasis on it is already present within marxism and the social sciences. Such an interpretation fits readily into existing schemas.

On the surface, this theoretical approach appears to meet the requirement of escaping the reductionism sometimes encountered within marxism. It insists on a distinct theory of social relations as they affect women specifically; it refuses to look at the subordination of women as the effect of somehow 'more basic' social relations such as private property. It is, therefore, open to accounts from psychoanalysis and anthropology. Simultaneously, by offering itself as analagous to the marxist concept of the relations of production, it appears to remain firmly within marxism — a commitment sought both because of sympathy with marxism's analytic specification of structural economic contradiction and principled anti-naturalism. At the same time, as this book has shown, the concept is by no means a challenge to the theoretical tenets of marxism; both the concepts of patriarchy and the specificity of human relations of production are crucially interlinked with existing marxist priorities.

Two primary positions associated with the way in which the concept has been taken up demonstrate the possible limitations with the idea of a specific level, that of 'the human relations of reproduction'. One of these is the way in which it sometimes appears as indistinguishable from biological essentialism.[5] It is by virtue of women's reproductive capacity that they are controlled or subordinated. Yet whatever the cause is said to be for this control — demographic factors or the requirements of private property — what it does not explain is why women should be controlled by men.[6] These arguments regularly make the assumption that men always control women and draw on underlying assumptions about a universal male psychology or inherent female capacities.

The second way in which the concept has been used has been a sort of doubling over of other implications of the term 'reproduction' within marxism. There are, for example, attempts to incorporate women's biological reproductive capacity into the idea of women's specific contribution to the reproduction of the economy.[7] The family is organised as a site of reproduction of labour power in the form of children. In addition, the labourer is reproduced outside the costs of capital, through the performance of domestic labour. These accounts all fail to explain sexual division. In a mode of argument reminiscent of those outlined in Chapters 5 and 6, they presuppose sexual division. It is a natural division which is utilised by the capitalist economy.[8] These arguments have been, however, important in drawing attention to the differential relationship between men and women to the economy, a direction which is now being more usefully pursued.

Other, apparently less reductionist, accounts have run into similar problems. For example, the suggestion that the family might be the site of ideological reproduction of the capitalist mode of production assumes no less the functionality of the family for capitalism, again ultimately depriving it of any specificity. It offers no account of why or how sexual division arises, and ultimately reduces the family to being a function of capital.

Patriarchy

The most insistent analysis of the specificity of the relations of human reproduction has been in terms of patriarchy.[9] In fact, the revival of various patriarchal theories has been a major contribution to the endeavour to produce an adequate analysis of the position of women. However, like discussions of the specificity of relations of human reproduction, the accounts of patriarchy tend to be similarly characterised by a surprising lack of attention to what patriarchal relations are and how they operate.

Variously, patriarchal relations describe the oppression of all women by all men (what is often also referred to as sexism), a particular kind of kinship structure, or finally a residual ideology of male dominance. This latter is thought to have arisen from a kinship organisation which has since been superseded.

Patriarchy has a loose currency. It is generally employed to designate a problem — a contradiction between men and women, the recognition of a gender division which implies power and demands explanation. There can be no doubt as

270

to the political importance of this insistence; it has given a theoretical basis for arguing for the specificity of women's oppression.

But this book has made a series of related arguments which have indicated that there are aspects of the patriarchal theory which should be treated with caution. We have seen, in fact, that the notion of the patriarchal family is often a stumbling block to the development of an understanding of the construction of sexual division in historically specific terms. Within marxism, the integral relation between the patriarchal family and other concepts led to a mode of theorisation where the specificity of sexual division within the family did not appear. Within psychoanalysis, it was the conceptualisation of the patriarchal family which constantly pulled back the radical implications of psychoanalytic theory, committing psychoanalysis to a universalising account of the procreative family. Mobilised as an explanation of sexual relations, it often resorts to wild generalisations.

There are two points which must be made in relation to the term patriarchy. The first is that if the term is to be developed at all rigorously as describing a real structure of social relations, it appears to be limited in crucial ways. For one thing, the arrangement of the contemporary family retains few of the features of a classic patriarchal structure. Changes in family law have slowly begun to undermine the conception of father as absolute head of the family, financially, legally and politically responsible for his wife as a dependent. Descent is neither reckoned nor controlled exclusively by the father; our culture has no strict laws of residence. Historically, there have been definite transitions in family forms and we need ways of describing rigorously the forms taken by familial arrangements at particular historical moments. It is the same problem as that facing the anthropologist. The application of the term 'patriarchal' to all aspects of male control and dominance can obscure the differences between familial forms, differences which are vitally important if any understanding of sexual relations is to be constructed. We need ways of talking about shifts from male dominance within the patriarchal family to male dominance outside the family.

In addition, the term 'patriarchal' describes a form of

power which does not do justice to the complexity of the problem of sexual division and society. It limits what can be said in terms of the production and redefinition of sexual identities in a number of forms. It does not do justice to the subtle workings of discrimination. For the term 'patriarchal' implies a model of power as interpersonal domination, a model where all men have forms of literal, legal and political power over all women. Yet many of the aspects of women's oppression are constructed diffusely, in representational practices, in forms of speech, in sexual practices. This oppression is not necessarily a result of the literal overpowering of a woman by a man.

The concept of patriarchy then has to be treated with caution. It does not deal sufficiently with the diffused workings of power in relation to sexuality, for example in representational structures. Nor does the term show sufficiently the contradictory effects of practices. There is, for example, no homogeneous relationship between the state and the patriarchal family as is sometimes suggested under this concept. As a result of determinate social conditions, practices often construct contradictory notions of the family and act according to these different categories.[10]

None of these points is destined to challenge the fact that sexual division in our society confers power on men, regardless of whether individual men are themselves powerful. However, these comments are destined to raise questions about an uncritical use of the term patriarchy. In the early part of this book it was shown how the concept laid a blanket explanation of sexual relations across all cultures, a blanket explanation which did not stand the scrutiny of a detailed knowledge of different societies. For example, the most usual explanation of patriarchy as either cause or effect of individual property relations was shown to be false; there was no demonstrable necessary correspondence between individual private property, male power and patrilinear descent. Theories which tried to prove this correspondence invariably ended up presupposing essential sexual charactersitics; men would necessarily seek to 'own' their biological offspring; women would necessarily be subordinated on account of their reproductive capacity. There is no doubt that the forms of control which our society exercises on its reproduction are crucial in the subordination of women. However, these controls are not universal; societies may differ in what relationship there is between reproduction, sexual activity and the social position and value attributed to women.

One of the most productive ways of thinking about patriarchy in recent years has been that emerging from the combination of ideas from psychoanalysis and structural anthropology. This combination has insisted on the need to explore the psychological mechanisms by which sexed subjectivity is constructed in our culture. It argues that 'patriarchy' is sustained by the whole construction of sexual identity and desire, not necessarily by the literal overpowering of one interest group, women, by another, men. As such it has had to ask the question of how sexual construction and sexual division is related to other aspects of our society. However, it is not altogether clear that this structuralist 'rereading' of psychoanalysis avoids making essentialist claims about notions of sex.

It is certainly true that there are some important implications for understanding sexuality within structuralist interpretations of psychoanalysis. On the one hand, the idea of a pre-given sexual disposition has been displaced by Freud's theory of sexual construction; on the other hand, the structuralist interpretation of phylogenetic theory apparently abolished the need for psychoanalysis' universal history of the family. Instead it argued that Freud was trying to deal with the fact that kinship itself was made up of relations of difference like language. Lévi-Strauss suggested that it was these systems of classification and difference which underlay kinship systems. He argued for an analogy to be drawn between kinship and linguistic relations, as described by structural linguistics. They are made up of the same elements: systems of difference, signs, relations of exchange.

In this way both Lévi-Strauss and Lacan insist that the universals described by Freud are the universals of differentiation, constitutive of culture. They are not the universals of emotions, but an outline of the primacy of the complex, that is, culture, over the instinctual. The question is whether the emphasis on the fact of the systematicity of kinship rules — so valuable in arguing against functionalism[11] — is in fact useful for understanding sexual relations in society.

There are serious flaws within the structuralist approach as it now stands. In stressing the systematicity of kinship, Levi-Strauss described it as a system of communication. It guaranteed the possibility of reciprocity and therefore integration between self and others. In this system of communication, women are exchanged as signs. It is on this element that many feminists have attempted to reintegrate an explanation for the subordination of women. They say that it is the fact that women are exchanged by men in the kinship system which explains their apparently universal subordination.[12]

The way in which Lévi-Strauss explains that it is women who are exchanged needs to be carefully scrutinised. He assumes a natural promiscuity of men and an inevitable shortage of 'desirable' women; this makes women the most 'valuable' possession of the group. There is no theoretical necessity in his argument that it should be women who are exchanged. Nor does he assume that the exchange of women entails forms of subordination — legal, political, economic or intersubjective. This assumption has been added by the subsequent feminist interpretations.

Lévi-Strauss's argument is problematic in several ways. Anthropological evidence disputes his universalising generalisation that all marriage customs involve the exchange of women. In addition, it will be apparent that the assumptions of kinship as intellectual systems are assumptions deeply entrenched in philosophical anthropology. Joined with the Freudian account of the necessity for sexual renunciation, Lévi-Strauss's becomes an especially poignant variant of the negative critique of culture.

Finally, it can be argued that Lévi-Strauss's hypothesis of women's 'value' undermines his reliance on Saussurean linguistics. Saussurean linguistics argues that language is simply a system of differences.[13] There is no pre-given meaning which is free-floating and freely apprehended by the individual. Language is simply signifiers (sound-images) whose differential arrangements construct signifieds (the concept); the relationship between signifier and signified is arbitrary, agreed through social convention. In such a system there is no room for presupposing elements as valuable. The relations of difference the signifying system of a culture, construct how elements signify as valuable. The construction takes place within a socially signifying system.[14]

When Lévi-Strauss talks of the 'value' of women, he ignores the assertion that value is determined only by the conventions agreed within a given culture. By assuming a pre-existent value for women, structuralism remains committed to universalising assumptions about sexual division; men and women are assumed to have definite attributes. Thus, the appropriation of structuralism as a description of the political control of women by men, that is, patriarchy, is also problematic. It neglects the idea that sexual identity is constructed as part of the meanings which a given society inscribes.

In addition, there is a danger of returning to the same problematic traced by Jones and Malinowski in the 1920s. What is invoked is the idea of sexual forms *conditioned* by social forms (the political power of men) in a relation of straightforward determinacy. In fact, structural anthropology is potentially a theory which contradicts the idea of the universality of sexual and psychic forms. It is clear to most contemporary anthropologists that forms of marriage and sexual behaviour *do* vary. Even the prohibitions against incest take widely different forms, rarely confined to the bilateral prohibitions characteristic of Western culture. Structuralism is not concerned to dispute this but to establish, in the face of functionalism, that kinship relations do display a certain systematicity. This is because they are coincident with the fact that society is significatory, classifying and requires structures of differentiation. The incest prohibition and marriage outside immediate groupings are seen as practices synonymous with the fact that all human cultures are signifying and have classificatory structures. Through a rereading of Freud, it has been suggested that anatomical difference is a crucial element by which classificatory systems are operative. In fact, Freud and Lévi-Strauss asserted that this link had fatal consequences for the sexual life of humanity.

275

It is this last part of the statement which has allowed structuralism to return to the same problem of universal claims about sexual and psychic structures. For both Lévi-Strauss and Freud made claims about the universal link between anatomical difference, classificatory systems and the organisation of the *sexual* field which are, in fact, deductions based on our own culture. It is not surprising that the ideas should have been presented in this way. For the level of classification and differentiation — the elements necessary for language — never appear as abstract and neutral, separate from the cultures in which they are realised. The meanings given to anatomical difference are determined by the ways in which the sexual is organised, the meanings and values surrounding sexual division, by the power of various groups. Nor does it seem useful to look for one primary cause in the production of these meanings which are produced by their interrelation. Freud and Lévi-Strauss both generalised from the equation found in our culture between anatomical difference and sexual division; this is the mechanism by which in our culture sexuality is submitted to the polarity of anatomical distinction. This, however, is a mechanism of a specific and delimited culture and may not be a universal phenomenon.

Structuralism can indicate how all societies are signifying systems. It can therefore provide a way of understanding how meanings are arrived at and function within a particular culture. More especially, combined with psychoanalysis, this trajectory has been able to indicate the crucial way in which sexuality is constructed neither as a natural element nor an element simply determined by other more material factors. There is, however, nothing universal about the forms taken by differentiation, including sexual differentiation.

Structuralism, in fact, warns against making universal assumptions about dominance and subordination between men and women. Anatomical difference acquires its significance only in relation to other elements in the culture and it is not a universal fact that sexuality will be enforced around this polarisation. The sexual division of labour may also have different meanings in different cultures; women's widespread exclusion from ritual and public life may not have identical meanings within cultures whose power structure is different from our own. The meanings of the division between public and governmental, private and domestic may not be analogous in other cultures. To suggest hesitation over universalising claims is not to dispute that the subordination of women is widespread. It is to introduce a note of caution against thinking that men and women have a history separable from specific cultures.

The specificity of the sexual domain

Attempts to theorise sexual relations frequently end up presupposing aspects of sexual division and presupposing male and female sexual identities. This indicates that adequate questions relating to sexual relations cannot be asked either from within existing discourses or simply by adding elements from one theory to another. These discourses have mutually exclusive ways of defining sexual relations and sexual division, definitions which are crucial to other aspects of the theory. Thus in mergers between theories it invariably happens that radical ways of thinking about sexual relations are submerged.

Does this mean that existing theories are doomed to remain in splendid isolation? Does it mean that nothing can be usefully exchanged between theories, except perhaps criticisms? It should be clear from this conclusion that it is claimed that many of the theories studied do make propositions of importance for feminism. Moreover, these theories *do* have important implications for one another. But this is not because they can supply each other with missing elements.

The implications are that they displace the possibility of certain forms of arguments and therefore demand drastic changes in how the problems are formulated and considered. Thus the Freudian insistence on initial bisexuality and the construction of hetero-sexual identity cannot be accepted as a possible element of a theory which otherwise depends on assumptions of essential sexual division. The Freudian hypothesis, if taken seriously, must leave no room for theories which take sexuality as a given. It must displace any argument

277

in which sexual identity of sexual behaviour is thought to arise out of a sexual predisposition.

Not only must there be a rejection of essentialist ideas of sexual identity, but we can also conclude that searches for the one single cause of women's subordination also end up in trouble. To look for single histories ends up presupposing the sexes to be definite interest groups. Instead, we have begun to see the necessity for looking at the way in which the sexual relates to other aspects of a culture, the changes over periods of history and the way in which the sexual is organised in relation to anatomical difference. In our culture, the way in which sexual relations are entered into, and conducted, the organisation of sexual relations in other aspects of the society, all entail the subordination of women to men. It is this organisation of the sexual domain which creates and sustains the power of men. Yet we cannot investigate the mechanisms of this without insisting that the organisation of the sexual domain is not to be reduced to some single cause or explanation.[15] The subordination of women in our culture is contingent on a complex history.

The clarification of sexual terms

The implications of the preceding studies of sexual relations suggest that future studies might usefully rethink their terms. Any future study should make no presuppositions about the sexual identities of men and women. Nor does it seem useful to attempt to construct a universal history of the relations between the sexes. For, to produce this history, different sexual identities would have to be assumed without exploring how these are constructed with different meanings in different cultures. While future studies of sexual relations might usefully hold back from universalising hypotheses, there is no need to abandon general questions. At certain moments, the insistence on the general and systematic nature of kinship relations helped to advance the debate, and has allowed us to argue for the specificity of the sexual domain. We are confronted with the need to explore general questions without resorting to wild generalisations or universalising hypotheses which have to assume the very phenomena which we wish to explore.

278

It will be necessary to examine, in any future study of sexual relations the historical changes in the construction of sexual identity and how power is exercised within the sexual domain. This will require abandoning once and for all ideas of fixed, natural sexual instincts and identities. But it will also require that we do not make the mistake which sometimes accompanies this proposition. This mistake is in reducing the sexual domain to a reflection of other social practices, a reduction which inhibits the investigation of the historical construction of sexuality.

One of the conclusions which this book has been able to draw is that terms used to describe the sexual domain have been all too readily conflated. Thus we have seen how sex, sexuality, sexual identity, sexual division and sexual relations are treated as synonymous, or at least practices resting coherently on one another. Various theoretical discourses have focused on one or another of these phenomena, leaving the rest to be claimed by other discourses. The splitting up of the field of theoretical exploration has allowed a hegemony of universalising explanations. This book has also hinted that these various phenomena are in fact theoretically separable. Sex could be confined to a description of the act where sensual aims and gratification are enacted. Sexuality could be used to describe the representation of activities surrounding sensual aims and gratifications, representations which may be to yourself or which may be presented by various discourses like the law or medicine. Sexual identity is the public presentation of sensual aims and objectives as integrated into the personality. Sexual division describes the division of labour, roles and activities according to sexual classification. Sexual relations are those activities where sensual aims and objectives are integrated into relations (usually public) with other people.

This separation of terms is more than just a theoretical exercise. A closer examination of the differences between these terms will reveal that there has been an ideological work to merge these terms to work coherently on the combined axis of anatomical division and sexual instinct. It is the fact that *sexed* groups are constructed on anatomical division and our sexual identities are enmeshed around these divisions which is the primary mechanism by which men are able to exercise power over women.

The terms dealing with the domain of the sexual have been conflated and this has blocked historical investigations of the construction of sexual identity. This conflation reflects the mechanism by which, in our culture, sexual behaviour and identity are tied to anatomical division. Anatomical division is seen as equivalent to sexual identity and has been privileged as the fundamental symbolic category in sexuality.

Sexual division, however, is not a fixed, unchanging transhistorical division where men and women have timelessly pursued different objectives. Sexual division varies greatly between cultures. And even within our own culture, definitions of appropriate work and identities for men and women has changed historically. For example, in the seventeenth century it was not considered fit for gentlewomen to breastfeed their children.[16] It took a drive against the wet-nurse in favour of the idea of natural motherhood to persuade gentlewomen to breast-feed. It does seem the case that anatomical division is a significant division in almost every culture but it may not have the same meanings as it does in our own. Here, the idea of sexual division implies division of labour, roles and activities. A hierarchy is implied where women's activity is devalued, and women's 'sexual identity' becomes the basis for their subordination to men.

In our culture we refer to the classificatory divisions based on anatomy as sexual divisions. This is because anatomy has become synonymous with sexual identity and activity. Thus sex is assumed to be an act between men and women who are united for a purpose — pleasure or reproduction. What lies behind this assumption is that the sex act is about penetration. What is arbitrarily precluded is the fact that sex may be the enjoyment of sensual satisfaction with either sex and that the enactment of sensual gratifications may not be with other persons. In other words, we can produce a definition of sex which is far away from the idea of the satisfaction of an instinct, generated by the interests and desires consequent on anatomical distinction. Once we reject the idea of sex as exclusively the combination of sexed groups, we begin to

280

see how the idea of sexed groups is indeed an ideological construct. It means a group defined by their combination in the act of sex and their different activities.

A cursory examination of the notion of sexed groups and the ideologies carried by this reveals that the classification of different activities and needs of men and women around the sex act has been a crucial factor in the control of women. A study of nineteenth-century legal and medical attitudes towards sexual crimes[17] reveals that aspects of women's contemporary subordination were constructed through the ideology of different sexual needs and activities. The statutes concerned with sexual crimes passed throughout the nine- teenth century assumed that only men had an active sexuality. Therefore only men could be punished for sexual crimes. The statutes equally supposed that women's sexuality was passive, if not altogether entirely absent. However, when it came to the processes or workings of the law, women were only guaranteed protection if they were morally and sexually respectable, that is, virgins or respectable married women. In cases of rape, women were (and still are) not guaranteed protection if they are prostitutes or known to be sexually 'promiscuous'. These processes of the law made it clear that in fact women were assumed to have a sexual response — they were assumed to give off sexual messages to which men could not help but respond. It was therefore up to women to protect themselves by only allowing the responsible expres- sion of their sexual messages. Men's sexuality was thought to be a physical need akin to any other bodily function; it was seen as an almost automatic response which would take the initiative (even aggressively) in order to find out whether women were responsive. It is for this reason that women are not guaranteed protection against rape and that men are often treated leniently; rape is sometimes simply seen as normal sexual expression gone too far, becoming 'reckless' of women's permission.

These legal and medical ideologies of the sexual act and the different male and female activities connected to this reveal how the notion of 'sexuality' is discursively construc- ted. When 'sexuality' is mentioned in everyday conversation, it tends to refer to an individual's most intimate characteris- tics, their sensual aims, objectives, satisfactions and how this affects their personality. We tend to be obsessed with what is our 'true' sexual identity. But the idea of a 'true' sexuality is very problematic. For one thing, Freud has shown that the choice of object to satisfy sexual desire is not something immanent to a person; it is not a natural need which arises spontaneously from the individual. There is nothing pre-given about the objects and activities which compel a person through her life. The sensations — pains and pleasures — are decided by personal histories, the way in which sexual activities mesh with personal and social factors. For example, in our culture there is a preferencing of the heterosexual object choice but again Freud has suggested that this preference should not be taken for granted but should be explained. Social policies inscribe the heterosexual unit at the heart of the organisation of the social field; there are punishments and restrictions meted out on those who do not conform. But to recognise that there are general structures governing the form of expression of sexuality does not exhaust what can be said about sexuality. Many discourses suggest that individuals' 'true' sexuality is constrained by these cultural generalities; even within the dominant forms, the way of experiencing or organising that object choice can differ greatly. Different forms of sexuality may be experienced with different partners.

The idea of a true and fixed, albeit hidden, sexuality is more than an inadequate representation of the diversity of object and activity experienced by an individual. The ideology of a true single sexuality has been a crucial mechanism in what has been called the 'incitement to discourse' around sexuality. Foucault, in *The History of Sexuality*,[18] has suggested that there is no true fixed individual sexuality, but rather a multitude of discourses defining and proliferating 'sexualities'. He suggests that Western society has been increasingly characterised by an incitement to classify, describe and talk about sexuality. Contrary to popular mythology, he has indicated that the Victorian era was not a period marked by sexual repression from which we are only just beginning to recover. Instead, he suggests that the last two centuries have been witness to a discursive explosion around the issue of sexuality. This discursive explosion was connected with rapid industrialisation and its consequence of urban overcrowding. Combined with imperialist expansion and racialist preoccupations, a configuration of concerns was produced around hygiene and the reproduction of the population. Foucault suggests that a primary means in the controlling of the population was the interrogation, detailing and policing of sexuality. There was no one single discursive production of a sexuality but the production of sexual definitions across discourses around health, education, parenting, and in social policy such as in housing, etc. The nuclear family, in fact, was privileged as a solution to the restructuring of the population. It was constructed as an institution crossed by numerous legal, medical and educational investigations and recommendations about sexuality. But it was not an institution which was the guardian of a single sexuality. Instead, it was crossed by a series of different incitements and prohibitions. For example, sexual satisfaction between the married partners would be positively encouraged, so much so that all sorts of violence against women might be condoned so long as the husband was seen to be receiving sexual satisfaction. Sex between siblings and between generations, however, would be subjected to fairly strict taboos.

Foucault's argument shows how there is not one single sexuality enforced in our culture, but rather how discourses produce a series of sexual definitions. Discourses around sexuality are operative on the idea of sexual identity. This is the sense of identity constructed through a definite practice or discourse around sexual expression. Sexual identity is the public representation of sensual aims and objectives as integrated into the personality. Identity is a discursive construction. This process of construction entails the modes of subjectivity constructed in discourse; consequently these modes are multiple and any individual would be subject to the workings of any number of discursive constructions. Foucault, correctly, rejects the idea of the individual as substantive of instinct, need or behaviour. Instead, he is interested in the possibilities for individualisation in discourse, or subjection in discourse. As far as Foucault is concerned, it is the lure of the true sexual identity or disposition which constructs the possibilities of power within discourse. This is because the subject is produced by a discourse through recognising their identity within that discourse. The imperative

283

within the nineteenth century for medical classification of sexual types, such as the nymphomaniac, the homosexual, etc. was a proliferation and detailing of sexual activities. Constantly defining and expanding categories of perversion and pleasure became the means by which the body and its activities were increasingly harnessed to social objectives through the connection between sexual pleasure, identity and their discursive definition.

This description is useful for it shows how power can be exercised through the production of sexual identity. Where it is limited is in paying insufficient attention to the centrality of anatomical difference in the production of sexual identities and especially the different powers entailed in these identities. Foucault talks generally of the submission of the body to the workings of power, and the ways in which a particular 'bio-politics' produced a discursive imperative whereby pleasure was submitted to scrutiny and constraint through the mechanism of sexuality. He neglects the fact that at the heart of the 'explosion' of sexualities was the production of a very distinctive social unit, based on heterosexual dependency. It is through this unit, and the identities which it presupposes, that the consistent subordination of women is secured in our contemporary society.

Power is exercised in our society not by the literal control of one group by another. There are different distributions of power and position according to different practices. These practices need not be as tangible as literal economic advantage; power can be exercised by the form of language, the ability to control or manipulate situations, to exclude and marginalise groups. Power can also be given by social policies which on the surface appear to be indifferent to power groups. Actually, social policy in the form of how benefits are paid, who gets tax relief, what kinds of housing is built and who is provided with housing — all these practices prefer certain forms of living. In our society, the preferred unit is the heterosexually committed couple who are assumed to have children. Since the end of the last century, state intervention and social policy has constructed this unit which is not a neutral unit. For it is maintained by a definite ideology and concomitant practices which make women dependent on men. Benefits and provisions are given to women when this unit breaks down. It is assumed that when the unit functions, the man provides for his family, even though this bears little relation to reality.

This unit works to the absolute disadvantage of women. Women are never individuals in their own right in social policy. They are not entitled to benefits in their own right as individuals, but only as dependants of men, or as women who have lost the support of men. This plays into other social practices, such as those which determine economic forms. Women are constantly consigned and consign themselves to low-paid ghettoised employment because of ideologies about the role played by a woman's wage in the family income, or women's labour within the home.

This unit, which is to the direct disadvantage of women, works not through direct coercion, but because it appears to correspond to the sexual needs arising from the sexual identities of men and women. This social unit is maintained by appearing as the natural expression of sexual and emotional needs and activities. Because it is the only structure in which our society recognises dependency between individuals, it becomes the easiest way in which dependency can be expressed. The population appears to enter voluntarily into the structures and ideologies, which are actually enforced, because the sexual identities of men and women are constructed as leading logically to this structure.

Women's subordination is secured because identity is constructed as sexual identity, and sexual identity is the mechanism by which men and women combine in a unit which subordinates women. In our society, the public relations based on sexual connection are not enforced through kinship structures. They are not conditioned by property or material considerations in any very direct sense. The family has not been the basic property-owning structure for a long time. In a developed capitalist country, the ownership of property is secured in the hands of companies and legal entities; individuals may benefit but the ownership and control of the means of production does not require coherent family groups. Since the last century most of the last vestiges of the family as unit of ownership have disappeared. When women were granted the right to property within marriage, it was a sign that the family and legal descent was no longer relevant to property considerations.[19] In this context, where the sexual relations are no longer secured by the intervention of relatives or community, sexual identity and sexual need has been elevated to the driving force behind the formation of social units. Because our culture privileges sexual identity as the truest part of our beings, we are secured voluntarily in a social unit which subordinates women.

It is for this reason that we have to break up the traditional ways of viewing sexual relations in our culture. It is on the equation anatomical division, sexed group, sexual identity that a structure of power is operative. We therefore need ways of deconstructing and exploring how sexual identity is secured in this society. This book has been able to conclude that in our society there is an ideological investment to effect the equation between anatomical division and sexual identity. This equation, with its consequences for the lived subjective experiences of sexuality, is the mechanism by which women are subordinated to men.

We are now in a better position to clarify and understand the problem with which this book started. It is appropriate to talk about women as a sexed group in our society. Feminism has been right to recognise that women are subordinated as a sex, but that there is no natural sexual identity of women. The reason why it is appropriate to talk in this way is because our culture has centralised anatomical division as a division constituting sexual interest groups. Sexual identity has been constructed as flowing from anatomical identity and on this have been built ideologies of appropriate desires and orientations.

This book has explored the way in which traditional investigations of sexual relations have inhibited our understanding of the part played by sexual identity in women's subordination. The direction taken by feminist investigations has laid the foundation for understanding and therefore changing this structure.

Notes

Introduction

1 This description of a theoretical problematic is drawn from Louis Althusser, *Reading Capital*, London, New Left Books, 1974.

2 *Ibid.*, p. 27.

3 See, for example, Evelyn Reed, *Women's Evolution*, New York, Pathfinder Press, 1975.

1 The dissolution of the patriarchal theory

1 The best-known of these works is Millar's *Observations Concerning the Distinction of Ranks in Society*, London, 1771.
   See also P. Lafitau., *Les Moeurs de Sauvages Ameriquains comparées aux moeurs des premiers Temps.*, Paris, 1724.

2 It was Sir Robert Filmer who had developed a version of the patriarchal order in *Patriarcha* (1630); he argued 'that the power of the monarch derived from literal paternity of his people, so that the authority of the parent and the authority of the statesmen were one and the same. All forms of social obedience were construed in terms of the patriarchal family . . . and, indeed, so were all forms of social organisation' (K. Tribe, *Land, Labour and Economic Discourse*, London, Routledge & Kegan Paul, 1978, p. 39). Tribe goes on to argue that this theory became the main theoretical buttress of the monarchy and Tory Party throughout the seventeenth century. Locke challenged Filmer over his theory of the relation between the paternal and political power. Yet he still retained a notion of the patriarchal household as the basis of political and civil society, and the possession of property.

3 This is argued by R. Meek, in *Social Sciences and the Ignoble Savage*, Cambridge University Press, 1976. He draws attention to

the way in which a particular conception of the development of human society had become dominant by the middle of the eighteenth century. He calls this conception the 'four stages theory'.

In its most specific form, the theory was that society 'naturally' or 'normally' progressed over time through four more or less distinct and consecutive stages, each corresponding to a definite mode of subsistence, these stages being defined as hunting, pasturage, agriculture and commerce. To each of these modes of subsistence, it came to be argued, there corresponded different sets of ideas and institutions relating to law, property and government, and also different sets of customs, manners and morals (p. 2).

4 J. Myres, 'The Influence of Anthropology on the Course of Political Science', *University of California Publications in History*, vol. IV, no. 1, 1916, p. 54.

5 The following writers used an approach to comparative law similar to that of Maine. All the studies were confined to Indo-European society. Fustel de Coulanges, *The Ancient City*, Boston, Mass., 1874; R. Skene, *The Highlanders of Scotland*, 1837; R. Sohm, *The Institutes of Roman Law*, Oxford, Clarendon Press, 1892; W. Stokes, *Hindu Law*, Madras, J. Higginbotham, 1865.

6 H. Maine, *Ancient Law* (1861), reprinted Everyman's Library, London, Dent, 1917, p. 73.

7 *Ibid.*, p. 74.

8 This summary of Maine's theory is advanced by D. McLennan, in *The Patriarchal Theory*, London, Macmillan, 1885, p. 4.

9 *Ibid.*, pp. 180–204.

10 F. Le Play, *L'Organisation de la Famille*, Tour, 1884; M. Kovalevsky, 'Tableau des origines det de l'évolution de la famille et de la propriété', *Skrifter ufgina af Lovenska Stiffelsen*, no. 2, Stockholm, 1890; E. De Lavaleye, *Les Communautés de famille et de village*, 1889; V. Bogišić, *De la forme dite Inokosna de la famille rurale chez les Serbes et les Croates*, Paris, Thorin, 1884.

11 Maine, *op. cit.*, p. 73.

12 Lafitau, for example, in *Les Moeurs des Sauvages Ameriquains comparées aux moeurs des premiers Temps*, Paris, 1724, eulogises the social and political superiority of women in terms very similar to those employed by Bachofen much later (see Chapter 2).

It is in the woman that the nation, the nobility of blood, the geneological tree, the order of generations and the conservation of the families truly consists. It is in that all real authority resides. . . . The men on the other hand are entirely isolated and confined to themselves, their children are strangers to them, and everything perishes with their own death.

13 Myres, *op. cit.*, p. 57.

14 J. B. Tavernier, *Les six voyages de J. B. Tavernier*, Paris, 1676.

15 Buchanan, *A Journey from Madras through the Countries of Mysore, Canada, and Malaba* (3 vols), London, 1807.

16 Pinkerton, *A collection of the best and most interesting voyages and travels in all parts of the world* (17 vols), London, 1808–1814.

17 J. Mackenzie, *Ten Years North of the Orange River, 1859–1869*, Edinburgh, 1871; D. Livingstone, *Narrative of an Expedition to the Zambesi and its Tributaries, 1858–64*, London, 1865; J.D. Hunter, *Manners and Customs of Several Indian Tribes Located West of the Mississippi*, Philadelphia, 1823.

18 Gallatin, *Archaeologia Americana*, Philadelphia, 1820 onwards; T. Schoolcraft, *Travels*, 1825; *Notes on the Iroquois*, 1846.

19 Meek, *op. cit.*, has described the impact of this encounter. He claims that social scientists turned with relish to areas which, unlike the Americas, had escaped, 'corruption' by contact with Western imperialising regimes. They appeared to offer a more viable chance of studying mankind in a primitive state.

20 McLennan, *op. cit.*

21 *Ibid.*, p. 25.

22 *Ibid.*, p. 27.

23 J. J. Bachofen, *Myth, Religion and Mother-Right*, selections from Bachofen's writing including from *Das Mütter-recht* (1861). London, Routledge & Kegan Paul, 1968. This quotation, as the subsequent ones, comes from the extracts from *Das Mütter-recht*, p. 77.

24 *Ibid.*, p. 109.

25 *Ibid.*, p. 80.

26 *Ibid.*, p. 109.

27 *Ibid.*, p. 78.

28 For an account of this, see P. Brown, and L. J. Jordonova, 'Oppressive Dichotomies', in *Women and Society*, Cambridge Women's Studies Group, London, Virago, 1981.

29 J. F. McLennan, *Studies in Ancient History*, London, Quaritch, 1876–7; comprising a reprint of *Primitive Marriage*, 1861, p. 6.

30   *Ibid.*, p. 6.

31   E. B. Tylor, *Primitive Culture*, quoted in R. Lowie, *The History of Ethnological Theory*, New York, Holt, Rinehart & Winston, 1937, p. 3.

32   J. F. McLennan, *op. cit.*, p. 9.

33   *Ibid.*, p. 113.

34   L. H. Morgan, *Ancient Society*, New York, Henry Holt, 1877, pp. 525–6.

35   *Ibid.*, p. 505.

36   *Ibid.*, p. 463.

37   *Ibid.*, p. 465.

38   M. Kovalevsky, 'Tableau des origines et de l'évolution de la famille et de la propriété, *Skrifter ufgina af Lovenska Stiftelsen*, no. 2, Stockholm, 1890.

39   *Ibid.*, p. 9.

40   *Ibid.*, p. 9.

41   Here Kovalevsky cited the work of Morgan on the Iroquois Indians and Fison and Howitt's study of the Australians.

42   Kovalevsky, *op. cit.*, p. 10.

43   H. Maine, *Dissertations on Early Law and Custom*, London, John Murray, 1883, p. 287.

44   *Ibid.*, p. 202.

45   *Ibid.*, p. 205.

46   *Ibid.*, p. 217.

47   *Ibid.*, p. 218.

2   The meaning of mother-right

1   A. Lang, and J. J. Atkinson, *Social Origins and Primal Law*, London, Longman, 1903, p. viii.

2   See, for example, texts ranging from R. Lowie, *Primitive Society*, New York, Harcourt, Brace, 1927, p. 52; to E. E. Evans Pritchard, *The Position of Women in Primitive Society and Our Own*, Fawcett Lectures, 1955–56, p. 3; and, more recently, E. Fee, 'The Sexual Politics of Victorian Social Anthropology', in *Clio's Consciousness Raised*, ed. M. Hartmann and L. Banner, New York, Harper, 1974.

3   Evans Pritchard, *op. cit.*, p. 3.

4   J. Lubbock, *The Origin of Civilisation and the Primitive Condition of Man*, London, Longmans, 1870, p. 3.

5   For a discussion of this, see M. Foucault, *The Order of Things*, London, Tavistock, 1970, pp. 250–302.

6   W. H. R. Rivers, *Social Organisation and Kinship*, 1924 lecture, reprinted London, Athlone Press, 1968, p. 95.

7   J. Weeks, *Sex, Politics and Society: the Regulation of Sexuality since 1800*, London, Longman, 1981, p. 19.

8   *Ibid.*, pp. 19–20.

9   For an account of this period — both the development of state intervention in the social field and the growth of working-class political participation, — see Helen Lynd's excellent book, *England in the 1880's* (1945), reprinted London, Frank Cass, 1968. She lists the various forms of intervention and debate over the possibilities of legislation: debate over the possibilities of protective legislation, debate over the land question; intervention around the area of health and housing. She points to a period of forty years where a series of acts were passed by which the state intervened in the organisation of the social: acts giving the Board of Trade control over railroads, 1845; the ten-hour factory act of 1851; the health act, 1858; the Joint Stock Company Act, 1862; the Bankruptcy Act, 1869, the Civil Service and Elementary Education Acts of 1870; the Mines Regulation Act, 1872; the public health Act; the Cross Housing Act; the Factory Act, the Public Health Act all in 1875; and, in 1883 the Contagious Diseases Prevention Act.

10   Lubbock, *op. cit.*, p. 104.

11   E. B. Tylor, 'The Matriarchal Family System' in *Nineteenth Century*, July, 1896.

12   E. Crawley, *The Mystic Rose* (1902), revised edn, London, Macmillan, 1927.

13   Tylor, *op. cit.*, p. 84.

14   R. S. Rattray, *Ashanti*, Oxford, Clarendon Press, 1932, p. 84.

15   A. Sachs and J. Wilson, *Sexism and the Law*, Oxford, Martin Robertson, 1978, pp. 3–67.

16   E. Westermarck, *The History of Human Marriage*, London, Macmillan, 1891, p. 19.

17   C. N. Starke, *The Primitive Family*, International Scientific Series, 1872.

18   E. B. Tylor, *Anthropology*, London, Macmillan, 1881.

19   Lang and Atkinson, *op. cit.*

20   Crawley, *op. cit.*

21 Tylor, 'The Matriarchal Family System', p. 82.

22 B. Malinowski, *The Family Among the Australian Aborigines*, University of London Monographs in Sociology, vol. 2, 1913, p. 184.

23 *Ibid.*, p. 184.

24 S. Hartland, *Primitive Paternity*, London, David Nutt, 1909, vol. 1, p. 254.

25 S. Hartland, 'The Evolution of Kinship', 1922, in *The Frazer Lectures*, Oxford, Clarendon Press, 1922, p. 9.

26 R. Briffault, *The Mothers*, London, Allen & Unwin, 1927, vol. 3, p. 507.

27 See A. Türel, *Bachofen-Freud zür Emanzipation des Mannes vom Reich der Mütter*, Berne, 1939. This book makes the links between Bachofen's and Frend's evolutionary schemas explicit.

28 Schouten was a seventeenth century Dutch explorer whose pronouncement on paternity was often quoted, *Voyage aux Indes Orientales*, Amsterdam, 1757, pp. 458-9.

29 J. F. McLennan, *Studies in Ancient History*, London, Quaritch, 1871.

30 D. McLennan, *The Patriarchal Theory*, London, Macmillan, 1885, p. 216.

31 Three books were particularly influential here: L.H. Morgan, *Ancient Society*, New York, Henry Holt, 1877; L. Fison, and A. W. Howitt, *Kamilaroi and Kurnai*, Melbourne, 1880; W. B. Spencer, and F. Gillen, *The Native Tribes of Central Australia*, 1899.

32 S. Hartland, *Primitive Paternity*, vol. 1, p. 325.

33 J. Frazer, *Totemism and Exogamy*, London, Macmillan, 1910, vol. 4, p. 131.

34 S. Hartland, *Primitive Paternity*, vol. 2, p. 98.

35 H. Ellis, *Women and Marriage*, London, W. Reeves, 1888, p. 5.

36 B. Russell, *Marriage and Morals* (1929), Harmondsworth, Penguin, 1961, p. 23.

37 Kovalevsky, *op. cit.*, p. 59.

38 C. Letourneau, *The Evolution of Marriage and the Family*, Contemporary Science Series, London, Walter Scott, 1889, p. 347.

39 J. Corin, *Mating Marriage and the Status of Women*, London, Walter Scott, 1910.

40 Tylor, 'The Matriarchal Family System', p. 83.

41 *Ibid.*, p. 86.

42 *Ibid.*, p. 96.

43 *Ibid.*, p. 93.

44 *Ibid.*, p. 93.

45 *Ibid.*, p. 94.

46 An article where this problem is made explicit is, Carveth Read's, 'No Paternity' in *Man, The Journal of the Royal Anthropological Institute*, 1918.

47 R. Briffault, 'Family Sentiments' in *Zeitschrift für Socialforschung*, Frankfurt, vol. II, 1933, p. 358.

48 *Ibid.*, p. 359.

49 *Ibid.*, p. 359.

50 V. F. Calverton, 'The Compulsive Basis for Social Thought', *The American Journal of Sociology*, vol. XXXVI, Chicago, 1931.

51 *Ibid.*, pp. 696, 697, 702.

52 E. Westermarck, *Three Essays on Sex and Marriage*, London, Macmillan, 1834, p. 334.

53 Briffault, *Family Sentiments* p. 359.

54 See the writings of Dora Russell.

55 See H. Bosanquet, *The Family*, London, Macmillan, 1906.

3. Sexual antagonism: theories of sex in social sciences

1 This was a title of one of the chapters in Tylor's book *Anthropology*, London, Macmillan, 1881.

2 C. Darwin, *The Origin of Species* (1859), London, Dent, 1971, p. 81.

3 *Ibid.*, p. 81.

4 C. Patteson, *Evolution*, London, Routledge & Kegan Paul, 1978, pp. 146–7.

5 Darwin, *op. cit.*, p. 87.

6 *Ibid.*, p. 89.

7 *Ibid.*, p. 24.

8 P. Geddes, and A. A. Thompson, *The Evolution of Sex*, London, Walter Scott, 1891, p. 4.

9 *Ibid.*, p. 4.

10 *Ibid.*, p. 4.

11 Brooks, quoted by Geddes and Thompson, *op. cit.*, p. 5.

12   Geddes and Thompson, *op. cit.*, p. 9.

13   A. H. Huth, *The Marriage of Near Kin*, London, J. and A. Churchill, 1875.

14   *Ibid.*, p. 214.

15   R. Briffault, *The Mothers*, London, Allen & Unwin, 1927, vol. 1, p. 204.

16   J. Frazer, *Totemism and Exogamy*, London, Macmillan, 1910, vol. 4, p. 9.

17   *Ibid.*, vol. 4, p. 98.

18   E. Durkheim, 'La Prohibition de Inceste et ses origines' in *L'Année Sociologique*, Paris, 1890.

19   Lord Raglan, *Jocasta's Crime*, London, Methuen, 1933, p. 43.

20   *Ibid.*, p. 46.

21   *Ibid.*, p. 48.

22   For account of the eugenicist theory and politics, see J. Weeks, *Sex, Politics and Society*, London, Longman, 1981; G.R. Searle, *Eugenics and Politics in Britain 1900–1914*, Noord hof International, 1976; A. Davin, 'Imperialism and Motherhood,' *History Workshop* no. 5., Spring, 1970; G. Stedman-Jones, *Outcast London*, Oxford University Press, 1971.

23   P. Gaskell, *The Manufacturing Population of England*, London, Baldwin & Cradock, 1833.

24   A. W. Blyth, *Tenement Dwellings*, Transactions of the Society of Medical Officers of Health, 1882–3, p. 82.

25   Gaskell, *op. cit.*, p. 133.

26   Simon, *2nd Annual Report to the City of London from the Medical Health Officer*, 1840, pp. 118–19.

27   V. Bailey, and S. Blackburn, 'The Punishment of Incest Act 1908; A Case Study of Law Creation', *Criminal Law Journal*, 1979.

28   J. Weeks, *Sex, Politics and Society. The regulation of sexuality since 1800*, London, Longman 1981, p. 30.

29   Bailey and Blackburn, *op. cit.*

30   C. Perkins Gilman, *Women and Economics* (1898), reprinted New York, Harper Torchlight Books, 1966, p. 33.

31   For an account of these arguments in British politics see, especially, Weeks, *op. cit.*

32   G. H. L. F. Pitt-Rivers, *The Clash of Culture, and the Contact of Races*, London, Routledge, 1911, p. 246.

33 R. Lowie, *Primitive Society*, New York, Harcourt Brace, 1921, pp. 167–8.

34 E. Crawley, *The Mystic Rose* (1902), reprinted London, Macmillan, 1927.

35 *Ibid.*, vol. II, p. 77.

36 E. Westermarck, *The History of Human Marriage*, London, Macmillan, 1891, p. 157.

37 R. Briffault, *op. cit.*, vol. 3, p. 518.

38 W. Heape, *Sex Antagonism*, London, Constable, 1913, p. 1.

39 *Ibid.*, p. 1.

40 *Ibid.*, p. 1.

41 *Ibid.*, pp. 1–2.

42 *Ibid.*, p. 2.

43 *Ibid.*, p. 3.

44 *Ibid.*, p. 3.

45 *Ibid.*, p. 4.

46 *Ibid.*, p. 102.

47 *Ibid.*, p. 43.

48 *Ibid.*, p. 48.

49 *Ibid.*, p. 49.

50 *Ibid.*, p. 208.

51 *Ibid.*, p. 34.

52 *Ibid.*, p. 207.

53 Frazer, *op. cit.*, vol. 4, p. 166.

54 P. Lafargue, *The Evolution of Property from Savagery to Civilisation*, 1890, p. 10.

55 H. Spencer, *Works*, vol. 6, p. 629.

56 L. T. Hobhouse, *The Material Culture and Social Institutions of Primitive Peoples* (1915), reprinted, London, Routledge & Kegan Paul, 1965.

57 M. and M. Vaerting, *The Dominant Sex*, trans. Eden and Cedar Paul, London, Allen & Unwin, 1923.

58 *Ibid.*, p. 185.

59 *Ibid.*, p. 77.

60 *Ibid.*, pp. 85–6.

61 Jane Harrison, *'Homo Sum'; being a Letter to an Anti-Suffragist from an Anthropologist*, National Union of Women's Suffrage Societies, 1913, p. 11.

62 For an account of interventions around sexual definitions of this period see, amongst others, Weeks, *op. cit.*; M. Foucault, *History of Sexuality*, London, Allen Lane, 1978; J. Donzelot, *The Policing of Families*, London, Hutchinson, 1980; E. Wilson, *Women and the Welfare State*, London, Tavistock, 1977.

4 The impasse on kinship

1 B. Malinowski, 'Must Kinship be Dehuamnised by Mock-Algebra?' *Man*, February 1930.

2 For an account of the consolidation of anthropology as a distinct academic discipline, see S. Feuchtwang, 'The Colonial Formation of British Anthropology' in T. Asad, ed., *Anthropology and the Colonial Encounter*, London, Ithaca Press, 1973. Feuchtwang traces the consolidation of academic anthropology throughout the 1920s, a development marked by Malinowski's readership at the LSE created in 1923, and the appointment of Radcliffe-Brown to a chair of Anthropology at Cape Town University.

3 Malinowski, *op. cit.*, p. 20.

4 *Ibid.*, p. 20.

5 Malinowski was referring to the writings of A. A. Radcliffe-Brown and Brenda Seligmann in England, A. Kroeber and R. Lowie in America.

6 Malinowski, *op. cit.*, p. 20.

7 *Ibid.*, p. 21.

8 F. Boas, 'Evolution or Diffusion?' *American Anthropologist*, vol. XXVI, 1924, p. 342.

9 See C. Ritchie, *Darwinism and Politics*, London, Swann Sonneschein, 1889. An example of the use of evolutionary theories for a defence of political conservatism.

10 R. Lowie, *Primitive Society*, New York, Harcourt, Brace, 1927, p. 5.

11 Lowie wrote:

It is natural to suppose that like phenomena must have like causes and accordingly it would become the ethnologist's duty to determine these: a priori they might be supposed to lie in racial affinities, or the similarity of geographical environment, or some other fundamental condition shared by the cultures compared. Practically however . . . it is not so easy to isolate such determinants amidst the tremendous complexities of cultural data and to demonstrate they are the significant factors. Indeed some ethnologists have abandoned all hope of ever unravelling them.

12 *Ibid.*, p. 177.

13 *Ibid.*, p. 178.

14 *Ibid.*, p. 178.

15 *Ibid.*, p. 184.

16 *Ibid.*, p. 186.

17 *Ibid.*, p. 196.

18 *Ibid.*, p. 162.

19 *Ibid.*, p. 158.

20 Malinowski, *op. cit.*, p. 22.

21 Lowie, *op. cit.*, p. 159.

22 *Ibid.*, p. 159.

23 *Ibid.*, p. 55.

24 *Ibid.*, p. 58.

25 Malinowski, *op. cit.*, p. 22.

26 *Ibid.*, p. 22.

27 *Ibid.*, p. 22.

28 Lowie, *op. cit.*, p. 60.

29 B. Malinowski, *The Family Amongst Australian Aborigines*, University of London Monographs in Sociology, vol. 2, 1913, p. 183.

30 Malinowski, 'Must Kinship be Dehumanised by Mock Algebra?' p. 25.

31 *Ibid.*, p. 25.

32 *Ibid.*, p. 25.

33 Malinowski, '*The Family Amongst Australian Aborigines*', p. 170.

34 Malinowski, 'Must Kinship be Dehumanised by Mock Algebra?' p. 25.

35 Lowie, *op. cit.*, p. 15.

36 B. Malinowski, 'Must Kinship be Dehumanised by Mock Algebra?' p. 23.

37 A. A. Radcliffe-Brown, *African Systems of Kinship and Marriage*, Oxford University Press, 1950, p. 82.

38 The idea of a general articulating principle will be criticised more thoroughly in the following chapter, and in the conclusion.

39 Kroeber, *op. cit.* see n. 38.

40 *Ibid.*, p. 378.

41 *Ibid.*, p. 378.

42 *Ibid.*, p. 378.

43 *Ibid.*, p. 378.

44 *Ibid.*, p. 380.

45 These criticisms have, for example, been made of the recent writings of Paul Hirst and Barry Hindess.

5 The concept of the family in marxist theory

1 F. Engels, *The Origins of the Family, Private Property and the State* (1884), London, Lawrence & Wishart, 1972.

2 V. I. Lenin, *The State*, Peking, 1919, Foreign Language Press, p. 3.

3 *Ibid.*, p. 21.

4 *Ibid.*, p. 21.

5 K. Marx, *Das Kapital* (3 vols): vol. 1, 1967; vol. 2, 1885; vol. 3, 1894; London, Lawrence & Wishart, 1974.

6 D. Ryzanov, *Karl Marx und Friedrich Engels*, 1929, p. 210.

7 M. Adler, *Engels als Denker*, Berlin, 1920, pp. 48–9.

8 K. Kautsky, 'Die Enstehung der Ehe und Familie', *Kosmos*, Stuttgart, 1882.

9 H. Cunow, *Die Verwandschafts Organisationen der Australnager, Ein Beitrag zur Entwicklungsgeschichte*, 1894; H. Cunow, 'Zur Urgeschichte der Ehe und Familie', *Erganzungshefte zur Neuen Zeit*, no. 14, Stuttgart, 1912.

10 Both Cunow and Kautsky criticise Engels for introducing factors outside the schema of materialist causation. Cunow took issue with Engels for his separation of women's child-bearing capacities into an independent element in the determination of human history. The social forms of sexual relationships he argued, were determined by the conditions of material production alone. Kautsky was particularly critical of Engels's psychologism. By this he referred to the fact that Engels appears to presuppose the psychology of the monogamous nuclear bourgeois family to account for the history of its emergence. These criticisms foreshadowed those made by recent marxist feminist writings on Engels.
H. Cunow, 'Zur Kritik der Engels'schen Urgeschichtskonstruktion',

in *Die Marxische Geschichts*, pp. 138–42. K. Kautsky, *Die Material-istische Geschtsauffassung*, Berlin, 1927, vol. I, pp. 323–4.

11 See, in particular, the work of L. Althusser, and the so-called neo-Althusserians. L. Althusser, 'Marxism and Humanism' in *For Marx*, Harmondsworth, Penguin, 1969; A. Cutler, B. Hindess, P. Hirst, and A. Hussain, *Marx's Capital and Capitalism Today*, London, Routledge & Kegan Paul, 1978.

12 K. Marx, 'Critique of Hegel's Doctrine of the State' (1843), in *Early Writings*, ed. L. Colletti, Harmondsworth, Penguin, 1975.

13 L. Colletti, Introduction to Marx, *Early Writings*, p. 36.

14 K. Marx, 'Critique of Hegel's Doctrine of the State', p. 167.

15 K. Marx, 'Critique of Hegel's Doctrine of the State' 1843, *Early Writings*, p. 63.

16 These early writings are characterised by several deep-rooted assumptions about the family and its relation to society, namely, the assumption of the family as procreative unit; the supposition of a natural division of labour based on a natural division between the sexes; that patriarchy is the original family relation; and finally that the patriarchal family contains latent forms of slavery, i.e. the natural rights of the patriarch to offspring and produce of offspring's labour.

17 See n. 11.

18 Engels, *The Origins*, p. 71.

19 *Ibid.*, p. 71.

20 *Ibid.*, pp. 71–2.

21 See, for example, the article, 'Patriarchy and Relations of Pro-duction' by R. Harrison, and R. McDonough, in A. Kuhn and A. Wolpe, eds, *Feminism and Materialism*, London, Routledge & Kegan Paul, 1978.

22 Engels, *The Origins*, p. 83.

23 Engels here adopts a position on the primacy of the collective which is typical of socialist and anarchist writers of the period. Kropotkin for example in *Mutual Aid*, (1902, reprinted Harmonds-worth, Penguin, 1939), even extended the hypothesis back into the animal kingdom. He engaged in dialogue with the conservative – Huxley, who had derived a theory of the origins of society based on Darwin's theory of the struggle for survival and the survival of the fittest in the animal kingdom. Against this, Kropotkin advanced his own observation of animal behaviour, arguing that mutual aid and selfless co-operation is readily observable in all forms of social behaviour amongst animals.

24 Engels, *The Origins*, p. 100.

25 *Ibid.*, p. 101.

26 Morgan's definition of a gens, it will be remembered, was a 'group of consanguinei' bearing the gentile name.

27 Engels, *The Origins*, p. 147.

28 K. Marx, *The Ethnological Notebooks of Karl Marx*, ed. L. Krader, Assen, von Gorcum, 1974, p. 18.

29 Engels, *The Origins*, p. 125.

30 See, B. Brown, 'The Natural and Social Division of Labour', *M/F*, no. 1, 1978.

31 Engels, *The Origins*, p. 161.

32 Engels is in argument with classical historians and, indeed, writers like Maine who suggest that the gens is a grouping made up of individual families. On the contrary, it was expedient for Engels to stress that the gens had a different basis for unification;

> Under the gentile family constitution the family never was an organisational unit and could not be so, for man and wife necessarily belonged to two different gentes. The whole gens was incorporated within the phratry and the whole phratry within the tribe; but the family belonged half to the gens of the man and half to the gens of the woman. In public law the state also does not recognise the family; up to this day, the family only exists in private law. And yet all our histories have hitherto started from the absurd assumption which since the 18th century in particular has become inviolable, that the monogamous single family which is hardly older than civilisation, is the core around which society and the state have gradually crystallised. (p. 164)

33 In *The Origins*, Engels traces three principal forms which have characterised the transition from gentile to political organisation. The Athenian state springs directly out of the class oppositions which developed within the gentile constituion itself. In Rome, gentile society becomes a closed aristocracy surrounded by plebs who had no rights but only duties. It is the victory of the plebs which breaks up the old constitution based on kinship and erects the state on the ruins of the gentile constitution. Finally, in the case of the Germans, the state emerges as a consequence of large-scale conquests which can no longer be governed by the gentile constitution.

34 Robert Lowie in *The Origins of the State*, New York, Harcourt

Brace, 1927, argued against the marxist assumptions of the qualitatively different nature of gentile and political society. He shows
how American Indian social organisation in fact exhibited both
forms: territorial and gentile bonds are frequently found co-
existing. Moreover, 'police' forces are sometimes found with gentile
organisations.

35 F. Engels, *The Origins*, p. 125.

36 *Ibid.*, p. 128.

37 *Ibid.*, p. 128.

38 *Ibid.*, p. 233.

39 See, for example P. Q. Hirst and B. Hindess, *Pre-Capitalist Modes
of Production*, London, Routledge & Kegan Paul, 1977:

> The structure and mechanism of complex redistribution involves
> the organisation of the social formation into groups structured
> internally by kinship relations, e.g. between cadet and elder,
> and combined into larger units, villages, tribes, etc., through a
> wider network of marriage exchanges.

40 See M. Molyneux, 'Androcentrism in Marxist Anthropology',
Critique of Anthropology, nos 9/10, 1977.

41 See C. Delphy, *The Main Enemy*, Women's Research and Resources
Centre Pamphlet, 1970–1.

42 This position can only be sustained if it is agreed that capitalist
social relations can be specified as abstract general principles which
inform all manifestations of the social formation. However, if this
position is challenged, it remains to approach the actual history of
capitalist social relations. Here the importance of sexual division,
the organisation of the family, etc., are inescapable determinants
on the form taken by the development of capitalist social relations.
This argument has been suggested by B. Taylor and A. Phillips, in
'Sex and Skill', *Feminist Review*, no. 6, 1980.

43 For an early critique of this see B. Russell, *German Social
Democracy*, London, Longman, 1896. For a contemporary
critique, see Culter *et al.*, *op. cit.*

44 This is the reason given by Maxine Molyneaux, op. cit., who resists
carrying her critique of androcentrism in marxist anthropology
towards designating women as a class.

45 See Cutler *et al.*, *op. cit.*

6 The woman question and the early marxist left

1 See M. Molyneaux, 'Socialist Societies Old and New', *Feminist
Review*, no. 8, 1981.

2 P. Lafargue, *La Question de la Femme*, Paris, Editions de L'Oeuvre Nouvelle.

3 Quoted in W. Thönnessen, *The Emancipation of Women*, London, Pluto Press, 1973, p. 35.

4 V. I. Lenin, Quoted in *The Woman Question: Selected writings of Marx, Engels, Lenin and Stalin*, International Publishers Co., 1951, p. 47.

5 J. V. Stalin, 'International Women's Day 1925', quoted in *The Woman Question*, p. 44.

6 The re-evaluation of the place of feminism within socialism and the relationship between the two is now under investigation.
    Barbara Taylor's 'The Feminist Theory and Practice of the Socialist Movement in Britain 1820–45', PhD, University of Sussex, is an important exploration of the relationship between feminism and socialism in pre-marxist socialism. Other studies can be found in: S. Rowbotham, and J. Weeks, *Socialism and the New Life*, London, Pluto Press, 1977; S. Rowbotham, *Stella Brown, Socialist and Feminist*, London, Pluto Press, 1978; J. Weeks, *Sex, Politics and Society*, London, Longman 1981.

7 K. Marx, *Das Kapital*, London, Lawrence & Wishart, 1974, vol. 1, p. 391.

8 For a full account of the context and politics surrounding this see J. Walkewitz, *Prostitution in Victorian England*, Cambridge University Press, 1980.

9 E. Marx, and E. Aveling, *The Woman Question*, London, Swann Sonnenschein and Co., 1885–6.

10 I. Lafleur, 'Five Socialist Women: Traditional Conflicts and Socialist Visions in Austria 1893–1934', in M. Boxer, and J. Quartaert, *Socialist Women*, New York, Elsevier, 1978.

11 'Was Bebel den Proletarierinnen gab', *Gleichheit*, XX, no. 10, February 1910, pp. 150–1.

12 J. Quartaert, 'Unequal Partners in an Uneasy Alliance, Women and the Working Class in Imperial Germany', in Boxer, and Quartaert, *op. cit.*, p. 117.

13 The Exceptional Laws against Social Democracy 1878–90, when all party organs were banned.

14 See, for example, Eliza Butler's *The Tyranny of Greece over Germany*, Cambridge, 1935.

15 See C. Alzon, *Femme Mythifiée, femme mystifiée*, Paris, Presses Universitaires de France, 1978. In an otherwise reactionary book,

Alzon provides a summary of ouvrierist attitudes to the woman question within socialism.

16 L. Otto-Peters, *Das Richt der Frauen auf Erwerb*, Hamburg, 1866, p. 103.

17 See, for example, H. P. Bleuel, *Sex and Society in Nazi Germany*, New York, Lippincott, 1973.

18 An account of these theories of mother-right and history can be found in E. Fromm, 'The Theory of Mother-Right and Social Psychology' (1934), in *The Crisis of Psychoanalysis*, Harmondsworth, Penguin, 1973.

19 Quoted in Thönnessen, *op. cit.*, p. 20.

20 *Ibid.*, p. 32.

21 K. Marx, quoted in Thönnessen, *op. cit.*, p. 33.

22 A. Bebel, *Woman under Socialism* (1883), trans. D. De Leon, New York, Schoken Books, 1971.

23 The Erfurt Programme, 1891.

24 A. Kollontai, 'Sexual Relations and the Class Struggle' in *Selected Writings*, London, Allison & Busby, 1977, p. 248.

25 *Ibid.*, p. 249.

26 Recent writing includes. e.g. C. Porter, *Alexandra Kollontai*, London, Virago, 1980. B. Farnsworth, 'Alexandra Kollontai, in Boxer, and Quartaert, *op. cit.*

27 Kollontai, *op. cit.*, p. 245.

28 A. Russell, Appendix on Social Democracy and the Woman Question in B. Russell, *German Social Democracy*.

29 *Ibid.*, p. 176.

30 *Ibid.*, p. 180.

31 *Ibid.*, p. 182.

32 This position which predominated amongst the Fabians, and was exemplified by writers like H. G. Wells, was also espoused by writers like Havelock Ellis and Ellen Kay.

33 A. Russell, *op. cit.*, p. 183.

34 For an account of these divisions and their relation to the theorisation of class interest see B. Hindess, 'Marxism and Parliamentary Democracy' in A. Hunt, ed., *Marxism and Democracy*, London, Lawrence & Wishart, 1980.

35 A. Russell, *op. cit.*, p. 183.

36 *Ibid.*, p. 187.

7 The patriachal family in Freudian theory

1 J. Mitchell, *Psychoanalysis and Feminism*, London, Allen Lane, 1974.

2 E. Zaretsky, *Capitalism, the Family and Personal Life*, London, Pluto Press, 1976.

3 J. Kristeva, *On Chinese Women*, London, Marion Boyars, 1977.

4 Lévi-Strauss writes that Freud's *Totem and Taboo* is both 'an example and a lesson':

> Freud successfully accounts, not for the beginning of civilisation but for its present state; and setting out to explain the origin of a prohibition, he succeeds in explaining certainly not why incest in consciously condemned but how it happens to be unconsciously desired. It has been stated and restated that what makes *Totem and Taboo* unacceptable, as a prohibition of incest and its origins, is the gratuitousness of the hypothesis of the male horde and of primitive murder, a vicious circle deriving the social state from events which presupposes it. However, like all myths, the one presented in *Totem and Taboo* with such dramatic force admits of two interpretations: The desire for the mother or the sister, the murder of the father and the son's repentance, undoubtedly do not correspond to any fact or group of facts occupying a given place in history. Perhaps they symbolically express an ancient and lasting dream. (*Elementary Structures of Kinship* (1949), Boston Beacon Press, 1969.)

5 *Das Jahrbuch der Psychanalyse*, replaced in 1913 the original psychoanalytic organ, the *Jahrbuch für psychoanalytische und psychopatholoishe Forschung*. The latter was founded in 1908, edited for the first five years by Jung. After the split between Jung and Freud, Freud himself became the director, with Abraham and Hitchmann. *Imago* was founded in 1912. Its aim was the application of psychoanalysis to the mental sciences and it was edited by Rank and Sachs.

6 Arguments based on the constitutional nature of sexual 'disturbbance' can be found in any number of medical and social discourses of the period. Lombroso and Ferrero's theory of constitution as the basis of the female criminal type in their *The Female Offender*, Criminology Series, vol. 1, 1895 was typical of this period.

Virchow's *Das Weib und die Zelle* was a much-quoted medical authority on mental disorders among women, claiming that these arose from constitutional defects.

7 S. Freud, 'Three Essays on Sexuality' (1905), *Standard Edition* vol. VII, reprinted in Penguin Freud Library, vol. 3, 1977, p. 155.

8 *Ibid.*, p. 57. This footnote was added in 1910.

9 A. L. Kroeber, 'Totem and Taboo: an Ethnological Psychoanalysis', *American Anthropologist*, vol. 22, 1920.

10 S. Freud, *Totem and Taboo, Standard Edition* vol XIII, pp.160–1.

11 S. Freud, and J. Breuer, *Studies on Hysteria, SE* vol. XI, reprinted in the Penguin Freud Library, vol. 3.

12 S. Freud, *On the History of the Psychoanalytic Movement, SE* vol. XIV, pp. 17–18.

13 S. Freud, *The Interpretation of Dreams* (1900), *SE* vol. V, p. 620.

14 S. Freud, *From the History of an Infantile Neurosis* (1914–15), *SE* vol. XVII, reprinted in (ed.) M. Gardiner, *Siegmund Freud and the Wolf Man*, Harmondsworth, Penguin, 1973, p. 181.

15 *Ibid.*, p. 198.

16 *Ibid.*, p. 200.

17 *Ibid.*, p. 221.

18 *Ibid.*, p. 221.

19 *Ibid.*, p. 260.

20 S. Freud, *From the History of an Infantile Neurosis*, p. 285.

21 S. Freud, 'The Sexual Theories of Children' *SE* vol. IX, p. 212.

22 E. Jones, 'The Reception of Totem and Taboo' in the *International Journal of Psychoanalysis*, quoted by M. Robert, *From Oedipus to Moses*, London, Routledge & Kegan Paul, 1977, p. 147.

23 It is this concept which draws Freud's schema so close to Bachofen's. Bachofen hypothesised an advance in intellectuality with the recognition of paternity and the triumph of patriarchy. For Freud, the advance is achieved by the possibility of a social form where psychic anxiety can be successfully expressed. It should be noted that Freud saw the neurotic resolution of monotheistic religion as a stage in the development of mankind towards a truly rational philosophy, that is science.

24 S. Freud, *Moses and Monotheism*, 1938, *SE* vol. XXIII, edition referred to, London, Hogarth Press, 1974, p. 43.

25 For a discussion of Rank's book and the general application of psychoanalysis to mythological phenomena, see the following chapter.

26 E. Jones, *op. cit.* p. 147.

27 S. Freud, *Moses and Monotheism*, p. 99.

28 *Ibid.*, pp. 88–9.

29 *Ibid.*, p. 118.

8 Psychoanalysis and anthropology: the interpretation of social practices

1 A. L. Kroeber, 'Totem and Taboo: an Ethnological Psychoanalysis', *American Anthropologist*, vol. 22, 1920, p. 55.

2 C. Kluckhohn, 'The Impact of Psychiatry in American Anthropology in the Last 100 Years' in *One Hundred Years of American Psychiatry*, New York, American Psychiatric Association and Columbia University Press, 1944.

3 O. Rank and H. Sachs, *The Significance of Psychoanalysis for the Mental Sciences* (1913); English translation, Nervous and Mental Diseases Monograph Series, no. 13, New York, 1916.

4 Evidence of this perspective can be found in European marxist writing of the inter-war period, especially in England and Germany. In England writers like Eden and Cedar Paul championed psychoanalysis as the branch of psychology most likely to be of profit to a marxist study of society. This position was advanced in *An Outline of Psychology*, the first of the Plebs Text Books, produced in 1921, and based on the idea of workers' education advanced by Proletkult in the USSR. Eden and Cedar Paul translated Marxist tests prolifically, but they also translated important books in the area of psychology and sex psychology. They translated the Vaertings' *The Dominant Sex* (see chapter 3).

The close links between marxism and psychoanalysis were evident from the way in which psychoanalysis entered Britain. It was introduced by the Fabians, Virginia and Leonard Woolf who published the Psychoanalytic Library with the Hogarth Press. That tradition was upheld throughout the 1930s with the Left Book Club publishing several books on the subject of psychoanalysis and marxism (see, for example, R. Osborne, *Freud and Marx* and *The Psychology of Reaction*.)

These books were characteristic of a whole genre of marxist psychology in Europe. Most influential of this tendency were books like Aurel Kolnai's *Psychoanalysis and Sociology*, London, Allen & Unwin, 1921 (an attack on anarchism as 'maternal' and regressive), and Paul Federn's *Zur Psychologie der Revolution: Die Vaterlöse Gesellschaft*, (*The Psychology of Revolution: Fatherless Studies*), Berne, 1927, where it is argued that the collective attitudes of the working class would prohibit patriarchal fascist attitudes.

The influence of such attitudes on the Frankfurt school should be apparent. Their study of Authoritarianism and the Family attempts to develop the idea of a marxist psychology; M. Horkheimer, ed., *Studien uber Autorität und Familie*, Paris, Alcan, 1936.

Finally, it is worth mentioning the extent which this perspective influenced a whole movement towards radical studies of society. The work of Mass Observation grew directly out of the dream of a human science, influenced by anthropology, psychoanalysis and marxism which would provide a way of understanding and interpreting society. See *The First Year's Work of Mass Observation*, ed. T. Harrison and C. Madge, with an introductory essay by B. Malinowski, Lindsay Drummond, 1937–8. For a short account of the intellectual influence on Mass Observation see T. Jeffrey, 'Mass Observation — A Short History', Centre for Contemporary Cultural Studies Stencilled Paper.

5 S. Freud, *Totem and Taboo* (1912–13), *SE* vol. XIII, reprinted London, Routledge & Kegan Paul, 1968, p. 156.

6 The orthodox position on female sexuality was much disputed throughout the 1930s, dominating debates in *The International Journal of Psychoanalysis*, see E. Jones, 'Early Female Sexuality', vol. 16, 1935. M. Bonaparte, 'Passivity, Masochism and Feminity', in ibid.; K. Horney, 'The Denial of the Vagina', vol. 14, 1933; H. Deutsche, 'Female Sexuality', in ibid. For an account of these debates see Juliet Mitchell and J. Rose, *Female Sexuality in the Lacanian School* (forthcoming).

7 Rank and Sachs, *op. cit.*, p. 13.

8 *Ibid.*, p. 13.

9 E. Jones, 'The Theory of Symbolism' (1917), in *Papers in Psychoanalysis*, London, Tindall and Cox, 1923.

10 K. Abraham, *Dreams and Myths*, Nervous and Mental Diseases Monograph No. 15, New York, 1913, p. 38.

11 W. H. R. Rivers, 'Dreams and Primitive Culture', Bulletin of the John Rylands Library, vol. IV, nos. 3–4, February–July 1918.

12 O. Rank, *The Myth of the Birth of the Hero*, English edn, London, Vintage Books, 1964, p. 9.

13 E. Silberer, *Problems of Mysticism and Its Symbolism*, New York, Moffat Yard & Co., 1917.

14 T. Reik, *Ritual* (1928), English edn, with introduction by Freud, London, Hogarth Press, 1931. R. Money-Kyrle, The Meaning of

Sacrifice, 1930. G. Röheim, *Australian Totemism*, George Allen & Unwin, 1925.

15 Abraham, *op. cit.*, p. 37.

16 O. Rank, *Das Inzest-Motiv in Dichtung und Sage*, Leipzig, 1912, p. 277.

17 E. Jones, 'The Madonna's Conception through the Ear', in *Essays in Applied Psychoanalysis*, London, Hogarth Press, reprinted in 2 vols, 1951.

18 *Ibid.*, p. 355.

19 E. Jones, 'The Symbolism of Salt', in *ibid*.

20 Reik, *op. cit.*, p. 49.

21 *Ibid.*, p. 51.

22 *Ibid.*, p. 53.

23 *Ibid.*, p. 87.

24 E. Jones, 'Mother-right and the Sexual Ignorance of Savages', in *Essays in Applied Psychoanalysis*, p. 128.

25 Rivers, *op. cit.*, p. 30.

26 J.C. Flügel, *The Psychoanalytic Study of the Family*, London, Hogarth Press, 1921, p. 175.

27 *Ibid.*, p. 140.

28 *Ibid.*, p. 120.

29 E. Jones, 'Mother-right and the Sexual Ignorance of Savages'.

30 Here Malinowski was clearly influenced by Durkheim's views of collective representations and society.

31 B. Malinowski, *Sex and Repression in Savage Society*, Routledge, 1926, p. 2.

32 *Ibid.*, p. 81.

33 *Ibid.*, p. 4.

34 *Ibid*.

35 *Ibid.*, p. 9.

36 *Ibid.*, p. 82.

37 *Ibid.*.

38 E. Jones, 'Mother-right and the Sexual Ignorance of Savages', p. 163.

39 *Ibid.*, p. 163.

40   *Ibid.*, p. 166.

41   *Ibid.*, p. 169.

42   *Ibid.*, p. 170.

43   *Ibid.*, p. 173.

44   Malinowski, *Sex and Repression*, p. 155.

45   E. Fromm, 'The theory of mother-right and its significance for Social Psychology', (1934), reprinted in *The Crisis of Psychoanalysis*, Harmondsworth, Penguin, 1973.

46   W. Reich, *The Invasion of Compulsory Sex Morality* (1931), English edn, Harmondsworth, Penguin, 1975.

47   Many of the criticisms made by someone like Fromm remain extremely interesting. This analysis of Freud's interpretion of the Oedipus myth and the little Hans case are still exemplary counter-readings, exposing Freud's patriarchal assumptions. See, E. Fromm, 'The Oedipus Complex and the Oedipus Myth' in R. Anshen, ed., *The Family, its Function and Destiny*, New York, Harper & Bros, 1949; E. Fromm, 'The Oedipus Complex: Comments on the Case of Little Hans', in *The Crisis of Psychoanalysis*.

48   M. Bonaparte, 'Notes on Excision', *Psychoanalysis and The Social Sciences*', vol. 11, 1950.

49   G. Röheim, *Australian Totemism*, p. 143.

50   G. Röheim, *The Riddle of the Sphinx*, London, Hogarth Press, International Psychoanalytic Library, 1934, p. 280.

51   *Ibid.*, p. 202.

52   *Ibid.*, p. 282.

53   G. Röheim, 'Psychoanalysis and Anthropology', *Psychoanalysis and The Social Sciences*, vol. 1, 1949, p. 435.

54   F. Boas, *American Anthropology*, vol. XXII, 1920.

55   C. Du Bois, 'Some Anthropological Perspectives on Psychoanalysis', *Psychoanalytic Review*, vol. XXIV, 1931.

Conclusion: sex and social relations

1   An example of the divisions between these explanations can be found in the collection of essays on *Rationality*, ed. B. Wilson, Oxford, Basil Blackwell, 1979.

2   The first criticisms of this wage form were raised in the domestic labour debate. For a summary of this see E. Kaluzynska. 'Wiping the Floor with Theory', *Feminist Review*, no. 6, 1980. Recently the criticisms of the family wage have become more extensive, see

309

Hilary Land, 'The Family Wage', *Feminist Review*, no. 6, 1980;
B. Campbell, 'Divided we Fall', *Red Rag*, 1980.

3   See J. Ellis, 'On Pornography', *Screen*, vol. 21, no. 1, 1980.

4   I would like to acknowledge discussions with Diana Adlam in t
    the formulation of the following section.

5   An example of this would be C. Meillasoux, *Femmes, Greniers,
    Capitaux*, Paris, Maspero, 1975.

6   This point has been made by O. Harris, F. Edholm, and K. Young,
    in 'Conceptualising Women', *Critique of Anthropology*, no. 9/10,
    1977.

7   This position is characteristic of the domestic labour debate. For
    references, see Kaluzynska, *op. cit.*

8   This presupposition becomes glaringly obvious when it is realised
    that in its early stages the domestic labour debate frequently had
    to presume that the waged labourer was male and the domestic
    labourer an unwaged female.

9   A spate of recent writings have discussed the issue of patriarchy.
    Briefly, these can be found in the debate over patriarchy between
    Sheila Rowbotham, on one side, and Barbara Taylor and Sally
    Alexander, on the other, in the *New Statesman*, 1979/80. Veronica
    Beechey provides a summary of recent uses of the term in 'On
    Patriarchy', *Feminist Review*, no. 3, 1979. Diana Adlam's 'Capitalist
    Patriarchy and Socialist Feminism', *M/F*, no. 3, 1979, criticises the
    use of the term patriarchy in contemporary debates.

10 For an examination of the relation between the state and the family
    from this perspective see, F. Bennet, R. Heys, and R. Coward, 'The
    limitations to Financial and Legal Independence' in *Politics and
    Power*, no. 1, London, Routledge & Kegan Paul, 1980.

11 See the opening section of C. Lévi-Strauss, *The Elementary
    Structures of Kinship*, London, Eyre & Spottiswoode, 1969.

12 See G. Rubin, 'The Traffic in Women', in R. Reiter, ed., *Towards
    an Anthropology of Women*, New York, Monthly Review Press,
    1975.

13 This is best exemplified by Saussure himself in his *Course in
    General Linguistics* (1906), printed by Fontana, 1974. Here he
    argues: 'Language is a system of independent terms in which the
    value of each term results from the simultaneous presence of
    others.' The argument has been made by E. Cowie, in 'Women as
    Sign', *M/F*, no. 1, 1978.

14 This theory is summarised in R. Coward, and J. Ellis, *Language and*

Materialism, London, Routledge & Kegan Paul, 1977.

15 The implications of this approach are particularly searching for marxism's insistance that all aspects of society are structured by and reflect a general abstract principle. Marxism as a tradition paying attention to structural contradictions around economic relations of production is still important. However, it is now clear that the problem of sexual division can only be ignored if an account of the economic mode of production is conducted either in totally abstract terms (paying attention only to the wage form, exchange and circulation) or in totally reductionist terms (paying attention only to the forces generated by the division of labour and capital.

16 See R. Trumbach, *The Rise of the Egalitarian Family*, London, Academic Press, 1978.

17 See S. Edwards, *Female Sexuality and the Law*, Oxford, Martin Robertson, 1981.

18 M. Foucault, *The History of Sexuality*, London, Allen Lane, 1978.

19 See A. Sachs and J. Wilson, *Sexism and the Law*, Oxford, Martin Roberton, 1978.

Bibliography

Abraham, K., *Dreams and Myths*, Nervous and Mental Diseases Monograph No. XV., New York, 1913.

Adlam, D., 'Capitalist Patriarchy and Socialist Feminism', *M/F*, no. III, 1979.

Adler, M., *Engels als Denker*, Berlin, 1920.

Althusser, L., 'Marxism and Humanism', in *For Marx*, Harmondsworth, Penguin, 1969.

Althusser, L., *Reading Capital*, London, New Left Books, 1974.

Alzon, C., *Femme Mythifiée, femme mystifiée*, Paris, Presses Universitaires de France, 1978.

Aveling, E., and Marx, E., *The Woman Question*, London, Swann Sonnenschein & Co., 1886.

Bachofen, J.J., *Myth, Religion and Mother-Right*, selections of Bachofen's writings including *Das Mutter-recht* (1861), London, Routledge & Kegan Paul, 1968.

Bailey, V., and Blackburn, S., 'The Punishment of Incest Act, 1908: a Case Study of Law Creation', *Criminal Law Journal*, 1979.

Bebel, A., *Woman under Socialism* (1883), trans. D. De Leon, New York, Schocken Books, 1971.

Beechey, V., 'On Patriarchy', *Feminist Review*, no. III, 1979.

Bennett, F., Heys, R., and Coward, R., 'The Limitations to Financial and Legal Independence', in *Politics and Power, No. 1*, London, Routledge & Kegan Paul, 1980.

Bleuel, H. P., *Sex and Society in Nazi Germany*, New York, Lippincott, 1973.

Boas, F., 'The Occurrence of Similar Inventions in Areas widely apart', in *Science IX*, 1887.

Boas, F., 'Evolution or Diffusion', *American Anthropologist*, vol. XXVI, 1924.

Bogišić, V., *De la forme dite Inokosna de la famille rurale chez les Serves et les Croates*, Paris, Thorin, 1884.

Bonaparte, M., 'Notes on Excision', *Psychoanalysis and the Social Sciences*, vol. II, 1950.

Bosanquet, He., *The Family*, London, Macmillan, 1906.

Boxer, M., and Quartaert, J., *Socialist Women*, New York, Elsevier, 1976.

Briffault, R., *The Mothers*, London, Allen & Unwin, 1927.

Briffault, R., 'Family Sentiments', *Zeitschrift für Socialforschung*, vol. II, 1933.

Brown, B., 'The Natural and Social Division of Labour', *M/F*, no. I, 1978.

Buchanan, C., *A Journey from Madras through the Countries of Mysore, Canara and Malaba* (3 vols), London, 1807.

Butler, E., *The Tyranny of Greece over Germany*, Cambridge University Press, 1935.

Calverton, V.F., 'The Compulsive Basis for Social Thought', *The American Journal of Sociology*, vol. XXXVI, 1931.

Colletti, L., *Introduction to the Early Writings of Karl Marx*, Harmondsworth, Penguin, 1975.

Copans, J. and Seddon, (eds), *Marxism and Anthropology*, London, Frank Cass, 1978.

Corin, J., *Mating Marriage and the Status of Women*, London, Walter Scott Publishing Co., 1910.

Coward, R., 'Sexual Liberation and the Family', *M/F*, no. I, 1976.

Coward, R., and Ellis, J., *Language and Materialism*, London, Routledge & Kegan Paul, 1977.

Cowie, E., 'Women as Sign', *M/F*, no. I, 1976.

Crawley, E., *The Mystic Rose* (1902), revised edn, London, Macmillan, 1927.

Cunow, H., *Die Verwandschafts Organisationen der Australnager; Ein Beitrag zur Entwicklungsgeschichte*, 1894.

Cunow, H., 'Zur Kritik der Engels' schen Urgeschicktskonstruction' in *Die Marxiste Geschichts*.

Cunow, H., 'Zur Urgeschichte der Ehe und Familie', *Erganzungshefte zur Neuen Zeit*, no. 14, Stuttgart, 1912.

Bibliography

Cutler, A., Hindess, B., Hirst, P., and Hussain, A., *Marx's Capital and Capitalism Today*, London, Routledge & Kegan Paul, 1978.

Darwin, C., *The Origin of Species* (1859), London, J.M. Dent, 1871.

Darwin, C., *The Origin of Man* (2 vols), London, John Murray, 1871.

David, A., 'Imperialism and Motherhood', *History Workshop No. 5*, Spring 1978.

De Coulanges, F., *The Ancient City*, trans. Boston, Mass., 1874.

De Lavaleye, E., *Les Communautés de famille et de village*, 1889.

Delphy, C., *The Main Enemy*, Women's Research and Resources Centre Pamphlet, 1970-7.

Donzelot, J., *The Policing of Families*, London, Hutchinson, 1980.

Du Bois, C., 'Some Anthropological Perspectives on Psychoanalysis', *Psychoanalytic Review*, vol. XXIV, 1937.

Ellis, H., *Women and Marriage*, London, W. Reeves & Co., 1888.

Ellis, H., *Studies in the Psychology of Sex*, vol. IV, Philadelphia, 1905-10.

Ellis, J., 'On Pornography', *Screen*, vol. XXI, no. 1, 1980.

Engels, F., *The Origins of the Family, Private Property and the State* (1884), London, Lawrence & Wishart, 1972.

Engels, F., *Briefwechsel mit M. Kausky*, Vienna, 1955.

Ennew, J., 'The Material of Reproduction' in *Economy and Society*, vol. VIII, no. 1, February 1979.

Evans Pritchard, E.E., *The Position of Women in Primitive Society and our Own*, Fawcett Lectures, 1955-56.

Federn, P., *Zur Psychologie der Revolution: die Vaterlöse Gesellschaft*, (The Psychology of Revolution: Fatherless Studies), Berne, 1927.

Fee, E., 'The Sexual Politics of Victorian Social Anthropology', in Hartmann, M., and Banner, L. (eds), *Clio's Consciousness Raised*, New York, Harper, 1974.

Feuchtwang, S., 'The Colonial Formation of British Anthropology', in Asad, T., (ed.), *Anthropology and the Colonial Encounter*, London, Ithaca Press, 1973.

Filmer, Sir R., *Patriarcha*, 1630.

Firth, R., 'Marriage and the Classificatory System of Relationship', *Journal of the Royal Anthropological Institute*, vol. LX, 1930.

Fison, L., and Howitt, A.W., *Kamilaroi and Kurnai*, Melbourne, 1880.

Flandrin, J.-L., *Families in Former Times*, Cambridge University Press, 1980.

Flügel, J.C., *The Psychoanalytic Study of the Family*, London, Hogarth Press, 1921.

Foucault, M., *The Order of Things*, London, Tavistock, 1970.

Foucault, M., *History of Sexuality*, London, Allen Lane, 1978.

Frazer, Sir. J., *Totemism and Exogamy*, London, Macmillan, 1910.

Freedman, D., 'Totem and Taboo: a Reappraisal', in Muensterberger, W. (ed.), *Man and his Culture*, London, Rapp & Whiting, 1969.

Freud, S., and Breuer, J., *Studies on Hysteria, The Standard Edition of the Complete Psychological Works of Sigmund Freud*, ed. J. Strachey, 1953–74, 24 vols (*SE*), *SE* II, reprinted in Penguin Freud Library, vol. III.

Freud, S., *The Interpretation of Dreams*, (1900), *SE* vol. V.

Freud, S., *The Psychopathology of Everyday Life* (1904), *SE* vol. VI, Reprinted in Penguin Freud Library, vol. V.

Freud, S., *Three Essays on Sexuality* (1905), SE vol. VII, reprinted in Penguin Freud Library, vol. 3, 1977.

Freud, S., *Leonardo da Vinci, and a memory of Childhood*, 1910, *SE* vol. IX

Freud, S., *The Sexual Theories of Children* (1908), SE vol. IX, reprinted in Penguin Freud Library, vol. VII.

Freud, S., *Totem and Taboo* (1912–13), *SE* vol. XIII, reprinted London, Routledge & Kegan Paul, 1968.

Freud, S., *On the History of the Psychoanalytic Movement*, *SE* vol. XIV.

Freud, S., *From the History of an Infantile Neurosis* (1914–15), *SE* vol. XVII, reprinted in Gardiner, M. (ed.), Siegmund Freud and the Wolf Man, Harmondsworth, Penguin, 1973.

Freud, S., *Group Psychology and Analysis of the Ego*, *SE* XVIII *Moses and Monotheism*, 1938, *SE* vol. XXIII, Hogarth Press Edition, 1974.

Fromm, E., *The Crisis of Psychoanalysis*, Harmondsworth, Penguin, 1973.

Fromm, E., 'The Oedipus Myth and the Oedipus Complex' in Anshan, R.H. (ed.), *The Family; its Function and Destiny*, New York, Harper & Bros, 1949.

Gallatin, *Archaeologia Americana*, Philadelphia, 1820 onwards.

Gardiner, M., *Sigmund Freud and the Wolf Man*, Harmondsworth, Penguin, 1973.

Bibliography

Geddes, P., and Thompson, A.A., *The Evolution of Sex*, London, Walter Scott Publishing Co., 1891.

Harris, D., Edholm, F., and Young, K., 'Conceptualising Women', *Critique of Anthropology*, nos. 9/10, 1977.

Harrison, J., *Prolegomena to the Study of Greek Religion*, Cambridge University Press, 1903.

Harrison, J., *Homo Sum; being a Letter to an Anti-Suffragist from an Anthropologist*, National Union of Women's Suffrage Societies, 1913.

Harrison, T., and Madge, C., *The First Year's Work of Mass Observation*, Introduction by B. Malinowski, Lindsay Drummond, 1937–8.

Harrison, R., and McDonough, R., 'Patriarchy and Relations of Production', in Kuhn, A., and Wolpe, A.M. (eds), *Feminism and Materialism*, London, Routledge & Kegan Paul, 1978.

Hartland, S., *Primitive Paternity*, London, David Nutt, 1909.

Hartland, S., 'The Evolution of Kinship' (1922), in *The Frazer Lectures*, Oxford, Clarendon Press, 1922.

Heape, W., *Sex Antogonism*, London, Constable, 1913.

Hirst, P.Q., and Hindess, B., *Pre-Capitalist Modes of Production*, London, Routledge & Kegan Paul, 1977.

Hobhouse, Wheeler and Ginsberg., *The Material Culture and Social Institutions of Primitive Peoples* (1915), reprinted London, Routledge & Kegan Paul, 1965.

Horkheimer, M., *Studies über Autorität und Familie*, Paris, Alcan, 1936.

Huth, A.H., *The Marriage of Near Kin*, London, J. and A. Churchill, 1875.

International Journal of Psychoanalysis, International Psychoanalytic Library, 1920 onwards.

Jones, E., *Papers in Psychoanalysis*, London, Tindall & Cox, 1917.

Jones, E., *Essays in Applied Psychoanalysis*, London, Hogarth Press, 1951.

Jung, C.G., *Collected Papers in Analytical Psychology*, London, 1916.

Kaluzynska, E., 'Wiping the Floor with Theory', *Feminist Review*, no. VI, 1980.

Kautsky, K., 'Die Enstehung der Ehe und Familie', *Kosmos*, Stuttgart, 1882.

Kautsky, K., *Die Materialistische Geschtsauffassung*, Berlin, 1927.

Kidd, D., *Kaffir Socialism and the Dawn of Individualism*, London, 1908.

Kluckhorn, C., 'The Impact of Psychiatry in American Anthropology in the last 100 Years', in *One Hundred Years of American Psychiatry*, New York, American Psychiatric Association and Columbia Press, 1944.

Kollontai, A., *Selected Writings*, London, Allison & Busby, 1977.

Kolnai, A., *Psychoanalysis and Sociology*, London, Allen & Unwin, 1921.

Kovalevsky, M., 'Tableau des origines et de l'évolution de la famille et de la propriété', *Skrifter ufgina af Lovenska Stiftelsen*, no. 2, Stockholm, 1890.

Krader, L. (ed.), *The Ethnological Notebooks of Karl Marx*, Assen, von Gorcum, 1974.

Kristeva, J., *On Chinese Women*, London, Marion Boyars, 1977.

Kroeber, A.L., 'Totem and Taboo: an Ethnological Psychoanalysis', *American Anthropologist*, vol. 22, 1920.

Kroeber, A.L., Review of Lowie's *Primitive Society*, *American Anthropologist* vol. XXII, 1920.

Kropotkin, Prince, *Mutual Aid* (1902), reprinted Harmondsworth, Penguin, 1939.

Lafargue, P., *The Evolution of Property from Savagery to Civilisation*, 1890.

Lafargue, P., *La Question de la Femme*, Paris, Editions de l'Oeuvre Nouvelle, 1902.

Lafitau, P., *Les Moeurs des Sauvages Ameriquains comarées aux Moeurs des premiers Temps*, Paris, 1724.

Lang, A., and Atkinson, J.J., *Social Origins and Primal Law*, London, Longmans, 1903.

Lenin, V.I., *The State*, Peking, Foreign Language Press, 1919.

Lenin, V.I., *Woman and Society*, selections in *The Woman Question, Selected Writings of Marx, Engels, Lenin and Stalin*, International Publishing Co. 1951.

Le Play, F., *L'Organisation de la Famille*, Tours, 1884.

Letourneau, E., *The Evolution of Marriage and the Family*, Contemporary Science Series, London, Walter Scott, 1889.

Lévi-Strauss, C., *Elementary Structures of Kinship* (1949), Boston, Beacon Press, 1969.

Lévi-Strauss, C., *Totemism*, Harmondsworth, Penguin, 1973.

Livingstone, D., *Narrative of an Expedition to the Zambesi and its Tributaries, 1858–64*, London, John Murray, 1865.

Bibliography

Lombroso C., and Ferrero, *The Female Offender*, Criminology Series, vol. I, London, Unwin, 1895.

Lowie, R., *Origins of the State*, New York, Harcourt Brace & Co., 1927.

Lubbock, J., *The Origin of Civilisation and the Primitive Condition of Man*, London, Longmans, 1870.

Lynd, H., *England in the 1880s* (1945), reprinted London, Frank Cass, 1968.

Mackenzie, J., *Ten Years North of the Orange River, 1859–1869*, Edinburgh, Hamilton, 1871.

McLennan, D., *The Patriarchal Family*, London, Macmillan, 1885.

McLennan, J.F., *Studies in Ancient History*, London, Quaritch, 1876–7.

Maine, H., *Ancient Law* (1861), reprinted Everyman's Library, London, Dent, 1917.

Maine, H., *Dissertations on Early Law and Custom*, London, John Murray, 1883.

Maine, H., *Popular Government*, London, John Murray, 1885.

Malinowski, B., *The Family amongst Australian Aborigines*, University of London Monograph in Sociology, vol. 2, 1913.

Malinowski, B., *Sex and Repression in Savage Society*, London, Routledge, 1926.

Malinowski, B., 'Must Kinship be Dehumanised by Mock-Algebra?' in *Man*, February 1930.

Marrett, R.R., 'The Beginnings of Morals and Culture', in *The Outline of Modern Knowledge*, London, Gollancz, 1932.

Marx, K., 'Critique of Hegel's Doctrine of the State', (1843), in *Early Writings*, ed. L. Colletti, Harmondsworth, Penguin, 1975.

Marx, K., *Pre-Capitalist Economic Formations* (1857–8), ed., E. Hobsbawn, London, Lawrence & Wishart, 1965.

Marx, K., *Das Kapital* (3 vols): vol. 1, 1867; vol. 2, 1885; vol. 3, 1894; London, Lawrence & Wishart, 1974.

Marx, K., and Engels, F., *The German Ideology* (1846), London, Lawrence & Wishart, 1970.

Meek, R., *Social Sciences and the Ignoble Savage*, Cambridge University Press, 1976.

Meillasoux, C., *Femmes, Greniers, Capitaux*, Paris, Maspéro, 1975.

Millar, J., *Observations concerning the Distinctions of Ranks in Society*, London, 1771.

Mitchell, J., *Psychoanalysis and Feminism*, London, Allen Lane, 1974.

Molyneux, M., 'Androcentrism in Marxist Anthropology', *Critique of Anthropology*, nos. 9/10.

Morgan, L.H., *Ancient Society*, New York, Henry Holt & Co., 1877.

Myres, J., 'The Influence of Anthropology on the Course of Political Science', *University of California Publications in History*, vol. IV, no. 1, 1916.

Osborne, R., *Freud and Marx*, London, Left Book Club, 1932.

Osborne, R., *The Psychology of Reaction*, London, Left Book Club, 1937.

Patteson, C., *Evolution*, London, Routledge & Kegan Paul, 1978.

Paul, E., *An Outline of Psychology* (1921), London, Plebs Textbooks.

Perkins Gilman, C., *Women and Economics, 1898*, reprinted New York, Harper Torchlight Books, 1965.

Pinkerton, *A Collection of the best and most interesting voyages and travels in all parts of the world* (17 vols), London, 1808–14.

Pitt-Rivers, G.H.L.F., *The Clash of Cultures and the Contact of Races*, London, Routledge, 1911.

Pitt-Rivers, G.H.L.F., *Weeds in the Garden of Marriage*, London, Noel Douglas, 1931.

Porter, C., *Alexandra Kollantai*, London, Virago, 1980.

Radcliffe-Brown, A.A., *African Systems of Kinship and Marriage*, Oxford University Press, 1950.

Raglan, Lord, *Jocasta's Crime*, London, Methuen, 1933.

Rank, O., *The Myth of the Birth of the Hero* (1914), English edn, London, Vintage Books, 1964.

Rank, O., and Sachs, H., *The Significance of Psychoanalysis for the Mental Sciences*, (1913) English translation in Nervous and Mental Diseases Monograph Series, No. 13, New York, 1916.

Rattray, R.S., *Ashanti*, Oxford, Clarendon Press, 1932.

Read, C., 'No Paternity', *Man, The Journal of the Royal Anthropological Institute*, 1918.

Reich, W., *The Invasion of Compulsory Sex Morality* (1931), English edn, Harmondsworth, Penguin, 1975.

Reik, T., *Ritual,* (1928), English edn with an introduction by S. Freud, London, Hogarth Press, 1931.

Ritchie, C., *Darwinism and Politics*, London, Swann Sonnenschein, 1889.

Rivers, W.H.R., 'Dreams and Primitive Culture', *Bulletin of the John Rylands Library*, vol. VIm bis, 3–4, February–July 1918.

Bibliography

Rivers, W.H.R., *Social Organisation and Kinship*, 1924 lecture, reprinted London, Athlone Press, 1968.

Röheim, G., *The Riddle of the Sphinx*, London, Hogarth Press, International Psychoanalytic Library, 1934.

Rosen, A., *Rise Up Women*, London, Routledge & Kegan Paul, 1974.

Rowbotham, S., versus Taylor, B., and Alexander, S., 'Debate over Patriarchy' in *New Statesman*, 1979/80.

Rowbotham, S., *Stella Browne*, London, Pluto Press, 1978.

Rubin, G., 'The Traffic in Women', in R. Reiter, (ed.), *Towards an Anthropology of Women*, Monthly Review Press, 1975.

Russell, A., Appendix to B. Russell, *German Social Democracy*.

Russell, B., *German Social Democracy*, London, Longmans, 1896.

Russell, B., *Marriage and Morals* (1929), Harmondsworth, Penguin, 1968.

Ryzanov, D., *Karl Marx und Friedrich Engels*, London, 1927.

Sachs, A., and Wilson, J., *Sexism and the Law*, Oxford, Martin Robertson, 1978.

Saussure, F. de, *Course in General Linguistics* (1906), London, Fontana, 1974.

Schoolcraft, T., *Travels*, 1825.

Schoolcraft, T., *Notes on the Iroquois*, 1846.

Schouten, W., *Voyage aux Indes Orientales*, Amsterdam, 1757.

Searle, G.R., 'Eugenics and Politics' in *Britain, 1900–1914*, Leyden, Noordhof International, 1976.

Seligmann, B., 'Incest and Descent', *Journal of the Royal Anthropological Institute*, vol. LIX, 1929.

Shorter, E., *The Making of the Modern Family*, London, Fontana, 1977.

Silberer, E., *Problems of Mysticism and its Symbolism*, New York, Moffat Yard & Co., 1917.

Skene, R., *The Highlanders of Scotland*, 1837.

Sohm, R., *The Institutes of Roman Law*, trans. Oxford, Clarendon Press, 1892.

Spencer, W.B. and Gillen, F., *The Native Tribes of Central Australia, b* 1899.

Starke, C.N., *The Primitive Family*, International Scientific Series, 1872.

Stokes, W., *Hindu Law*, Madras, J. Higginbotham, 1865.

Tavernier, J.B., *Les six voyages de J.B. Tavernier*, Paris, 1676.

Taylor, B., 'The Feminist Theory and Practice of the Socialist Movement in Britain 1820–1845', PhD for Sussex University, 1980.

Taylor, B., 'Lords of Creation', *New Statesman*, March 1980.

Taylor B., and Phillips, A., 'Sex and Skill', *Feminist Review*, no. VI, 1980.

Thompson, G., *Aeschylus and Athens*, London, Lawrence & Wishart, 1941.

Thönnessen, W. *The Emancipation of Women*, London, Pluto Press, 1973.

Tribe, K., *Land, Labour and Economic Discourse*, London, Routledge & Kegan Paul, 1978.

Türel, A., *Bachofen — Freud zür Emanzipation des Mannes vom Reich der Mütter*, Berne, 1939.

Tylor, E.B., *Anthropology*, London, Macmillan, 1881.

Tylor, E.B., 'The Matriarchal Family System', in *Nineteenth Century*, July 1896.

Vaerting, M. and M., *The Dominant Sex*, translated from the German by Paul, E. and C., London, Allen & Unwin, 1923.

Walkewitz, J., *Prostitution in Victoria England*, Cambridge University Press, 1980.

Weeks, J., *Sex, Politics and Society: the Regulation of Sexuality since 1800*, London, Longman, 1981.

Westermarck, E., *The History of Human Marriage*, London, Macmillan, 1891.

Westermarck, E., *Three Essays on Sex and Marriage*, London, Macmillan, 1934.

Wilson, B., (ed.), *Essays on Rationality*, Oxford, Basil Blackwell, 1979.

Wilson, E., *Women and the Welfare State*, London, Tavistock, 1977.

Zaretsky, E., *Capitalism, the Family and Personal Life*, London, Pluto Press, 1976.

Index

Index

Kollontai, Alexandra, 141, 150, 168, 177–81
Kovalevsky, Maxim, 24, 42
Kroeber, A.L., 126, 127, 249

Lacan, J., 206, 207, 266, 273
Lafargue, P., 164
Lafitau, P., 27
Lang, A., 47, 57
Lassalle, Ferdinand, 173
Lenin, V.I., 132–3, 150, 164, 165
LePlay, Frederick, 24, 25
Lévi-Strauss, C., 206, 207, 217–18, 273–6
Locke, John, 24
Lowie, R., 108–10, 126
Lubbock, J., 28, 29
Luxemburg, Rosa, 177

McLennan, J.F., 28, 29, 31, 35–8, 42, 44, 47, 52
Maine, Henry, 17–18, 19, 20, 21–6, 28, 29, 30, 42, 43–5, 47, 55, 56
Malinowski, B., 47–8, 103–4, 112, 115–16, 117–18, 119, 236–45, 246, 248, 249
marriage: customs as 'survivals' from primitive cultures, 35–8; distinction not always drawn between function of marriage and mating, 89; as economic structure, 155–6, 168; notions of influenced by theories of natural selection, 87; and population exigencies, 87
Marx, Karl: *Das Kapital*, 133, 138, 139, 157, 173; dispute with Hegel, 136–8; early view of the family, 134, 135; *German Ideology* and the *Grundrisse*, 138–9, 151; lack of overall philosophical and social theory, 133; the 'woman question', 164, 167; women's labour, 173, 174–5; *see also* marxism
marxism: concept of the family in, 130–62, 187; Engels and significance of matriarchal gens, 142; family, labour market and 'true sex love', 166–7; and feminism, 130–1;

142, 164; importance for understanding position of women, 14–15; Kollontai's reply to feminist and suffragist movements, 178; and nineteenth century discussions on sexual relationships, 10–11; patriarchal power and class relations, 159–60; and patriarchy, 7; social divisions and classes, 156–8; and social position of women, 140, 141; and theories of sexual identity, 4; and the 'woman question', 163–87; *see also* Marx, Karl
mating: and marriage, 89, 98; unregulated, 40, 57
matriarchy: idea of universal precedence of, 11–12; importance of concept, 9; matriarchal inversion of patriarchal structures, 27; primitive, 31–5; struggle over patriarchy and matriarchy, 12
matrilineal societies: in Freudian theory, 194; Malinowski's studies, 237, 239–40; matrilineal descent, 37–8, 40, 41, 52–6, 61, 62, 112–13; seen as primitive version of Western patriarchal society, 39
Mead, Margaret, 250
Mill, J.S., 182
monogamy, 38, 40, 70, 71, 150, 151
Morgan, Lewis Henry, 28, 31, 39–42, 44, 47, 50, 52, 84, 95, 126, 141, 142–3, 149
mother-right: importance of societies in social theory, 19; meaning of, 46–74; from mother-right to matrilineal descent, 52–6; overwhelming evidence of, 42–5; property and transition to father-right, 63
myths, 191, 224–35

nature/culture debate, 4–7, 13, 262
natural selection: and prohibition of incest, 80–7; and sexual selection, 76–80

Oedipus complex, 192–3, 197, 201–2, 204, 205, 206, 237–45